THE QUAKERS

a new look at their place in society

THE

QUAKERS

a new look at their place in society

by JOHN SYKES

J. B. LIPPINCOTT COMPANY

Philadelphia and New York

1959

250

For Joey
some years hence

CONTENTS

CONTENTS

ACKNOWLEDGEMENTS

I wish to thank Miss Helen Morfey and Mr P. Pulzer for their help in research. I also wish to thank the Librarian and Assistant Librarian at Friends House for their invaluable assistance at each stage of the book's production. I am grateful to their Library Committee for permission to quote extensively from John Nickall's edition of *The Journal of George Fox,* Cambridge University Press, 1952. Unless otherwise stated, all quotations from Fox's *Journal* are taken from that edition. Where MS sources are quoted these refer to documents in the Library of the Society of Friends, unless given otherwise.

PART I. A FIRST DESCRIPTION

RELATIONSHIP WITH GOD

(a) Introduction. The Essence of Quakerism

THE popular view of Quakers is too inclined to label them as a good, simple, slightly eccentric, middle-aged group of people who, rather like a maiden aunt, manage not to get too involved in the disasters of our time, but then are suddenly at hand with a cup of tea, a stretcher, and a kindly word. They are seen as survivors from a more liberal age that had the independence of mind and the funds to practise Christian charity. For many, not only for those who still picture them in traditional dress, warning their children against the theatre, they are remote, almost museum pieces, at best a continuing, though numerically negligible, coterie with high ethical standards and a habit of waiting together in silence for Divine inspiration and comfort. They do not seem to be afflicted enough, spiritually or otherwise.

Such notions, whatever truth they contain, do not take us very close to the actual experience of Quakers, suggesting rather that this was long ago perfected, inwardly and towards the world, wrapped up like a bar of Cadbury's chocolate, and handed down through successive generations to the present members of their Society. The fault for this lies partly with them; for through most of their three centuries of history they have fostered a Quaker legend of unremittingly staid aspect, disowning those who did not conform, coming before the public either as sages of the moral life or as well-established angels of mercy. Discounting all that did not fit in they have pitched their account of themselves too high, so that even to-day the Society of Friends is widely thought of as a closed shop to all but the most worthy of the worthy.

This is far from being true; but such ideas, diffused and embellished in the public mind, may deter people from exploring the inner reaches of Quaker experience. Though they feel afflicted by the general loss of faith in the habits and language and visible symbols involved in man's religious life, they may decide that the necessary and urgent work of revitalisation could hardly begin there. However deeply they realise the need to keep the centre of one's being open to the forces of eternity, to God, and that all relevant techniques and disciplines may have some power to assist them, and that from among these one will take them furthest according to their particular condition, they may never look for it within Quakerism.

Yet this, an effective spiritual method, for a wide range of personalities, is exactly what lies, beneath all the accretions and misconceptions through which the public gaze must filter, at the core of the experience of the Society of Friends. It is this that first sent them crying the news of their discovery up and down England, and to America, in the days of Oliver Cromwell's Commonwealth; and steeled them against subsequent persecution; and later, as the mummifying breath of respectability settled about them, burned more quietly in their retired meetings to spark forth in individual lives. It is the genesis of those activities such as the crusade against slavery, the work in prisons and adult education, the continuing work of reconciliation in a war-attuned world, for which they are respected, often for which they are only known, by the public. It has not formed all their attitudes, for many forces have been at work, but it has modified each of them. It is still the heartbeat of Quaker existence; and it is open to all who wish to try it out and who apply themselves to it properly.

For instance, those enquiring souls who, depressed by the seeming irrelevance of much in Western religious practice, who run to the East for enlightenment, to the resources of Yoga and Zen Buddhism, might well ponder if there were not nearer home techniques that can yield the same felicities and can possibly ground the personality in modes more serviceable for daily living. If for reasons of faith they cannot surrender to the experience of the Catholic Church, to its knowledge of the way of interior prayer, then without its walls but within Christianity, within the silent prayerful group that composes a Quaker meeting for worship, workaday, practical in make-up yet infused with the most ardent mystical longings, they may well find what suits their need. They do not have to be Christians to participate, though most of those present will call themselves Christians; the experience transcends any set of words used to reflect or explain it.

It is at this point therefore that one should begin to study Quakers: here at the centre of their corporate life, the start of all their works and testimonies, and the connecting thread throughout their history. Nothing that has ever happened to them, in particular the changing moods of their Society, as dramatic sometimes as a prima donna's, can be elucidated without reference to it. One must understand the meeting for worship.

For in fact, at different stages of their history Quakers have been very different people, with different backgrounds and problems to solve, reflecting the age in which they lived. Superficially, they have been more typical of the age, and also of England or the United States, and latterly of other countries, than of any central Quaker thesis; hence the confusion of ideas about them.

Yet all, in attending Meeting for Worship and knowing the power engendered through that, whether in vocalised concerns or profounder heart work, have been open to an experience that has worked upon them, and to varying extent drawn them to its centre, relating their lives to a single goal. There have been failures, there have been saintly figures, leaders and rebels and healers of discord, and the great company of practising Friends with chiefly their steadfastness to record: all have gathered in the silence of Meeting, a communion that now stretches back through ten generations.

(b) First approach to Meeting for Worship

The Quaker meeting house in central London is in a street of theatres, between shops, one of those shadowy doorways one easily passes by. A modest sign shows it to be the Westminster Meeting of the Religious Society of Friends, holding a public meeting for worship on Sunday mornings at eleven o'clock: an even more modest announcement of this appears occasionally in the press. It is the same throughout the United Kingdom and Eire, on the European Continent, in North America, and in the few far corners of the earth where Quaker meetings are regularly held—in India, Australasia, Africa, Singapore, Hong Kong, Jamaica, these meetings are not easy to find. It was not always so, but it is to-day.

Having found such a meeting, or chanced upon it, the newcomer will have even more difficulty in knowing what is going on. Through the foyer, busy with chatter, stands the appointed room: bare, but for rows of benches running in from all four walls to leave a small square at the centre, and there a table with flowers and a bible. By eleven the company has gathered here in silence, one of the four sets of benches being reserved for those called Elders, the others being open to all. The meeting is to last about an hour.

For one unprepared, unless sensitive to the extent of being swiftly drawn in, not much may appear to happen. The meeting is grounded in silence, but out of this vocal prayer or words of exhortation or reflection, the exact character of which is not easy to pin, may arise from any person present. The silence seems to intensify, or on this occasion it may go limp and a good deal or fidgetting appear towards the close. A stranger might be fortunate in attending what is called "a very good meeting", in reality the culmination of faithful attendance by a nucleus of members week after week, who are after all here applying themselves to the comprehensive work of a life-time and can only occasionally hope to break through to a high pitch of communion and fellowship. Or so it is to-day when religious devotions are generally pitched low for fear of falsity, and when, at least in the Society of Friends, there are fewer individuals able to carry the rest at a bound towards the heart of worship.

But, should the meeting be good, no stranger can be unaware of this. To some degree it will reach him. Some phrase or something in a tone of voice, or in the bearing of a speaker, or something in the quality of the silence, will take hold of him, releasing joy, and represent his ordinary affairs to him in a new perspective, better resolved. Loneliness or despair will fade; he has been taken a little out of himself; and the fact is that five minutes later this impression will not have gone again for good. It stays. He will be drawn to the others present. Such meetings at the least are the seedbed of friendliness. Already he may sense they can be far more.

In 1676, Robert Barclay, Scottish laird turned theologian, who had joined the Quakers ten years previously, wrote: " when I came into the silent assemblies of God's people, I felt a secret power among them, which touched my heart, and as I gave way unto it, I found the Evil weakening in me and the Good raised up, and so I became thus knit and united unto them, hungering more and more after the increase of this power and life . . ." [1]

Those were days when Quakers were still the talk of the land, when the manner of prayer could be the subject of a fine, or a whipping or a prolonged imprisonment, and people spoke raptly of their experience; yet equally in Victorian times, in a considerably toned-down atmosphere,

[1] *Apology*. Prop. 11, Sect. vii.

Caroline Stephen, daughter of Sir James Stephen, experienced, in 1812, as follows . . . " On one never-to-be-forgotten Sunday morning, I found myself one of a small company of silent worshippers, who were content to sit down together without words, that each one might feel after and draw nearer to the Divine Presence, unhindered at least, if not helped, by any human utterance. Utterance I knew was free, should the words be given; and, before the meeting was over, a sentence or two were uttered in great simplicity by an old apparently untaught man, rising in his place amongst the rest of us. I did not pay much attention to the words he spoke, and I have no recollection of their purport. My whole soul was filled with the unutterable peace of the undisturbed opportunity for communion with God, with the sense that at last I had found a place where I might, without the faintest suspicion of insincerity, join with others in simply seeking His presence. . . . And, since that day, now more than seventeen years ago, Friends' meetings have indeed been to me the greatest of outward helps to a fuller and fuller entrance into the spirit from which they have sprung: the place of the most soul-subduing, faith restoring, strengthening and peaceful communion, in feeding upon the bread of life, that I have ever known." [2]

The impact came as strongly, the joining of the timeless with a moment of time. Exactly so it could be to-day, or could have been at the start of the world.

But what in reality is happening in these meetings, week after week and through the centuries? Officially the Society of Friends claims . . . " Our manner of worship springs from our experience of God and gives expression to it " [3] . . . and again, seventy years later; . . . " In our life as a religious Society we have found it true that the spirit of man can come into direct contact with the Spirit of

[2] *Quaker Strongholds*, 1911, pp. 2–5.
[3] *London Yearly Meeting Epistle* 1857.

God and can thereby learn of God "[4] . . . and baldly, a few years ago, at a world conference of Quakers . . . " The Quaker faith is a religion of experience ".[5] At the start of the Society's existence its founder, George Fox, wrote . . . " Friends, meet together and know one another in that which is eternal, which was before the world was." [6]

What is this governing experience, from which all else derives? Though no words can exactly represent it, especially when in logical sequence, something of its nature and of its path can be suggested; and this much must be set down before the spread of Quaker life is followed, and the course of Quaker history.

(c) Analysis of Meeting for Worship

Worship, to use one set of words, is the longing for communion with God, for renewal from the source of Being, and is both the degree of that attainment and the means leading towards it. Thus the Quaker meeting prepares in silence for its supreme objective, towards which all else is relative, but can only approach this through stages or phases, each transformed by the next, that at their level have substance and value.

The first phase is that of settling down into the quiet of the Meeting. Both regular members and attenders are advised to arrive a little early, to have found a place by the appointed hour that ushers in the silence; then to relax in mind and body, to steady the breathing to an even pace, to link the hands and ankles and incline the head so that nerves and feeling may become tender; most important, to trust oneself to the fellowship of the group of which formally one is now a part. Already the very peace of the room, not centred in outward altar or pulpit but solely in the worshippers, helps to stay chattering thoughts and

[4] *Christian Practice*, 1954, p. 2.
[5] *Third World Conference of Friends*, 1952, Official Report.
[6] *Epistle* 149 (1657).

anxieties, or habit of expecting a service to proceed by formula through the work of others. Each is here to be drawn in, an involvement on which all depend.

An early Friend, Alexander Parker, wrote in 1659 . . . " So Friends, when you come together to wait upon God, come orderly in the fear of God: the first that enters into the place of your meeting, be not careless, nor wander up and down, either in body or mind; but innocently sit down in some place, and turn in thy mind to the light, and wait upon God singly, as if none were present but the Lord; and *here* thou art strong. Then the next that comes in, let them in simplicity of heart, sit down and turn in to the same light, and wait in the Spirit: and so all the rest coming in, in the fear of the Lord, sit down in pure stillness and silence of all flesh, and wait in the light. . . ." [7] This advice does not change through the centuries.

The second phase, also essentially one of preparation, has more body, and may be as far as a particular meeting on a particular occasion can go.

We can call it the phase of meditation; for here many will harness their minds to the repetition of a prayer, or Scripture, or some significant holy name, evoking as with a mantram its purifying grace. The more bhaktic volatile type of Christian finds uniquely in the name of Jesus a liberating almost an erotic power that sends him at a bound beyond this stage. Others, more phlegmatic, have to start by re-examining their past week's actions, which now in the context of the praying group appear in a new perspective to them, subject of new questions and release, as in a confessional. The silence is a great listener.

Some think along abstract lines, of moral issues, about the nature of things.

Yet all these ways, however fruitful, are but to rinse the mind and to tauten the chords of feeling. Prejudices,

---

[7] *Letters of Early Friends* (ed. A. R. Barclay, 1841), p. 365.

grievances, inflamed ambitions: all such things need to be loosened from the vital energy lodged in them. This phase of flexing and repositioning, a sort of mental and emotional massage, assists in that; though, as with all we are examining, it is nothing less than the work of a life-time.

George Fox said . . . ' Be still a while from thy own thoughts . . . desires and imaginations, and be stayed in the principle of God in thee . . . up to God." [8] As the river broadens towards the estuary we prepare to steer away from shore, with its familiar habits.

For some this naturally comes more easily—just as some imagine they cannot begin without a background of chant-ing and incense to lull the active surface of self; yet practice, without stress, with a Taoist flexibility towards all that intrudes, soon brings results: principally because the indivi-dual is not alone, he is part of a group, concentrating to the one end. Suddenly he will notice the profound stillness, and feel himself to be within it. Gone are distinctions of they and me, or of race or colour, or suchlike. There is one over-arching commitment, and beneath this great tenderness.

Now perhaps someone may speak. A wide range of ministry is possible, one never knows what to expect for every meeting is a fresh start, but it could do one of three things. It could simply extend the preceding silence, keep-ing the Meeting at the same pitch: through words as yet not greatly inspiring, a recital of thoughts with general application or some mild moral exhortation. This would make explicit an aspect of the silence, and be of use to someone present, perhaps through voicing a sense of obliga-tion only half-realised—for Catholics, the value of " the lower slopes "; but it would stop there. Others might follow in the same vein, embroidering the theme into a group sermon, and the Meeting could close on that note.

[8] *Journal*, p. 346.

It would have been a slightly less than average Meeting.

Less fortunate occasions go dead. This is when ministry is nothing better than a spilling over of loose thoughts, or an argument suited to a lecture room; or when, the silence opening for someone like a flower arching towards the light, or a girl towards her lover, the right ministry is withheld through personal trepidation and self-centredness. This is by no means uncommon, and was characteristic of the Society in its Quietist period. Already George Fox had noted it [9] . . . " Friends, you see how men and women can speak enough for the world, for merchandise, for husbandry, the ploughman for his plough, but when they should come to speak for God they quench the Spirit." He saw that they " after become dead and dull ", for " where it is quenched it cannot try things ".

It is this " trying of things " that is vital, the potential leap forward. Accepting that there must be dull occasions, personal failures, dry periods sometimes for years on end, it is the other on which we concentrate, nerved to take risks through innate need to develop, to transform ourselves and the life around us. It is the creative impulse. In a recent film Picasso, showing how he paints pictures, plunging beneath the surface to discover the essential components of a new structure, says that one must risk all, that he likes to risk all.

If that attitude seizes a Quaker Meeting, quickening out of what has gone before, released through the indefinably right words of a particular speaker (and there are some who can sound this note often, as if given the password for the day) or more usually through a sudden crystallisation within the silence itself, then the great leap forward is taking place and the Meeting is launched on its centremost and not unperilous exercise. In a matter of minutes or seconds the worshippers can move nearer to their goal than in all the previous half hour's patient cir-

[9] *Epistles* 275 (1669), 150 (1667).

RELATIONSHIP WITH GOD 25

cumambulatory meditation. They are at grips with phase three.

In wide terms what is happening is the most commonplace experience. All the time our conscious minds are being peppered with signals from beyond consciousness, most of them unnoticed, but a few taken up as bright ideas or flashes of wit, or intuition about other people. In times of crisis such as war, or personal suffering, or love, they overwhelm us; we imagine we are poets, or psychic. Indeed, it is the unusually receptive people like poets or religious prophets who unceasingly receive such messages, from sly insinuations of insight to gigantic visions with voices that become the stuff of revelation and myth; and their task is to control what they receive, to make it serviceable for others, as a means of widening consciousness and for readjusting daily life (even if it has to wait a generation till the rest of us learn how to make use of it). If they fail in this control they skid nearer to the fragile line dividing them from maniacs and idiots and the generally obsessed; saints and child murderers at moments are only a hair's breadth apart.

So greatly have all religions prized this disruption of ordinary consciousness that they have engineered vast means to promote it—using magic, drugs, drums, display, fasting, flagellation, hell fire, and various psychological refinements—then clamped down a set of rules to keep the results within control, usually for the health and progress of society, often for less worthy motives. Here again where control has failed, among primitive or unorganised sects, or at times of great social upheaval, madness has broken out—an example being those early Anabaptists (from whose later developments the Quakers derived) who, sure of their perfected condition granted directly by Holy Spirit, indulged in polygamy, set up a tyranny of " Saints ", and waded through blood towards their objective of Utopia on earth. Many of the early Puritans were close to a

psychopathic condition: the burden of the times, with its
rush of insight, was too great for them. Even Quakers,
though disowning all kindred Ranting elements, at first
trembled near the edge of delusion, as the episode of James
Naylor illustrates. He was not untypical of his colleagues
then; it was only after he had been branded for blasphemy
that the Society took itself in hand, and evolved the mature
group technique that we are now considering.

The gateway then through which all must pass who
are to experience any extension of consciousness, in itself
the condition of spiritual insight, the basis of religious
values, is fraught with danger. A slight advance is not
difficult to cope with, and brings its well known sense of
joy, but the hurtling advance by whatever means onto the
exposed plateau can, it would seem, without special control,
precipitate evil as well as good, the voice of the Devil in
place of that of God. It is not a journey to attempt alone.

The Quaker meeting for worship knows that it is involved in this same travail. In different epochs it has
utilised some of the more dramatic methods; to-day, apart
from the occasional ministry that can lift it clean out of
itself, it depends on the basic silent concentration towards
the moment of break-through. At all times the presence
and control of the group frames what is happening, easing
the task of the individual, helping him, as the inner signals
increase, to recognise those which lead him towards the
Light of God. Right ministry, from one practised, who has
repeatedly travelled this way, and returns boddhisatva-
fashion to help others, can speed and intensify the process.
Sometimes the words spoken are themselves trembling on
the edge of flight: fragmentary, urgent, indecisive, hints
of what is yet to come; or sometimes the moment of travail
is such that the meeting veritably sweats in silence. Barclay
noted, though in more fervent times . . . " Sometimes the
power of God will break forth into a whole meeting, and
there will be such in inward travail, while each is seeking

to overcome the evil in themselves, that by the strong contrary workings of these opposite powers, like the going of two contrary tides, every individual will be strongly exercised as in a day of battle, and thereby trembling and a motion of the body will be upon most, if not upon all, which, as the power of truth prevails, will from pangs and groans end with a sweet sound of thanksgiving and praise. And from this the name of Quakers, i.e. Tremblers, was first reproachfully cast upon us." [10]

To-day, such outward manifestations are not much known, and very likely the tension is less acute, for people are less burdened with a sense of depravity, but the sweat of travail is not unusual, nor the concerted leap forward of the Meeting. This is the start of the fourth phase.

By now the worshippers are drawn close, wired up one to another so that the Light dawning in one or two of them diffuses its power through the rest, helping them to the same stage: for it is the group experience that Quakers look for. Within the individual this Light may come through a Name such as that of Jesus, which, as earlier noted, is for him so charged with the love of God, unifying and transforming all things, that he may reach this point at a bound; and must then wait, contemplating his Saviour, or speak out of this full experience, till the other worshippers, through their several ways, catch up, and the Meeting move forward together. These others may experience the Light first through some other spiritually-charged Name, or through some phrase, idea, or picture that brings with it sense of an absolute reality, a power and joy that far transcends any meaning that could ordinarily be attached to it. To this the worshipper must cling, yielding himself to it utterly; for it is this and this alone that will bring him, as it developes, into the deepest fellowship with the others similarly employed, and towards the shared communion with God.

[10] *Apology.* Prop. ii, Sect. viii.

Suppose for a moment there could be a mistake, even now an intrusion of evil impulse bringing not grace but demonic possession : but then it would not be attended by joy, nor the certitude of the patiently-prepared worshipper, nor could it ever bring him into unity with the other present. This last has always been the main safety clause in the Quaker method. " Mind that which is pure in one another which joins you together, for nothing will join or make fit but what is pure, nor unite nor build but what is pure " . . . " In that dwell which doth bring out of the Shadows, types, traditions " . . . "All Friends everywhere in the Power of God dwell . . . for that brings all your souls into peace, into oneness, into God " . . . " I was commanded to turn people to that inward light, spirit, grace, by which all might know their salvation, and their way to God; even that divine Spirit which would lead them into all Truth and which I infallibly knew would never deceive any." [11] Thus repeatedly, shepherding his brethren, wrote and spoke George Fox.

With quiet certitude and a sense of the enveloping fellowship that claims him, then, the worshipper yields to the Light within : the illumination of thought and feeling, of both reason and conscience, come from among the shadowy material breaking into consciousness but now transforming his whole nature, and leading it. This is the Guide, the good Angel, the Atman, the Light of Christ within : what Quakers call also the Seed, the Witness, and That of God in every man. For Christians it is uniquely the Light of Christ; for they believe in a Jesus whose every action was so infused with Divine Light that he incorporated and made known to men the presence of the Eternal Christ, the mediating Spirit of God—" I am the way, and the truth, and the life; no one cometh to the Father, except through me." " He that hath seen me hath seen the

---

[11] *Epistles* 13 (1652), 72 (1654), 104 (1655), and *Journal*, p. 35.

Father." [12] For Mahayana Buddhists and Hindus, less anchored to history or to the single revelation, it is the eternal Buddha or Krishna aiding the mind to self-realisation. Moslems and Jews speak simply of God's Spirit, making Him known within. All are concerned with the one process: illumination, exercise of soul, and communion with God, the ground of Being.

One might claim that a Quaker meeting for worship could unite practitioners of all these religions, together with certain agnostics, so long as they were of a mystical bent, for beneath their terminologies or lack of them the experience aimed at is identical; and this to-day is in the minds of Friends who have held mixed meetings for worship in India, and also of some European Friends. [13] But by and large the Society sees itself as a purely Christian body and its meetings as the vineyard of Christ alone, and though it has wavered at times towards Deism such excursions have been pulled up short. It is not really conceivable that in the Western world of the last three centuries this could have been otherwise.

Leaving aside for the moment these formulations of experience, and returning to the experience itself, the Meeting in its fourth phase is centering down into a single unit, from which all irrelevant signals, thoughts, impulses, are dying away, displaced or transformed by the over-reaching power that reflects God's Spirit among the worshippers. This may happen entirely through the silence, or words may break forth, or they may have commenced in an earlier phase and served to usher in this one. Their note is sure, fresh, revealing something uniquely for the occasion; without fail they are sensitive to the inner condition of the small gathered group; and now often other voices follow, no longer so much embroidering a theme as swelling the one uprush of praise,

---

12 *John* 14.6, 14.9.
13 *Conference of European Friends*, Birmingham 1957, Report, p. 63.

the one blaze of understanding. Or a single voice may speak for all; or the Meeting, if the unity is profound, may lift its face in loving silence. This is the moment—of a few minute's duration, or longer, or only of a minute, but timeless—that heals individual hearts in a way that a whole year's striving may fail to do, that pulls in those still searching for their answers, and signals the irreducible fellowship of all men through the grace of God. Known, it can never again be doubted—"All Friends mind that which is Eternal which gathers your Hearts together up to the Lord and lets you see that ye are written in one another's Heart." [14]

It is the Pentecostal moment which early Quakers never tired of recording. "While waiting upon the Lord in silence . . . we received often the pouring down of the Spirit . . . and our hearts were made glad, and our tongues loosed, and our mouths opened . . . and the glory of the Father was revealed ",[15] and in the earliest records of a small Cumberland meeting, that also summarises the whole exercise . . . "And soe friends were settled upon Christ there Rock and foundation, were Diligent in Comeing to Meetings first day and week day, and an Exercisse and travill Entred the hearts of many for the more Enjoyment and Jnward feeling of the love of god we were often directed to wait for, that soe our hearts might be prpared to worship him in the spirit and in the truth, that an ofring of his own prpareing we all might know, which he would Except of; and as frds thus were deligent in the Jnward Exercise of true Silence, the lord was pleased in his own time to fill the hearts of many as with new wine, Jnsoemuch that sevrall friends Could not Contain, but speak forth a few words, that there spirits might be Eased. Great wass the tendrness and brokeness of heart in those days, for the Lord wass wittnessed to be near att hand by his Liveing

14 *Epistle* 24 (1653).
15 Edward Burrough's prefix to Fox's *The Great Mistery of the Great Whore Unfolded, etc.*

prsence from whence Refreshment Comes." [16]

There is yet another moment, the fifth phase, that occasionally comes towards the close of a Meeting, where Friends are practised and used to each other and diligent in attendance: a moment of total stillness of the spirit of the Meeting as a whole: the moment symbolically enacted at the climax of the Catholic Mass: among Friends recognised as the goal of their worship, to be enjoyed for itself though never sought after, a moment almost of group samadhi, of the displacement of all by God's Being, and Becoming. " God is himself blessed in the soul ",[17] wrote Meister Eckhart. " You are there ", the Zen master says, but equally can describe no further. " Be still, and know that I am God ".[18] This is the ultimate communion.

Having said this much about Quaker worship one must again stress that it is a method, a technique, for inducing the Light of God to flood into the conscious mind, a therapy and an occasion for praise, and sometimes, through grace, for the practice of His Presence; and that as with all methods it is open to failure for a hundred and one reasons. Meetings often stick halfway, sometimes never get going at all. There is no recital of creed, no outward sacrament, to sustain the Quaker on his way: he relies only on the silent pressure of the group feeling towards the Light, and upon occasion this fails. It requires the commitment of many years, and preferably of a familiar group (which explains why Friends beg of each other to be constant in attending Meetings) to see through such occasions to the experience that still abundantly awaits.

In any case, an individual simply through attending meetings and applying himself to the group exercise, lays himself open to the experience that palpably comes some-

---

[16] First Publishers of Truth (ed. N. Penney, 1907), p. 74.
[17] C. G. Jung, Psychological Types (trans. H. G. Baynes, 1923), p. 305. Also Meister Eckhart (colln. F. Pfeiffer, trans. C. de B. Evans, 1924), p. 271, has " God himself is happy in the soul ". Original German reads " Gott ist selber selig in der Seele ".
[18] Psalms 46.10.

times and all the time is more subtly working on his personality, conditioning him towards people and life: in essence this is the definition of a Quaker, the redeeming thread through otherwise rather odd pages of Quaker history.

There is a further point that should be clear. Few Quakers have private raptures or visions of a high mystical order; as Evelyn Underhill noted, there are no great Quaker contemplatives. But this follows from the group approach; any specially gifted individual surrenders himself to the group as a whole, helping it through the intermediate phases, then taking back from it his share of the deeper experience vouchsafed to all. The limit is the corporate vision.

The meeting for worship ends, with a word of thanksgiving or in silent prayer. There is a formal handshake between two of the Elders, an involuntary smile of relaxation, and notices of other meetings or concerns or social affairs are read out. The act of worship will have lasted an hour, about the limit an average group nowadays finds possible for concentration, though early Quaker meetings continued for hours at a stretch. " In such a meeting ", one recorded, " where the presence and power of God is felt, there will be an unwillingness to part asunder, being ready to say in yourselves, it is good to be here: and this is the end of all words and writings—to bring people to the eternal living Word." [19]

Always, after meetings, there is increased sensitivity, to each other, to further horizons within, to the oneness of all creation; the Light is seen to be available to all men, defining their unique equality—" doth enlighten every one that comes into the world ", as Fox unceasingly preached to the fury of those who had reserved it for a spiritual (and socio-political) Elect. " Liars, drunkards, whoremongers ", he cried, in a general warning to the people of Ulverston,

19 *Letters of Early Friends*, p. 366.

" and thieves and who follow filthy pleasures, you have all this measure in you . . . and this light will teach thee, if thou lovest it, it will teach thee holiness and righteousness, without which none shall see God; but hating this light, it is your condemnation. . . ." [20]

The continuing task is to stay tender to the Light, if it is faint to seek its increase; and to call it forth in other people, of all conditions, in the worst circumstances, knowing that to be possible. This is the basis of Quaker testimonies and Quaker work throughout the world, the corollary to the experience of Meeting for Worship. There is " that of God " in every man, the one redeeming power.

(d) Meetings in Different Epochs

The changes in Quaker meetings from one century to the next, the problems that arose and had to be solved so that the method could still function effectively, were caused by the wider changes taking place within English and American society and the degree of Quaker involvement in that. It is enough for the moment to trace the process as it impinged on the time of worship.

The Early Friends, the first Publishers of Truth as they called themselves, whom we date in England from 1652, never thought of themselves as a sect, a separate church or Society, but as an ever-increasing number of voices from among the people at large, proclaiming the good news of the Light of Christ within every man's make-up, to be sought there, not in creeds or sermons or visibly enacted sacraments. They commandeered the market places, raided what they termed the steeple houses to interrupt the services, held vast gatherings in fields: they were prophets, religious agitators, men and women who spoke and acted as if the world they knew and that of Galilee had merged. The Authorised Translation of the Bible, open to all after 1611, sang from their lips with free intermingling of Old

[20] Journal, p. 143.

and New Testament phrases as if the words were issuing for the first time, molten from a creative experience. They themselves, so complete was this possession, became the Apostles and the Hebrew prophets, not only exhorting in like manner but reproducing the same signs, minor miracles, and other vagaries of behaviour. It was testimony to the single direct and timeless presence of God.

In this fervent approach they reflected their day, which was one gone mad with revelation. The process of taking into the mind all the phenomena of faith hitherto externalised carried the Reformation man constantly to the edge of hysteria; all debated, tried to ease the strain; almost any gathering of English citizenry could run to a pitch one associates more with a Haitian voudoun possessed by " the loa ". These were revolutionary, psychic times, with the millenium around the corner.

Thus when the Quakers came preaching the logical extreme of inwardness, the stress already felt was intensified, and their audience either beat them black or blue or quaked over the dividing line. "Ah! the seizing of souls, and prickings at heart which attended that season: some fell on the ground, others crying out under the sense of opening their states, which indeed gave experimental knowledge of what is recorded (Acts 11.37)".[21]

Of William Dewsbury, one of the pioneer Quakers, it was written . . . " His Testimony was Peirceing and very powerfull, so as the Earth Shoke before him, The Mountains did melt at the power of the Lord, which exceedingly, in a Wonderfull manner, broke forth in these Dayes in our holy Assemblies, to the Renting of many hearts, & bringing Divers to Witness the same state, Measureably, as the Prophet or servant of the Lord did in Antient times, whose Lipps Quivered & Belly shook, that he might rest in the day of trouble. Oh! It was a Glorious Day . . . Many faces did gather Paleness, and the Stout hearted were made to

21 *The Memory of the Righteous Revived*, 1689.

Bow, and strong Oakes to bend before the Lord." [22]

More clinically, it is recorded of one convert that he "drove needles through his thumbs and lay as if dead for three quarters of an hour in public".[23] In some places rumour was enough to bring people over to Quakerism;[24] certainly the appearance of Fox was enough, with his formidable presence and glowing words. As his *Journal* everywhere afterwards comments . . . "the power of the Lord was over all". The ground, in fact, was well prepared for him.

These however, were public meetings, for "threshing among the world", to which came fashionable sightseers, angry divines, psychotics, spies, suppressed revolutionaries, as well as the average questioning highly wound up man of the day; it was from these gatherings that recruits were drawn for the "retired" meetings, or to form such meetings, to practise Quaker worship. Edward Burrough, reporting on the London campaign, writes . . . "We have thus ordered it since we came, we get Friends on the First days to meet together in several places out of the rude multitude, and we two go to the great meeting place which will hold a thousand people, which is always nearly filled, to thresh among the world; and we stay till twelve or one o'clock, and then pass away, the one to one place and the other to another place, where Friends are met in private; and stay till four or five o'clock." [25]

For a time these private meetings also were affected by the excitement without, brought in by newcomers who retelling their conversion experience, as was much their wont, induced in themselves and others of the company the attendant visible symptoms. In those early days it didn't take much to set the Meeting quaking, a quick means of plunging it into the realm of interior signals, among which

[22] *First Publishers of Truth*, p. 294.
[23] B. Bax, *Rise and Fall of the Anabaptists*, p. 374.
[24] *First Publishers of Truth*, p. 6.
[25] *Letter of Early Friends*, p. 27.

the more seasoned Friends would try to indicate the Light,
yet liable also to precipitate some highly dubious material,
as among Ranters. It was also this early lack of a sufficiently practised method that caused the more volatile
Meetings to split off from the emerging body of the Society
in a series of minor defections. The fault there naturally
was on both sides.

Yet, gradually, the method was shaping, the patient
application of the mind through silence and relevant
speech towards the unifying Light of God. Counsel was
given by all leading Friends: for instance, Edward Burrough in the year of the report quoted above writes . . .
"Dear Friends . . . all in silence wait, be swift to hear,
slow to speak, and all wait upon the Light in diligence . . .
take heed of forward wills in speaking, lest your minds be
drawn out from the movings of the Pure within." [26] And
Fox . . . "Concerning the silent meetings, the intent of all
speaking is to bring unto the life and to walk in and to
possess the same, and to live in and to enjoy it, and to feel
God's presence, and that is in the silence (not in the
wandring, whirling, tempestuous part of man or
woman) . . ." [27] Though soon a caution was needed about
silence—"For as our worship consisteth not in words, so
neither in silence, as silence; but it an holy dependence of
the mind upon God: from which dependence silence
necessarily follows in the first place, until words can be
brought forth, which are from God's Spirit." [28]

This caution, from another pen, had already become a
warning plea. . . "I beseech you in the bowels of tender
love, take heed of sluggishness, or carelessness or deadness
of spirit in your meetings . . ." [29] The pendulum had
swung over. The Meetings were starting to dry up.

[26] Works, p. 71.
[27] Gospel Truth Demonstrated, p. 103.
[28] R. Barclay, Apology. Prop. 11, Sect. ix.
[29] Isaac Pennington, Letter from Reading Gaol to "Friends in Truth in
Chalfont and thereabouts," 1671.

This was to be the characteristic of the next epoch, of the eighteenth century. Partly it was the aftermath of persecution, of disillusion with a world that would not listen, yet, going its way, now left them to themselves. The new generation of Quakers was inevitably less highly-charged than their pioneering fathers, their instinct was to pause and consolidate. Yet the principle factor reinforcing this trend, setting its seal on meeting for worship, was the growing respectability of Friends, through success in trade and rise in social status. Bourgeois rectitude was taking over: what was good for business was good for religion. The evolution of group control, that the early Quakers had reached experimentally but simply to strengthen their spiritual technique, and with continuing care for the individual voice, became the instrument of a conservative hierarchy pressing to bring all into line. Elders were instituted to keep an eye on Ministers (i.e. the Public Friends who preached Quakerism to the world at large, as well as being rather inclined to do more than their share in retired meetings), and Ministers were only named as such if they measured up to the new style, which was ponderous, rhapsodical, and keyed to self-abasement. The mind more and more was to be left untilled—except by precepts for a sober disciplined and useful tradesman's life; it was to take no active meditative rôle in the preparation for insight, but to be held utterly empty and humbled, in the silence now like a straitjacket round it, till the remote father figure of a God cast His Light down. Reinforcing this approach was the reading of the Continental Quietists, Molinos, Madame Guyon, Fénelon; also a tendency to swing back, especially among those who had been converts in youth from Baptists or Presbyterian churches, to the main stream of Puritan theology. Each factor reinforced the others to inhibit the open questing mind and the confidence reception of signals. The inner contact ceased to be made; meetings went dry.

The seating arrangements further emphasised these stultifying factors. Gone were the intimate circles of Friends
used to meeting in each other's houses, or in hired rooms
but with no prior disposition of places; now the meeting
house (and by 1700 there were 600 of them) provided a
raised gallery for the Elders and the nominated Ministers,
and facing that a set of benches for the other members and
attenders, separated, after 1678, into men on the one side
and women on the other. When from on high the Ministers
spoke, it was either to reveal their inward anguish, or to
castigate the world and the flesh (alas, tightening the screw
on their own minds further), or to extol silence. Some
meetings for years on end were held in unbroken silence.
The average member, other than Ministers (increasingly
the party men, so to speak) could not easily offer words.
He was constrained to a lonely travail—brilliantly reward-
ing in a few cases as with Job Scott, Sarah Grubb, or John
Woolman, for whom this added stress was the means to an
almost saintly attainment (and the slower development of
American Quakerism was also an influence on Woolman
and Scott); for the average person it was a time of decay,
because he was being famished of the free-flowing equally-
shared out-reaching activity of the group—the essence of
the Quaker method. The Society maintained its front,
indeed was constantly refurbishing it with new rules and
prohibitions, but was dying within.

" Goat's was dis . . . Goat's was long and dis " . . .[30] the
Gurney daughters complained in their diaries. The 1786
meeting in Goat's Lane, Norwich, typified the strangulation
being suffered by the Quaker method. The young people
found it disgusting. Their spiritual life was dammed back.

Change was inevitable, and in fact reflected a similar low
ebb and fresh impulse in the wider surrounding Protestant
world. The call of Wesley had shaken England; people
were again rolling on the ground, crying out they were

30 R. M. Jones, *The Later Periods of Quakerism*, London, 1921, p. 351.

saved through Jesus. Whatever the other social implications, this offered needed psychic release, like rain after drought. Quakerism was in turn affected.

At first the changed emphasis was preached by a few Friends who, having sounded in themselves the depths of Quietism, had conquered its inhibitions through renewed consciousness of Jesus as the Saviour who could raise them to the Light. This effected for them the essential break-through. They had caught the current impulse from Wesley, made it their own, and they now transmitted it, opening a new floodgate of the spirit to many a parched young Quaker. It was William Savery who awakened the soul of Elizabeth Gurney (later Fry) when his ministry brought him to Goat's Lane.

Other of like temper, thunderbolts striking into the timidity of meetings, were Thomas Shillitoe, David Sands, Rebecca Jones, Mary Dudley, and, the most striking of all, the aristocratic Stephen Grellet. "My mind", he wrote, "dwelt much on the nature of the hope of redemption through Jesus Christ. I felt the efficacy of that grace by which we were saved, through faith in Christ and His atoning blood, shed for us on Calvary's Mount." [31]

Such a message, passionately delivered, embellished with demonic elements in the portrayal of sin and outer darkness, leading up to the all-saving experience, resolved many an inward travail and shook meetings, that had almost ground to a halt, into a sudden deeper unity. It disrupted formal habits and started a useful buzz of questions, that led in particular cases to effective comprehension of the suffering of others—of slaves, lunatics, prisoners, the poor; and for individuals of a highly devotional tendency it offered the key to spiritual progress. This first evangelism was necessary medicine.

Unfortunately it became a dogma, a support for socially conservative tendencies. It increasingly stressed that per-

[31] *Memoirs*, Vol. 1, p. 47.

sonal salvation lay through faith in Christ's having purchased this once and for all on Calvary, through faith in
Scripture as the final imprint of God's revelation, through
acceptance that we can do nothing by ourselves but are,
until we have acknowledged the Cross, hopelessly de-
praved: and this dogma, the embodiment of all that was
smug and socially static and glib in the middle class
England of the day, was increasingly put forward as
Quakerism, a muzzle more menacing even than the previous century's inhibitory quietism.

Like the other it directed people's energies away from
the work they should be doing themselves in time of worship, as a group, creatively; it was more suited to kirk or
synod—it was indeed the old Puritan thesis designed for
an authoritarian church; it tried to clamp a single attitude
onto a method that by its nature was many-channelled,
exploratory, open. It led responsible Quaker worship down
yet one more side path, this time not only of a singular
emphasis but of outright travesty.

In England as a trend it was just contained till the pendulum started to swing back (and again from the play of
wider social forces: cultural, economic, political), but in
America it divided the Society. That development is
examined later, with its peculiar ramifications; for now
one can note that while one group, the Hicksites, clung in
the main to the Quaker experience, the other fell away
more and more into Evangelicalism. The further to the
west Friends went, the further those evangelically-inclined
carried their enthusiasms, till their meetings turned into
church services, with pastors and hymn singing and respon-
ses, and a church form of marriage ceremony, and, backing
all, a Presbyterian theology. They denied the experience
of Inward Light, seeing man as too sinful to attempt it;
salvation came through accepting the letter of the Bible,
as firmly as it had done for Calvin and Knox. They
dropped the name " Society of Friends ", preferring

" Friends' Church ". They wanted to be indistinguishable from the other surrounding American churches.

But this and much else, once the first straying step had been taken, in that particular historical context, was the inevitable outcome. To understand how far they went, compare this 1893 report with anything written by early Friends concerning the method of Quaker worship . . . " Revivals must have leaders, and evangelists were placed in charge; singing is indispensable to such a work, and meeting houses soon rang with songs of praise; the feeling of the people must be tested, and they were called to respond by rising or kneeling; the penitent form and inquiry room became a necessity, and they were brought into service. . . ." [32] This is the tenor of Billy Graham's approach.

At last in America also, after one of these Quaker pastors tried to introduce baptism, and so shocked Friends in Philadelphia, the high priests of American Quakerism, the pendulum began, but ever so slowly, to swing back towards centre. This has been its course since then.

In the present century the residual force of these exaggerated swings of the pendulum has been gradually absorbed, set in historical perspective, so that the original pattern could emerge again to be tried afresh in to-day's world. Education, social reform, war, the forces of industrial society, the scientific study of man, have all shaped the contemporary approach: bringing a renewed fellowship in meetings, a sense of the joining of equals (equally open to the signals of truth, equally dependent on one another—so that, for instance, nominated Ministers have been discontinued, and men and women sit again together) such as marked the first Quakers. One may be of an Evangelican turn, another blandly mystical, a third in a state of all-questioning doubt: the willingness now is to agree that these differences are related to individual make-up,

[32] *Friends' Review*, Vol. xlvii, p. 261.

may be vital to one though not his neighbour, and are transcended by the unifying experience of any meeting that can " settle down ". This approach is experimental, open to all, spiritually without limit: a window that gives onto Eternity.

If this were better understood by those in this age who are uncommitted, if Quaker statements of faith could search for language as all-inclusive as the method of worship itself, so that no man, whatever the religion his cultural background has imprinted on him, whoever be his avatar, need think himself excluded, then the validity of this group experience—demanding no more than the average mystical component in any one, and application, and patience through failures—might be known to many thousands more people. This, not only for its own sake, but through the attitudes it gives rise to in the increasingly urgent problems of the world, would be a profitable human step.

(e) Antecedents of Quaker Practice

George Fox records how in his early years he bearded a priest in a steeple house where an allowed disputation was in progress, a wrangling among the " professors ", as he called them, from the various Puritan sects . . . " I was rapt up ", he says, " as in a rapture, in the Lord's power; and I stepped up in a place and asked the priest, ' Dost thou call this place a church? Or dost thou call this mixed multitude a church?' But he did not answer me neither, but asked me what a church was. I told him the Church was the pillar and ground of Truth, made up of living stones, living members, a spiritual household which Christ was the head of, but he was not the head of a mixed multitude, or of an old house made up of lime, stones, and wood." [33]

This became his theme: [34] to bring people " off the

33 *Journal*, p. 24.
34 *Journal*, pp. 107, 114.

temples made with hands that they themselves might know they were the temples of God ", to show them " that God was come to teach his people by his spirit and to bring them off all their old ways, religions, churches, and worship, for all their religions, and worship, and ways were but talking of other men's words, for they were out of the life and spirit that they were in that gave them forth." He denounced " the state of apostasy that has been since the apostles' days " [35] and he and other early Friends spoke as if after centuries of darkness theirs were the first voices to be raised for the direct inward experience.

True, at that stage of the Reformation in England theirs was the most effective, uncompromising voice (soon gathering in the floating vote, so to speak, already inclined this way) that challenged institutional religion with its panoply of priest and Book. Down the Protestant scale from Episcopalian to Quaker, through intermediate links of Presbyterian, Congregationalist, and Baptist, the Quaker alone pleaded for the direct inspiration of the Holy Spirit as sufficient for man, his guide to interpretation of Scripture and for daily conduct, adding that if the inspiration was genuine it would necessarily show him good from evil and keep him in unity with other good souls. The witness, with so many Ranters about, was soon defined as a corporate one.

Even so, to the average Puritan, this was to stand one's relationship to Scripture on its head. " We must not try the Scriptures by our most spiritual apprehensions, but our apprehensions by the Scriptures ",[36] wrote Baxter from the heart of the new Puritan Establishment. " The Holy Spirit, by immediate inspiration, revealed unto the apostles the doctrine of Christ, and caused them infallibly to indite the Scriptures. But this is not that way of ordinary illumination now." [37]

[35] *Journal*, p. 109.
[36] *Works*, Vol. V, p. 559.
[37] *Works*, Vol. II, p. 104.

George Fox said it was. The same Spirit was at work in all, from the first man till the end of the world, and must be sought by each in turn ... " What had any to do with the Scriptures, but as they came to the Spirit that gave them forth? You will say, Christ saith this, and the apostles say this, but what canst thou say?" [38] His colleagues took up the same theme, for instance Isaac Pennington ... " We can truly say concerning the Scriptures that now we believe, not so much because of the relation of things concerning Christ which we have found in them, but because we have seen and received the thing which the Scriptures speak of." [39] Logically, this Quaker approach dispensed with all sacraments and ordained ministry: the church was a fellowship of believers stripped for the immediate prophetic experience. Each had his mite to contribute.

As they claimed, this was a return to the Pentecostal setting, and before that to the way of the Hebrew prophets, who had inveighed against kings and priests for tying the spiritual life of man to systems designed to uphold their own power—one might add, a conflict as old as society. They were making this same protest again, illustrating, by word and practice, what the purified life should be, in which they fondly hoped the whole of Christendom, the whole world, would shortly join. As it happened (and we can now add, inevitably) they formed part of a long line, a repeated knocking of the head against the wall of institutional religion by similar protesters and re-awakeners, from the days and the message itself of Jesus (to limit it to Christendom) till their own day.

These movements had gone by various names according to time and place—Montanists in second century Asia Minor, Donatists in fourth century North Africa, Paulicians in seventh century Armenia, Bogomils in tenth century Bulgaria, a proliferation of medieval sects such as the

[38] *Journal* (ed. 1901), Vol II, p. 512.
[39] *Works,* 1761, Vol. II, p. 6.

Waldenses, Albigenses, Catharists, Beghards, Lollards, Hussites, Taborites—all of which had challenged the Catholic Church, its priests and sacraments, its imported pagan philosophies and fetishes, its growing rôle in secular government with the perquisites of power, as unfit channels of the spiritual life; and had asserted the validity of fresh revelations directly open to those who would live in apostolic simplicity.

In reply the Inquisition had been instituted—in the first place to crush the Albigenses—for the entire feudal order was questioned by the mere breath of such heresies. Luther himself had started by repeating them, basing his protest on direct illumination, but then had retreated, frightened by the wider social implications; so that the residues of the older movements, now dubbed Anabaptist (a useful smear word, like Communist, for all awkward threads of revolt), had continued in opposition to both Catholic and Protestant Establishments. New Presbyter was but old Priest writ large. In fact, the attitude of Baxter to Fox had been determined a hundred years before, in the denial by Luther of the Prophets of Zwickau: the one side making peace with princes and using the Bible to bolster its authority, the other standing by the pure inward experience, whatever the resultant challenge to society.

Of course, the obvious dangers of this method, which later were to tease Quakers and had already, to quote the worst instance, been the undoing of the Paulicians, were all too apparent among Anabaptists. Some were afflicted with megalomania, some with a simple lust to destroy, others turned the instability of the times into weird private forms of excess: one can't altogether blame Luther, and one can remember George Fox turning on Ranters (who stemmed from this manic type of Anabaptist) with remarks such as " Repent, thou beast ".[40] The Messianic rule at Munster,

[40] *Journal,* p. 81.

the apogee of militant Anabaptism, was an awful warning
against self-styled Saints.

But this was only the extreme facet, exacerbated by the
prevailing violence into which the social struggle had
turned; other sides of Anabaptism were primarily engaged
in the inward search, pacific, ethical, content to prophesy
and leave the world to draw its conclusions. The teaching
of Hans Denck, in particular, directed men to their Inward
Light, which he saw as available to all human beings,
enabling them to find God.

Following him came the Mennonites and Collegiants of
Amsterdam, who held meetings for worship with silence
as their basis, gave equal right to men and women to
minister, and led outward lives of simplicity and neighbourly affection. This was a century before the rise of
Quakers.

Indeed, it was firstly the effects of this practice, mixed
with humanist speculation, mixed a little with the temper
of Calvanism, that worked on Puritan refugees from Queen
Elizabeth's England, and led on their return home to the
formation of Baptist and Independent congregations. Then,
with individual Mennonites, Collegiants, kindred Familists
and Boehmists, Ranters, and Seekers hugging the same
trail, to make London a hotbed of sectaries like Amsterdam,
to be mixed finally with the native strain deriving from
the Lollards, there began the cross-fertilisation of idea with
idea, of hope with despair, of dogma with doubt that prepared the ground first here, then there, for the reintegrating
message of Fox.

His first followers came from Baptists, then his first big
congregation from the Seekers—those who, in Penn's
words, " wandered up and down, as sheep without a shepherd, and as doves without their mates, seeking their
beloved, but could not find Him . . .(and) sometimes met
together, not formally to pray or preach . . . but waited
together in silence, and as anything rose in any one of

their minds, that they thought savoured of a Divine spring, so they sometimes spoke." [41]

These men and women were seeking an inspired reaffirmation of the quest of God within, of a Mediator who was a living presence and not just One who had died at Jerusalem; and Fox gave it to them, and in turn took over the ready-made group and its habits.

Other individuals and congregations joined, former Ranters and Familists and Independents, men from all the different sects: and who heard through him the call to the purely inward experience. They were all acting within their traditions. Quakers came from all these sources, with their roots, if somewhat intertwined, in a single age-old channel.

Fox himself, overwhelmed by his call and the huge task needing to be done, did not look for antecedents short of the Apostles; between, there had been centuries of apostasy. Yet in reality he was in the line of prophets, of practical mystics, and teachers such as had arisen in each generation, and continued afterwards to arise.

Though few could express themselves as he could, or found the stage so expectantly set. Close to the start of his *Journal* he records . . . "In the year 1648, as I was sitting in a Friend's house in Nottinghamshire (for by this time the power of God had opened the hearts of some to receive the word of life and reconciliation), I saw there was a great crack to go throughout the earth, and a great smoke to go as the crack went; and that after the crack there should be a great shaking. This was the earth in people's hearts, which was to be shaken before the Seed of God was raised out of the earth. And it was so; for the Lord's power began to shake them, and great meetings we began to have, and a mighty power and work of God there was amongst people, to the astonishment of both people and priests." [42]

[41] *Journal* (ed. 1891), p. xxv.
[42] *Journal*, p. 22.

Fox came at the right moment, was called into being by it. He was the prophet to his day. Seekers everywhere became Finders. The Quakers got off to a gallop.

CHAPTER II

SOCIAL BEHAVIOUR

(a) The Basis of Procedure

QUAKER worship, though an inward exercise, does not point to withdrawal from the world; it is group-centred, life-affirming, built on the interdependence of men for bringing into consciousness a heightened awareness of God's Spirit. Through this practice the heart is made tender to the equal value of all men's lives, to the need above all else, however difficult or new the situation, to keep way open between them for the spirit, or Inner Light, in each to seek and ultimately to find unity. This is the basis of Quakerly action.

There may be some reverse effect: in Meeting the sudden apprehension by a worshipper of his concern for a piece of social work or new social attitude, and decision concerning it, and later the actual doing of it, may speed his passage to the Light, and lift the entire Meeting with him; but this as a specific aid to contemplation is not sought by Friends. Their customary face is towards the world: there equally should God's Spirit be known. Their experience of Meeting sends them in search of it.

The first step naturally is one of procedure. Diversity and continuity of work require some sort of organisation, as do the taking and transmitting of decisions, view-points, gifts: those taking part need caring for. A Society comes into being.

To-day for the most part the Society of Friends keeps organisation to a minimum, as flexible and personal as it can—some of its members say, too much so; but this follows from its ever present need to be open to fresh insight, and from reaction to the authoritarianism that very nearly entombed it during its long middle period, and from consequent disinclination to pull any sort of strings together too tightly. It would rather be vague and dilatory than rigid. Even so, when pressed, it can be highly efficient; and at all times it is sensitive to the cry of the least member in the most remote group if his voice begins to carry weight with his fellows. By careful stages the whole Society comes to share his particular concern—a message is sent to the press or to Parliament, an individual or a team are fitted out to go wherever their service is required; or some new thought touching daily life is passed to all constituent meetings for study and response through local action.

This comes about in the following way. Each meeting for worship gathers monthly to consider its local activities and finance and other congregational matters in what is called Preparative Meeting: where at the same time its prime job is to prepare reports and subjects for discussion for the district Monthly Meeting, which is the real executive unit for these several local meetings, binding them in temporal affairs into a viable balanced body, and to which their members initially belong. Here for instance the records of births, deaths, and marriages are kept, applications for membership are considered, the allowing of new meetings for worship or the closing of moribund ones is decided, Elders (to care for the right holding of worship) and Overseers (to help with any personal problems, to visit families or the sick) are appointed for each congregation, and generally all church business and overall finance of the district is ordered. This is the ground floor of the Society, supporting the whole structure, the widest forum for the exercise of old and new ideas and of people willing to see them through.

Any idea adopted but concerning only the one district would be acted on from here; but should it concern the Society as a whole it would go forward to Quarterly Meeting, a larger gathering of several districts meeting for the sifting of viewpoints and co-ordination of Quaker work over a wider area, and from there, reviewed, rephrased or strengthened, to Yearly Meeting when in session (the representative gathering to-day for a country or section of a continent), or to the standing executive committee of Yearly Meeting, in England called the Meeting for Sufferings, which in turn has several subsidiary committees (for Peace, Friends' Service, Penal Reform, Race Relations, and so forth) to assist it. This is the focal point of the Society in touch with other Quaker groups the world over, and with the chief civil powers in its country, and through its own composition with its several units at district level. It can speak for the Society to the world, see that Quaker work goes forward, and advise the membership of new steps to be considered.

How is such responsibility shared? Any member of a Monthly Meeting can to-day take part, and is urged to do so, firstly in his local Preparative Meeting, then in his Monthly Meeting, then in the related Quarterly Meeting, and finally in the sessions of his Yearly Meeting; though, for the sake of those unable to attend, representatives are appointed, chosen by each group together for the next stage ahead; so that all concerns are sure to be voiced and all reports and requests passed back.

Meeting for Sufferings itself is composed of nominees from Quarterly Meetings together with any Elders from any Monthly Meeting able to attend; and the several central standing committees are also composed for the most part of Quarterly Meeting nominees, so that at any given moment (to take England) about one member in twenty of the total Quaker membership (twenty-two thousand in 1958) is sharing in central committee work. This, added to the work in districts, gives the Society of Friends a unity and resilience of approach towards both its own concerns and those brought to it from outside.

" The least member in the church hath an office, and is

serviceable; and all members have need one of another." [1]
" Do you individually take your right share in the attendance and service of these meetings so that the burden may
not rest upon a few?" [2] The emphasis here is still on the
group, and not only to ease the burden of the Society's
undertakings, but in order to find in this sphere also the
governing truth for each situation, open, as experienced
during worship, to the truly gathered assembly.

This necessarily begins in the taking of decisions. The
Quaker business meeting does not proceed by argument
leading to vote or veto. Those who wish speak their
mind on the subject under discussion, often with silent
pauses between; a recording clerk listens and notes any
unifying thread that may emerge; if it doesn't emerge he
may ask for further silence, or call on someone who has
not yet spoken; a minority view is not over-ridden or too
directly criticised, but accepted as an aspect of truth that
must be incorporated into the final decision, unless both it
and the views of the majority are transcended in the course
of discussion.

This in fact most often happens. The initial alignment
of individuals (far from crystallising into rigidity, or exag-
geration, each trying to score his point) is gradually shaken
free of elements not helpful to the developing central viewpoint, which finally may be different from anything envisaged at the start—sometimes, through the insight of a
single person who clarifies both the issue and the web of
feeling round it. This search for the " sense of the meeting ", as it is called, closely resembles the creative process
at work within an artist; as with him Friends look for the
underlying truth that simplifies and gives release, as though
each had come to the meeting to discover better who he
was and what his relation to life should be. This too is
a therapy, a useful preparation for engagement in a wider
sphere.

[1] George Fox, *Epistle* 264 (1669).
[2] *London Yearly Meeting Advices and Queries*, 1928.

Finally, the clerk reads out a minute that he feels reflects the degree of unity reached; a word here or there may be changed, and the minute accepted. It may not finally go as far as some present may have wished, but it involves no illusionary sense of progress; all will act on it this far, and orderly growth from here is possible.

Early Friends appear to have felt their way towards this method, leading out of their religious communion. Edward Burrough, by 1662, is advising London Quakers . . . " to proceed . . . not in the way of the world, as a worldly assembly of men, by hot contests . . . not deciding affairs by the greater vote . . . but in the wisdom, love and fellowship of God . . . by hearing and determining every matter coming before you, in love, coolness, gentleness, and dear unity. . . ." [3] The appeal is not just to reason, or to the set authority of leaders, but to the quest for right feeling among a group of equals.

This, however, has not always been so in the internal history of the Society. The inspired method had to follow a somewhat chequered course.

For a time it was fairly generally upheld. The first leaders were gentle and loving, were either the travelling evangelists like Fox and Dewsbury and Naylor, or the natural counsellors, the gurus (" one of two Friends who are most grown in the power and life, in the pure discerning in the Truth ")[4] within each local congregation, as formerly there had been among Seekers and Mennonites, and within the early Christian Church. To them, in 1653, William Dewsbury advised . . . " Be examples to the flock, and see that order be kept in the church . . . and you are to have a general meeting with other Friends near you, once in two or three weeks, as the Lord orders and makes way." [5]

These general meetings later became the regular Monthly

[3] *Letters of Early Friends*, p. 305.
[4] *Swarthmore MSS*, Vol. 3, (19).
[5] *Swarthmore MSS*, Vol. 3 (19). Also Smith's *Life of Dewsbury*, 1836, p. 63.

and Quarterly Meetings leading up to a Yearly Meeting, but not at first systematically, nor was there any uniform discipline.[6] It was through need to provide for family distress, from persecution or loss of livelihood or the bread-winner being away preaching, and to arrange marriages without priests and the settling of debts and disputes without lawyers, and to tackle backsliders and evolve a steady group witness—especially after the fall of Naylor—that the first church rules were put forth, in Yorkshire in 1656, but still most tentatively by the same modest self-effacing leaders.

The most stringent clause reads . . . " That if any person draw back from meetings and walk disorderly, some go to speak to such as draw back; to exhort and admonish such with a tender, meek spirit, whom they find negligent or disorderly. And if any, after admonition, do persist in the thing not good, let them again be admonished and reproved before two or three witnesses; that by the mouth of two or three witnesses, every thing may be established. And if still they persevere in them, then let the thing be declared to the church: and when the church hath reproved them for their disorderly walking, and admonished them in the tender and meek spirit, and they do not reform, then let their names and the causes, and such as can justly testify the truth therein, and their answers, be sent in writing to some whom the Lord hath raised up in the power of his Spirit to be fathers, His children to gather in the light,— that the thing may be known to the body; and with the consent of the whole body, the thing may be determined in the light."

And a postscript to this epistle reads . . . " Dearly beloved Friends, these things we do not lay upon you as a rule or form to walk by; but that all, with a measure of the light, which is pure and holy, may be guided: and so in the light walking and abiding, these things may be fulfilled

---

[6] *Letters of Early Friends*, p. 289.

in the Spirit, not in the letter; for the letter killeth, but the Spirit giveth life." [7]

These mild wise injunctions laid the onus on the individual's responsiveness to the insight of the group, and bespoke much patience with those who erred, and faith in the prevailing power of God's Spirit. Church unity would be strengthened as each grew towards the Light; the aim of leaders and of discipline was to assist gently in that development.

Ten years later, however, when persecution had broken the first spirited leadership, and contact between the scattered and battered congregations seemed too tenuous to maintain the Society's overall witness (though, to judge by the way they withstood persecution their high degree of individual freedom had been healthy enough), a centralising, authoritarian trend appeared. Fox's attitude was equivocal, for he prized the courage of the small congregations and he exhorted them now to ensure the proper share of each member in church government: yet, as he set about establishing a regular linkage of Monthly and Quarterly Meetings, he supported the increasing use of these as vehicles of a corporate discipline dictated by an élite of ministers and other weighty Friends in London.

The very tone of the 1666 Epistle sent out from Ministers in London to all meetings foretells this trend . . . " If any difference arise in the church, or amongst them that profess to be members thereof, we do declare and testify, that the church, with the Spirit of the Lord Jesus Christ, have power, without the assent of such as dissent from their doctrines and practices, to hear and determine the same . . . that if judgment so given be risen against and denied by the party condemned, then he or she, or such as so far partake of their sin as to countenance and encourage them

[7] *Letters of Early Friends*, pp. 277–8. Also consult Pennington's *True Church Government*, 1660.

therein, ought to be rejected, as having erred from Truth. . . ." [8]

The difference between this and the earlier epistle is clear. By the " church ", moreover, is increasingly meant the " elders ", as formal successors to the first counsellors, all now to be briefed from London. Quaker discipline was hardening under the stress of persecution, and as a new class of leader arose; a central caucus began to emphasise organisation and uniformity (for internal relief and legal defence, the collection of funds and information, no doubt, a very useful emphasis) to suit its own interpretation of Quaker truth and conduct. All meetings and all members were gradually pulled into line or disowned. A very great number, from now on, were disowned.

The next century, as we have seen previously, was internally a shuttered season; it was the heyday of unimaginative discipline in every detail of life. The organisation was assiduously tailored, membership and duties and beliefs defined in language the Puritan world could respect, but with little scope for the Society-wide practice of the " sense of the meeting " in reaching decisions. These came from select and closed sessions of Elders, guardians of the quiet name that suited both their more orthodox theology and their spreading commercial interests. Quakers were a challenge to no one : they used each level of church gathering to compile detailed answers to queries about their current condition and behaviour (a group confessional not dissimilar to that now demanded in China), and relayed these up the ladder to the exclusive Yearly Meeting at the top. Regulations and sound doctrine were the order of the day—the picture of Friends that still persists in so many people's minds; initiative and spontaneity were quietly discouraged. At one point two members per week were leaving the Society in England.

[8] *Leters of Early Friends*, p. 319. Also consult Barclay's *The Anarchy of Ranters*, 1691.

The turn came around 1860: with a revised Book of Discipline, a more restrained use of Advices and Queries, the throwing open of London Yearly Meeting to all its members, the allowing of Quakers to marry non-Quakers, and a general switch in church affairs from legalistic self-scrutiny to citizen concern with the surrounding world. It took another sixty years, to the aftermath of the First World War, for this new trend to be complete.

To-day, the Society benefits from the organization built up in its negative years, and from the spirit of freedom and equality in fellowship that early Quakers knew, and tries to use both to keep its authority centred in a controlled but ever-growing vision. All Friends are now responsible for the working of the present highly sensitive, open, yet closely linked-up system; and for what happens to it hereafter. Danger of inertia and renewed formalism can never be set aside, but, if cared for, this system, its source of strength in the ever-available " sense of the meeting ", offers a primary contribution to an increasingly authoritarian world.

Its guiding spirit is this . . . " Charity . . . seeketh not her own . . . but rejoiceth in the truth." [9]

(b) Characteristic Attitudes

Quaker simplicity in speech and dress, the refusal to swear a judicial oath or doff one's hat to anyone, the automatic assumption of equality between man and woman, servant and master, old and young (the first " Publishers of Truth " were mostly in their early twenties)—peculiarities, so called, still drawn on by the cartoonist—were there from the start, adopted by all, because they were in essence properties of the earlier groups from which Quakers sprang, stretching back through the centuries. Waldenses, Lollards, Catharists, Mennonites, refused oaths and preached equality and extreme simplicity of living. As with their equal objection to capital punishment and the use of war as an

[9] 1. Cor. 13.4–6.

instrument of State policy, and the Anabaptist rejection of tithes, it was in part social protest, from groups generally composed of artisans, tradesmen, scholars, small farmers, against the ruling Establishment. They were electing to contract out of the world into a preferable dispensation. This was a sizable factor among Quakers, many of whom had been Levellers in Cromwell's New Model Army, with their advanced and clear-cut social thinking, who in turn had derived from the sectaries of the previous decade and so back along the same channel; but the further irreducible factor, under any dispensation, and vital therefore to the entire tradition and thus among early Friends, was the search for a simple truthfulness in every human contact as the ideal basis of fellowship both in worship and daily life.

Thus George Fox and his colleagues, confronted on every side by Cavalier vanities and Roundhead hypocrisies, between which from one parish to the next there was little to choose, struck to the limit against both . . . " When the Lord sent me forth into the world ", writes Fox, " he forbade me to put off my hat to any, high or low; and I was required to ' thee ' and ' thou ' all men and women, without any respect to rich or poor, great or small." [10] In that age it was a powerful gesture, socially and morally. It struck home (as perhaps did casual sports dress and American slang, or the American approach to Royalty, on residual Victorian susceptibilities) and it hardened the official persecution.

There were some lively court scenes . . . "And they brought us into the court, where we stood with our hats on a pretty while, and all was quiet.

"And I was moved to say: ' Peace be among you '.

"And as last Judge Glynne, the Lord Chief Justice of England, a Welshman, said to the goaler:

" ' What be these you have brought here into court?'

" ' Prisoners, my lord ', said he.

10 *Journal*, p. 36.

" ' Why do not you put off your hats?' said the judge.

"And we said nothing.

" ' Put off your hats ', said the judge again.

" But we said nothing.

" Then again the judge:

" ' The court commands you to put off your hats '.

"And then I replied and said, ' Where did ever any magistrate, king, or judge from Moses to Daniel command any to put off their hats when they came before them into their courts amongst the Jews the people of God or amongst the heathen, or where did any of the heathen command any such thing in all their courts or their kings or judges? Or show me where it is written or printed in any law of England where any such thing is commanded; show it me and I will put off my hat.'

"And then the judge grew very angry and said, ' I do not carry my law books on my back.'

" Then said I, ' Tell me where it is printed in a statute book that I may read it.'

" Then said the judge, ' Take him away, prevaricator, I'll firk him.' " [11]

One senses a mixed motivation here, and love of scoring every point, always present in George Fox; but, besides this, Quaker plainness stood for a positive need to discard the conventional web of assumptions and behaviour, and then to experience a revivifying integrity through every word and deed. It was the crucial gesture for many converts, the most compact way of showing their choice, possibly in itself assisting in the final necessary shake-up of emotion involved in taking the plunge into Quakerism.

It led to much trouble in families. Thomas Ellwood, a young squire reached by Edward Burrough's preaching, braced himself first against his friends, other young gentlemen. When they doffed their hats and bowed and said, " Your humble servant, sir ", in embryo conveying the

[11] *Journal*, p. 243.

whole structure of their times (fine within artificial limits, but deadening to the newly-awakened spirit, as many young people find again to-day) he didn't respond till one of them said, " What, Tom, a Quaker?" " To which (he records) I readily and cheerfully answered, ' Yes, a Quaker '. And as the words passed out of my mouth, I felt joy spring in my heart, for I rejoiced that I had not been drawn out by them into a compliance with them, and that I had strength and boldness given me to confess myself to be one of that despised people." [12]

Next came the major test, with his father: he used " thee " instead of the conventional " you ", kept his hat on, and declined to attend family prayers. For which he had all his hats thrown away, one after the other, and got a thrashing in front of the servants.

But the gesture was decisive; from then on he was totally involved in the Quaker life.

Exactly one hundred and fifty years later, in 1809, Joseph John Gurney, banker and largely nominal Quaker, for his station and interests had drawn him towards Evangelical Anglicanism (and never entirely parted him from it) felt sudden need of submitting to what he saw as decided Quakerism, more particularly to the humbling sacrifice of " plainness of speech, behaviour and apparel." He resisted for a time but then one evening, invited to dinner by a neighbouring county family, felt he must face this personal test, and keep his hat on . . . " From this sacrifice, strange and unaccountable as it may appear, I could not escape. In a Friend's attire, and with my hat on, I entered the drawing-room at the dreaded moment, shook hands with the mistress of the house, went back into the hall, deposited my hat, spent a rather comfortable evening, and returned home in some degree of peace. I had afterwards the same thing to do at the Bishop's, the result was, that I found myself the decided Quaker, was perfectly understood to

[12] C. G. Crump, *The History of Thomas Ellwood*, 1900, p. 24.

have assumed that character, and to dinner parties, except in the family, was asked no more." [13]

This outward step, intensely valid for the whole company of early Friends and later for individuals such as Gurney, or his sister Elizabeth, who needed to signal and support their retreat from the style and assumptions of their social world, had already by the mid-eighteenth century become a dead symbol for Quakers generally. In the hands of the Elders it was a discipline to mark that all conformed. From being a means of release to Friends from one sort of restraint, it clamped down a worse one; they merely felt quaint in the garb of a previous century, with street boys shouting, " Quack, Quack!" after them. As a gesture it had served its purpose and, except among the Wilburite group of Friends in America, gradually fell into disuse. To-day Quakers, though they cherish the same simple directness of manner and word as their forbears and for the same reason, do not express this through any particular form of dress or language, or refusal to remove their hats to anyone at all but God. Many of them no longer own hats.

Side by side with these testimonies went refusal to swear an oath. This, with its implied refusal of allegiance to the ancient and pagan amalgam of priest-king-military commander was a deep-rooted challenge to the ordinary prejudice concerning the State and its dependent subjects, and brought the most vicious suffering onto the heads of Friends. They based their stand on Scripture (*Matt.* 5:34, and *James* 5:12) for those who themselves always pleaded Scripture, and they pointed both to the amount of perjury and the evil in any event of accepting a double standard of truth: one for the courts and one for the market place. Truth for them was the gateway to their whole conception of God and man. But to no avail: this particular stand branded them as outsiders, to be feared, and they were

13 J. B. Braithwaite, *Memoirs of J. J. Gurney*, 1854, p. 85.

slung into prison for years on end, had their goods confiscated, were deported.

Fox in his *Journal* constantly records this tendering of the oath in court—" Their last snare ", he calls it, " for they had no other way to get me into prison by; for all other things had been cleared. For this was like the Papists' sacrament and altar by which they ensnared the martyrs." [14]

Even after twenty years of preaching, after he had become famous in the land, he was still, in 1674, thrown back into gaol because he would not take the oath. It was this trial which finally led the young " Fabians " in the Society—William Penn, William Meade, Thomas Ellwood —to consult counsel's opinion in order to contest the verdict (which they did successfully), and to establish Meeting for Sufferings in the first place as a standing committee of legal defence for Quakers throughout England; a step which at once eased Quaker suffering, though it was at variance with the absolutist stand. Though, underlying the whole situation was the half-complicity of Catholic Kings, themselves by now outsiders in the State, and the appreciation by Whig merchants and City interests of the advantages of toleration, especially for such sober entrepreneurs as the Quakers were becoming. By 1687, James II could excuse Quaker constables from swearing allegiance; after the Act of Affirmation of 1695 Quakers were admitted as freemen of London. A simpler wording of this affirmation —in itself a further compromise, as the twenty-five years of debate about it within the Society showed—was hammered out by 1722, and the Government persuaded to legalise its use.

Thus in effect the Society of Friends came to terms with the Establishment; and except for a few last sufferings over tithes, a few last petty fines and distraints, settled down to a prosperous future and private pursuit of the good life. Until, a century and a quarter later, the mounting tempo

14 *Journal*, p. 461.

of wars and revolutions and the explosion of the modern industrial reality tore this privacy to shreds, and brought Friends face to face again, and salutarily so, with the commitments that necessarily followed from their beliefs. Of these commitments their attitude to war became the most crucial.

Another aspect of the early movement that together with love of truth and simplicity was seen to bring men into unity was recognition of their innate equality. All were servants of the Lord, and were to seek His Spirit in one another; the fellowship known in meeting for worship could be carried into all spheres of life, reaching beyond outward differences of ability or position, or race, or sex. This conviction freed much energy for worthwhile service; for instance it sent Mary Fisher, a housemaid, to preach to the Sultan of Turkey, and with quite some sagacity; it enabled Fox with the greatest naturalness to give advice to Oliver Cromwell . . . "And I was moved again to go and speak to Oliver Protector when there was a talk of making him King. And I met him in the Park and told him that they that would put him on an earthly crown would take away his life.

"And he asked me, ' What say you?'

"And I said again, they that sought to put him on a crown would take away his life, and bid him mind the crown that was immortal.

"And he thanked me. . . ." [15]

Ever since then Quakers have sought audience with kings and dictators and high State officials, and to-day regularly at the United Nations, usually at times when the course of events seem desperately confused and distorted, simply attempting through a sense of fellowship that can exclude no one to reach, through barriers of vanity and red tape, to the spiritual life within the ruler. For a few moments at least,

[15] *Journal*, p. 289.

through unity based on a real equality, a way to the truth may be cleared.

Towards their own servants and employees Friends maintained a benevolent paternalism, a clan relationship, which made time for all to come to worship and minister there if they so wished; and then ordered their several duties as advised in Ephesians vi: 5–9, which calls on both servants and masters to respect each other, seeing their relative functions as ways firstly of serving God, before whom all are equal. This mild feudal relationship, to-day still widespread in the world, was not in kind very different from that generally obtaining in Reformation England. The rising petite bourgeoisie to which Quakers mostly belonged, in vociferously asserting, on spiritual grounds, the universal equality of man, were so busily proclaiming it upwards that for a while they didn't explore to the full its application downwards; and, as the decades passed and their status improved and the overall discipline in the Society tightened, their attitude to those in trusteeship, so to speak—servants, workmen, even their poor— became increasingly static. Yet, at all times, the saving grace was the operation of meeting for worship that, keeping them open to fresh insight, allowed individuals to remind the Society of the full implications socially of the experience of equality spiritually.

The greatest measure of equality among them was certainly known in the first years, for persecution respected no one; and the prophetic gift then being the immediate claim to leadership, many simple labourers and servants took full share in all church matters; but, a little later, it became those of some material substance, those at least listed as contributors to the Society's poor relief, those who could afford to give their time, ordering it as they chose, and of a better education, who as Elders or church representatives were usually fixing the Society's behaviour, or as itinerant ministers were conditioning its vision. The stage was being set for to-day's condition, when Friends constantly bemoan, a little puzzledly, that there are so few working class people among them.

Even so, within this framework, great love and care, as within a family, was bestowed on the welfare of servants and apprentices, orphans, impoverished widows, and others needing help or instruction. Domestic training schemes and schooling, work houses and co-operative ventures to enable participants to stand on their own economic feet were an early and steady feature of Quakerism. Monthly Meetings would always find money to help old and young along, especially for good practical schooling (a practical measure assisting equality); the proviso being that the beneficiaries worked well and behaved themselves. Any sexual peccadillos were castigated. Epistles were constantly being written against the dangers of teenage flirting among Quaker dependants—but then, no one at all in the Society escaped strict moral supervision. On that point there was utter equality.

The Quaker holding of slaves, and traffic in them, falls however in a different category. So much attention is always given, and rightly, to Quaker initiative in the abolition of the slave trade in the western world, and equally within America of the institution of slavery itself, that it is overlooked that this reform had first to begin within the Society. Quaker tracts read . . . " It was not to be expected that such men (i.e. Quakers), with their keen sense of the right of the negro to enjoy liberty, could tamely and quietly behold all the wrong and injustice and cruelty around them without making an effort to put an end to it " [16]—yes, but it took them a century (in contrast to instantaneous action when their own vital freedoms were affected) to reach this standpoint. Friends in the American Colonies and West Indies were great plantation owners, shipowners, leading merchants, leading statesmen and judges, as well

[16] *Friends Ancient and Modern,* Tract No. 18, London, 1915.

as being men of lesser station. They set the tone not only in Pennsylvania, but in New Jersey, Rhode Island, and the Carolinas for the first half century or more—up till around 1750; and they traded in slaves and held slaves exactly as anyone else did then, and, decade after decade after decade, as their various Yearly Meeting Epistles show, the majority of them, with a good deal of sophistry, delayed reform and fought a rearguard action against abolition. It was the work above all of John Woolman, aided by one or two small meetings, that won the conscience of enough leading Friends, stirring the unease in their hearts beneath the evident prosperity, to bring the rest into line—an instance of the Society's discipline at last put to good use.

In approaching things thus one should remember that slavery, existing from earliest times in all parts of the world, though never accepted by Christianity as a natural state of man had even by the early Church been counted an inevitable evil, a requirement of vast empires in their over-all organisation, to be mitigated by Christian forbearance (again, Ephesians vi: 5–9) and thought of eternal reward or damnation. The interest was in men's souls. The medieval heretics reasoned better, and supported the claims of serfs, the successors to the earlier classes of slaves, for greater social rights; and eventually in England the Quakers inherited these radical attitudes, applying them to the immediate scene, which of course by then had greatly pro-gressed, serfdom having been replaced by money contracts for the most part. New issues claimed reforming zeal, and, to begin with, Friends valiantly struggled with these.

Beyond this, however, they were slow to make the required imaginative leap. They knew of the transatlantic slave trade, just getting into its stride, but they did not at first connect it in principle with the spiritual commitment they had inherited, nor with any direct spiritual call. At best their attitude was that of Fox, first in 1657, to " Friends beyond Sea, that have Blacks and Indian Slaves . . . Dear

Friends, I am moved to write these things to you in all plantations. God . . . is no respecter of persons . . . He hath made all nations of one blood . . . He doth enlighten every man that cometh into the world . . . And the gospel . . . is the power that giveth liberty and freedom, and is glad tidings to every captivated creature . . . And so, ye are to have the mind of Christ, and to be merciful, as your Heavenly Father is merciful." [17]

This, another echo of the passage in *Ephesians,* when set beside Fox's usual exhortations concerning a moral duty, is pretty lukewarm stuff. Doubtless, for the next century, Quaker slave owners heeded it, for they taught their slaves the gospel, cared for them above the average (as did the Catholic Portuguese in Brazil), and brought them to Meetings when possible, even at the risk in some districts of incurring a stiff fine. In fact one argument these Friends used against manumission was that their slaves would fall into worse hands. But it didn't reach to any truth beyond this.

Again, while visiting Barbados in 1671, Fox advised Friends there . . . " about training up their negroes in the fear of God, those bought with their money and such as were born in their families . . . and that their overseers might deal mildly and gently with them and not use cruelty as the manner of some is and hath been, and to make them free after thirty years' servitude. . . ." [18] Here, the advice that slaves should be freed, is the first step forward; and was repeated by William Penn in his will of 1701 . . . " I give to my blacks their freedom as is under my hand already "; but there was no immediate response on the spot.

The first resounding Colonial protest came (thus linking back to the tradition prior to Quakers) from a group of Rhineland ₒMennonites who, arriving in Pennsylvania, joined themselves to Friends and formed a subsidiary

[17] *Epistle* 153 (1657).
[18] *Journal,* p. 599.

meeting. They said, as early as 1688, . . . " To bring men hither, or to rob and sell them against their will, we stand against. In Europe there are many oppressed for con- science' sake; and here there are those oppressed which are of a black colour . . . This makes an ill report in all those countries of Europe, where they hear of it, that the Quakers do here handle men as they handle there the cattle . . . Pray, what thing in the world can be done worse towards us, than if men should rob or steal us away, and sell us for slaves to strange countries; separating husbands from their wives and children. Now this is not done in the manner we would be done by, therefore we contradict and are against this traffic in the bodies of men. . . ." [19]

Monthly, Quarterly, and Yearly Meetings duly considered this statement, but temporarised for eight years, and then only and very mildly to discourage the import of further negroes, so mildly that again after fifteen years they were found repeating the same injunction. The next year, 1712, William Southeby, a Friend, prayed the legislature to abolish slavery in Pennsylvania. His was an isolated voice.

Advice was now sought from London Yearly Meeting, to see how English Friends felt, and through them to learn about the Quaker conscience in the other American Colonies, all of which were in direct correspondence with London. There was little response. Too many fingers were in the pie. It must never be thought that the Quakers in America were at that stage different from the Quakers in England, any more than to-day a settler in Kenya is different from the man in London or Manchester : circumstances press differently, that's all, swaying prejudice; and at that time much of the Quaker wealth in England came from their trade with their fellows in the Colonies. The only protest against slavery was sporadic, from individuals, such as that of the Irish Quaker, William Edmundson, travelling in Maryland and Virginia, and that of Tom Hazard in

[19] S. W. Pennypacker, *The Settlement of Germantown*, Phila., 1899. p. 145.

Rhode Island, son of one of the largest slave-owning families in New England. A Quaker family.

The slow process continued. One small meeting, Chester meeting, in Pennsylvania, kept up its protest, gradually influencing Philadelphia Yearly Meeting to caution against the import of slaves and traffic in them by Friends. This was spread over twenty years. During this time there was also abolitionist pamphleteering by individual Friends, such as John Hepburn of New Jersey, William Burling of New York, Elihu Coleman of Massachusetts, but with no immediate effect; and when the tone became too peremptorary, as with Ralph Sandiford and Benjamin Lay, they were disowned for stirring up trouble. The most important advance was the minute of 1727 of London Yearly Meeting . . . " It is the sense of the meeting, that the importing of negroes from their native country and relations, by Friends, is not a commendable or allowed practice, and is, therefore, censured by this meeting." [20]

This much, at last, had been recognised; and it must be said in defence of the Society, throughout this whole snail-like process, that unity of voice was rightly considered the necessary basis of forward action, for if the Society had been split over slavery even less would have been accomplished; and ultimately the group conscience was to be roused, with maximum effect. It is sad only that Friends were so slow in putting conscience before pocket. The Light was visible all the time.

Another thirty years went by, and John Woolman, after seeing for himself the reality of slave-holding among Friends throughout the American Colonies, spoke out in the main centres, and firstly in Philadelphia Yearly Meeting, in 1758. He did not ask, " Is this evil?", but "Are you easy in your hearts doing it?" He appealed to the Inner Light in all. Just as to-day he could ask if we were

[20] F. J. Klingberg, *The Anti-Slavery Movement in England*, New Haven, 1926, p. 32.

easy basing our whole social existence on threats to use the hydrogen bomb; or on a system that raises our standard of living, year after year in the West, while Eastern peasants continue to starve.

He won Friends over, and that year's Epistle suggested that . . . "such Friends who have any slaves to set them at liberty,—making a Christian provision for them according to their ages." It was followed up by personal visits to each plantation. The tide swung over in the other Colonies. It took a further twenty years of unremitting effort, up to the outbreak of the Revolutionary War; but by then almost every slave held by Quakers had been freed, and to some extent compensated. Pressure then could be brought on State legislatures to abolish slavery: which was done in Pennsylvania in 1780, and Rhode Island in 1784. In the southern States, where this failed against the new cotton interests, Friends increasingly began to trek west. Their first unheroic era was closed.

From then on the crusade against slavery, both by British and American Quakers (though even now it had some niggling aspects) was fairly clear cut, requiring only time and perseverance and detached philanthropic concern. Though it is always most written about it is in fact, from a Quaker point of view, the less important phase. Others besides Friends were in the van; Rationalists and Evangelicals, even leading British policicians, were prepared to contest the still powerful slave trade lobby; and in America, though individual Friends (usually Hicksites), such as the Coffin family, bravely helped with the "Underground Railway" assisting fugitive slaves from the South, and in their case became enshrined in the pages of "Uncle Tom's Cabin", in fact the most powerful economic and political interests in the North were determined to end slavery. Individual Friends performed individual acts of merit, and the Society as a whole was atoning for a century's rather shameful record, but it was not now the testing time. That had gone before, and had been resolved by John Woolman.

Two factors, therefore, stand out in summary of the above story. First, Quakerism, not inheriting any highly-charged protest against slavery as it did against oaths or high living or sacraments, and unfortunately in any case seeing itself as the last word in saintly perception, did not for some time experience the necessary tension within its conscience to enable it to discard slavery, and go beyond both the practice of the day and that of *Ephesians* vi: 5–9. Insight it did receive, through individuals, but not for the group powerfully enough. It was operating, to all intents, within a new field.

But, secondly, it did ultimately put itself right from within; it learned, and then in complete unity. The Quaker method did work. Woolman could reach his fellows, especially when gathered in their religious meeting, taking them with him towards the Light. It was his utter humility and love that broke down self-interest, and let the spiritual signals through. Patiently, thus through fellowship, the labour was completed. It had been slow and grisly (though not in a long perspective of history) but it was solid at the finish.

By contrast, the American Civil War is still being fought to-day.

This particular chapter among Friends was to a very much less extent repeated with regards to their Peace Testimony, and to a similar extent in their attitudes towards the modern industrial order. The common factor would seem to be an inhibitory economic self-interest, the inertia of a comfortable status: and against that, by its nature bound to struggle to the last, the pleadings of spiritual insight, drawing the group, in unity, towards the new decisive step. Such heart-work, to mature, is slow.

There was a further instance of equality settled happily from the start among Friends, that between man and woman. Here Collegiants, Familists, Baptists had blazed the trail, and Fox, peculiarly susceptible to the spiritual life in women, welcomed their full participation in ministry and church affairs. " Encourage all the women ", he said, " of families that are convinced, and minds virtue, and loves the truth, and walks in it, that they may come up into God's service, that they may be serviceable in their genera- tion, and in the Creation . . . Let the Creation have its liberty." [21] And in this respect, among Friends, it had.

Women were very glad of this, for generally in Puritan society their status was declining; they enjoyed less freedom and power, even less instruction, than in medieval times. Milton's daughters were uninstructed; Knox's " Monstrous Regiment of Women " had been well digested, and any wilful lass was liable to be taken as a witch; even Bunyan wrote, " They are not the image and glory of God, as the men are." [22] To this Fox said, " Christ renews man and woman up into the image of God as they were in before they fell." [23]

He gathered a number of women preachers round him, such as Elizabeth Hooton, Mary Fisher, Mary Dyer, who travelled and ministered exactly as the men, and suffered with equal bravery. Elizabeth Hooton, from the Baptists, was the first; for twenty years she preached and was gaoled, and wrote from the gaols to the authorities, with a reform- ing organisational mind equal to that of Elizabeth Fry's, crying out for what should be done for the infamous con- dition of prisoners. Along with her daughter she braved the Puritan terror in Massachusetts, especially directed against Quakers . . . " being brought to the court, they ordered her to be sent out of their coasts, and to be whipped at three towns with ten stripes each. So at Cambridge she was tied to the whipping post and lashed with ten stripes, with a three-stringed whip, with three knots at the end. At

21 *Box Meeting MSS* (3). Deposited in Friends House Library.
22 *Complete Works*, 1862, p. 658.
23 *Gospel Truth Demonstrated*, p. 331. See also *Journal*, p. 39.

Watertown she had ten stripes more with willow rods: and to make up all, at Dedham, on a cold frosty morning, she received ten cruel lashes at a cart's tail. . . ." [24] But she survived, gave thanks to God, and returned with almost masochistic fervour to spread the Quaker message within the forbidden territory. She died, while on a mission with Fox, in Jamaica in 1671.

Mary Fisher, the maidservant who later preached to the Sultan in Turkey, experienced her baptism in the other Cambridge, in England itself . . . " they were led to the Market-Cross, calling upon God to strengthen their faith. The Executioner commanded them to put off their Clothes, which they refused. Then he stripped them naked to the Waste, put their Arms into the Whipping-post, and executed the Mayor's Warrant far more cruelly than is usually done to the worst of Malefactors. . . ." [25] This was the first flogging received by Friends in England, though by no means the last. The university scholars very definitely did not take to the unlearned appeal to the Light of God in simple people, that did not depend on scholarship, and was ready to dispense with lawyers and priests. Though, they might first have remembered Wyclif, himself a Fellow of Balliol, writing . . . " Universities and College degrees were instituted by pagan vanity and serve the Devil's purposes quite as much as God's." [26] Mary Fisher survived, however, braved Boston, braved the Turks, and finally married a master mariner.

Mary Dyer, in turn braving the Massachusetts magistrates, was hanged for her faith on Boston Common.

Meanwhile, the women who stayed at home did their share in a score of ways—seeing to the relief of the poor, the unemployed, the widows, the orphans, and those in prison; they supervised the settling of children in schools, and of maids and apprentices in employment—in fact

[24] W. Sewel, *History of the Quakers,* 1795, Vol. I. pp. 618–20.
[25] J. Besse, *Sufferings of the Quakers, etc.,* 1753, Vol. I, p. 84.
[26] Fleury, *Church History,* p. 103.

through them the sway and independence enjoyed by medieval guildsmen's wives were preserved through the Puritan era; and also increasingly they undertook the over-sight of marriage proposals and any subsequent marital difficulties. This, with the extreme simplicity of Quaker marriage procedure (which has survived in its original form till to-day), in a then generally licentious period, became necessary.

In London a Six Weeks' Meeting was composed jointly of men and women for such business, but otherwise the women had separate meetings—as Fox put it . . . " there is many things that is proper for the women to look into, both in their families and concerning women, which is not so proper for the men, which modesty in women cannot so well speak of before men as they can amongst their own sex ";[27] and eventually all over the country, following the London lead, separate women's meetings, on a monthly, quarterly, and yearly level were established, which never quite, during the long authoritarian sleep of the Society, lost touch as the men did with the social implications of Quaker faith; and ultimately all these meetings were merged with men's meetings, and so it is to-day.

In each decade there were outstanding Quaker women: this tradition never lapsed; so that, perhaps inevitably, in 1847, the first leaflet ever issued on women's suffrage was written by an English Quakeress, Anne Knight. A year later, in New York, a Hicksite Quakeress, Lucretia Mott, called for the first Woman's Rights Convention in all his-tory. This was the start throughout the world of the movement for women's suffrage. Friends however, though they worked for the movement, appealing to the world's conscience, till suffrage was granted, never approved of militant action. That was not the Quaker way. So the world took the fight out of their hands, and largely forgot their contribution.

[27] *Letters, Dreams, and Visions* (MS), p. 15.

So finally one can say that Quakers struggled, if need be without fear of suffering, for all moral and social views that gripped their conscience as fundamental, whether these were received with their first awakening to meeting for worship as the ground of spiritual insight, or were borne in on them gradually through its practice over the centuries, that gradually loosened their self-interest or earlier bias or inertia; but that even then they were mostly inclined to say what they themselves must do, or what the Society as such should do, tolerating divergencies, waiting for each to see the Light, taking steps forward only in the measure of unity achieved. This must seem very slow to modern world shakers. Yet at least it gives a useful deposit of insight freely arrived at, that uses no weapon but faith in this same insight in other people, to be reached through fellowship with them, to transform the situations confronting us. It can perhaps be best studied in the Quaker Peace Testimony.

(c) The Peace Testimony

That Quakers do not fight nor engage in preparation for war, nor can be tyrannised into doing so, is possibly the best known fact about them, and one which, when put together with their record in the relief of suffering and their missions of reconciliation, has won a certain puzzled respect. Their obstinate vocation is accepted—they are made that way, like musicians or monks; and they are recognised as a useful outlet for that part of the collective psyche that, even at the most murderous moments, wants to construct something better; and they assuage a little the guilt that accompanies all evil commitments. So they are tolerated, used, even awarded the Nobel Peace Prize; but in the final analysis are thought to be misguided.

But suppose there were no such people as Quakers, ready to give up war and to take the consequences of that decision, because only thus, they believe, can the splintered spirit of man be gathered, and acts of reconciliation take place, and however slow and immediately disconcerting and painful, the ultimate earthly fellowship be known? Suppose there was no one ready to stake everything on such a faith? It might then seem, however great our courage and strength and many-sided achievements, that something at the core of man was missing, something at the core of his religion, that the soul was darker than it need be. Perhaps to-day, the world drifting wide-eyed to self-destruction, even the toughest politician may be glad that such faith exists, quixotic though he calls it: because suddenly he may need to turn to it, as offering the last chance.

Among Friends themselves, all too aware of their own inconsistencies and failures, this Peace Testimony is not put forth as something that they more than other people are innately suited to express, or as followed through as it should be in all their social relationships: but as part of their constantly renewed attempt to extend the method that in meeting for worship brings those present into unity—that is, the search past habitual self and preconceived ideas for the shared experience of the Spirit of God, that perhaps could not be discovered singly but that transforms the feeling of those who discover it together, letting them see their true face in its eternal setting.

This is the Quaker approach to a misunderstanding of a conflict: to let in the most profound Light (which may call for developments not recognised before, and unexpected re-alignments) through readiness to meet in prayful simplicity with all those concerned. No compromise with evil is involved, nor with any set of arguments limited to a particular time or place: the attempt is to achieve unity on a level transcending individual attitudes, and so induce a fellow feeling that can sort through immediate difficulties. This is a way, a redemptive experience, always open for all to engage in, whatever their race or nation or creed: its antithesis is resort to war, in which primarily men do violence to God.

Quakers are no more than learners at using it, at some points more successful than at others. It took time, we have seen, for them to realise that slavery denied men spiritual unity; they have been equally slow to comprehend that modern organisation of industry involves a similar sort of denial, indeed that all violence, concealed or otherwise, is interactive within society. It also took time, though in this less, for them to formulate concerted opposition to war, and then to extend their rôle through relief work (the changing of the direction of group energy) and through acts of reconciliation between opposing nations and races, thus gradually establishing their present comprehensive tradition; and, even so, in several wars, for instance in the two recent major ones, individual Friends have fought, unsure in any other capacity.

Yet all along their response to insight, that has been almost a by-product of their search for spiritual unity, has given results that steadily have consolidated into an accepted central witness—the slave owners renounced their slaves and devoted themselves thereafter to the total abolition of the evil, the industrial employers instigated co-operative action with their employees that in embryo has brought a working spirit at least ahead of the generality, be it capitalist or socialist; and, now for nearly three hundred years, the Society of Friends as a whole has stood for renunciation of war, whatever the circumstances, in favour of a method based on their faith in God's Spirit at work in man. Even so their greatest trials, in a conceivably totalitarian world, that would sound their Testimony to its depths, may still lie before them. It is early as yet to say more than that they are learners, patient stumbling novice-practitioners of what should be thought of as all men's vocation, the discovery of the way of peace within as prelude to its pursuit without.

George Fox, in his first years of preaching, struck this authentic standard. Offered a captaincy in Cromwell's army, in 1651, he replied . . . " I told them I lived in the virtue of that life and power that took away the occasion of all wars . . . I told them I was come into the covenant of peace which was before wars and strifes were." [28] William Dewsbury, who joined him that year, had previously been a soldier, but had already in 1645 arrived individually at the same point, discovering that . . . " the enemies was within, and was spiritual and my weapons against them must be spiritual, the power of God. Then I could no longer fight with a carnal weapon against a carnal man." [29] So he had left the army.

These were the decisive experiences, rooted far deeper than argument, after which no man himself turned back to war, but began as best he could to explore the reconciling approach to life: for Friends, in those early years, before meetings were sufficiently established to give a sustaining sense of direction, and in the midst of the pell-mell chaos of religious challenge and counter-challenge, not always an easy task. Fox himself could be very aggressive in his utterances and writings, and in the way he looked to the Lord for vengeance, and in certain situations unforgiving towards opponents; yet he also showed a fine reconciling power (and always a sense of how others should behave!) and on several occasions a remarkable non-violent kind of strength. . . .

. . . " The constables took me and gave me a wisk over the shoulders with their willow rods, and so thrust me amongst the rude multitude which then fell upon me with their hedge stakes and clubs and staves and beat me as hard as ever they could strike on my head and arms and shoulders, and it was a great while before they beat me down and mazed me, and at last I fell down upon the wet

28 *Journal*, p. 65.
29 *Works*, 1689, p. 55.

common. There I lay a pretty space, and when I recovered
myself . . . I stood up again in the eternal power of God
and stretched out my arms amongst them all, and said
again with a loud voice, Strike again, here is my arms
and my head and my cheeks. And there was a mason,
a rude fellow, a professor called, he gave me a blow with
all his might just a-top of my hand, as it was stretched
out, with his walking rule-staff. And my hand and arm
was so numbed and bruised that I could not draw it in
unto me again but it stood out as it was. Then the people
cried out, 'He hath spoiled his hand, for ever having any
use of it more.' The skin was struck off my hand and a
little blood came, and I looked at it in the love of God,
and I was in the love of God to them all that had persecuted me.

"And after a while the Lord's power sprang through me
again, and through my hand and arm, that in a minute
I recovered my hand and arm and strength in the face
and sight of them all and it was as well as it was before,
and I had never another blow afterward." [30]

But Fox was also the leader of a movement whose members came from many sides, with varying emphases in their
convictions and varying degrees to which these had been
explored; a good number of them were still in the armed
forces. It took a further nine years for Quakers to be
unambiguously pacifist, this coming through a concordance
of pressures from among them and from events without.

To start with some of them agreed that Christians could
fight in a just cause (e.g. in Cromwell's army against the
King, or against Catholic or Islamic countries). Some like
Isaac Pennington felt that a true Christian could not fight,
but that where a professing Christian, or a Christian nation
so-called, were not yet convinced of this, then they should
continue to fight, in self-defence, until they saw Christian
truth clearer. This was quite a widespread view, trusting

[30] *Journal*, pp. 127-8.

to a gradual growth of insight; and because it is still canvassed to-day, one can note Pennington's further counsel . . . " It is not for a nation (coming into the gospel life and principle) to take care beforehand how they shall be preserved, but the gospel will teach a nation (if they hearken to it) as well as a particular person to trust the Lord, and to wait on him for preservation. . . ." [31] Put into a broader idiom to include non-Christian feeling, and given a rather more positive edge, wouldn't this speak to the faith of those who wish England to give up her hydrogen bombs? In the seventeenth century, as now, this island felt itself threatened by powerful neighbours. Quakers were not disregardful of this but nonetheless came to see that only a complete renunciation of arms would break the evil chain of war and its illusionary victories.

These various views, in turn yielding to the pacifist position, were reproducing what had happened before in the traditon from which Quakers stemmed; though now the absolute position was to become better established, to persist, because its holders were to be more determined in their stand, and more constructive, and so better tolerated. But the long line of Christian heresies—and before them, the Essenes—had all condemned the waging of war, some of them because it was waged by the unrighteous State or worldly Church, and some of them absolutely.

Usually what had happened was that the former protest was itself militant, but then suffering heavy persecution it changed to the latter's non-violence: thus, the quiet Donatists followed the fighting Circumcellions, the Waldenses noted the Albigenses's fate, the Bohemian Brethren that of the Hussites, the Mennonites at all costs eschewed another Anabaptist Munster, and the Quakers learned from the suppression of the Levellers, from whom they gathered disillusioned adherents. Fox admonished these last ones . . . " You would have unity and fellowship, before life was

[31] *Somewhat spoken to a Weighty Question*, 1661.

raised up in you ";[32] and John Lilburne, the chief Leveller, himself turned Quaker at the end, saying, " I have really and substantially found that which my soul hath many years sought . . . and that therefore confidently I now believe, I shall never hereafter be a user of a temporal sword more, nor a joiner with them that do so." [33] These, from one of the fathers of modern social democracy, were valuable words.

Also, as the Cromwellian régime, from which many Quakers had hoped the Millenium to sprout forth, visibly flagged and began to make way for a restoration of the monarchy, they became even more disillusioned with " carnal weapons " as a means of advancing God's King-dom, and the more ready therefore to abandon them. As Edward Burrough admitted . . . " We are now better informed than once we were, for though we do more than ever oppose oppression and seek after reformation, yet we do it not in that way of outward warring and fighting with carnal weapons and swords." [34] Burrough himself had formerly acquiesced in the execution of Charles I, seeing it as a judgment of God; and he had even exhorted the English army at Dunkirk, as late as 1659, to take no rest " till you have visited Rome . . . and avenged the blood of the guiltless through all the dominions of the Pope . . . and it would be to your honour to be made use of by the Lord to any degree." [35] But a year later he pulled in his horns, with the above address to Charles II, and another apology, in which he states of Friends . . . " we would have men's wickedness killed, and their persons saved, and their souls delivered; and this is the war we make." [36] It had not always been so circumscribed.

But to all these currents within the growing movement

[32] *A Word from the Lord*, 1654, p. 13.
[33] *The Ressurection of John Lilburne*, 1656, p. 14.
[34] *Works*, 1672, p. 671.
[35] *Works*, pp. 537–40.
[36] *Works*, p. 748.

that were clearly conditioned by outward events—and among them one should cite the Quaker soldiers, most of whom did not leave the army till they were dismissed from it—must be added the weight of inward conviction that was steadily gaining ground, equating pacifism with Quaker faith; and in this, above all, the preaching of Fox and Dewsbury and Naylor gave the lead. Fox would tell the individual convert " to wear his sword as long as he could ", putting beside this his own clearer vision of what the Quaker way should be, that would gather these several half-way views into " that which is new, that mind to guide all your minds up to the living God." [37] More specifically, as civil troubles increased, he warned Friends, in 1659 . . . " Keep out of plots and bustling and the arm of the flesh . . . All such as pretend Christ Jesus, and confess him, and yet run into the use of carnal weapons, wrestling with flesh and blood, throw away the spiritual weapons . . . And such as would revenge themselves be out of Christ's doctrine . . . All Friends everywhere, this I charge you . . . live in peace, in Christ, the way of peace, and therein seek the peace of all men, and no man's hurt." [38]

As early as 1655 he had assured Cromwell that . . . " I, who am of the world called George Fox, do deny the carrying or drawing of any carnal sword against any, or against thee, Oliver Cromwell, or any man ";[39] and he constantly reiterated this Quaker pledge, necessarily in times of disturbance and plots when Quakers and other dissatisfied radicals, such as Fifth Monarchy Men (the ancestors of Jehovah's Witnesses), seemed indistinguishable to the authorities. When actually in 1660, on the restoration of the monarchy, there was a Fifth Monarchy revolt, which caused the wholesale imprisonment of Friends, the first united Quaker declaration concerning their Peace Testimony was issued, and this has stood ever since.

[37] *Epistle* 77 (1654).
[38] *Journal*, p. 357.
[39] *Journal*, p. 197.

It said . . . " We utterly deny all outward wars and strife, and fightings with outward weapons, for any end, or under any pretence whatever; this is our testimony to the whole world. The Spirit of Christ by which we are guided is not changeable, so as once to command us from a thing as evil and again to move unto it; and we certainly know and testify to the world, that the Spirit of Christ, which leads us unto all Truth, will never move us to fight and war against any man with outward weapons, neither for the Kingdom of Christ nor for the Kingdoms of this world." [40]

Thus Quakers reached unity on this vital application of their faith, and maintained it as a Society through the succeeding centuries, and gradually developed it through their work of relief and reconciliation. Towards individual Friends who, in the stress of war, abandoned it, a varying amount of sympathy was shown—sometimes they were disowned outright, as generally in England before this century, and as during the American War of Independence, which led to a small Philadelphian group of fighting Free Quakers being formed; sometimes they were readmitted on expression of regret for having fought, as mostly among Hicksites during the American Civil War; and, during this present century, there has been a tendency towards still greater leniency, possibly because the Society as a whole is by now so surely grounded in its Testimony, upheld by almost all Friends, that the right course with the dissenting few is felt to be one of tenderness, in the hope they will later see more clearly, rather than abrupt disownment. But this is a policy only possible where the great majority are strong in their witness, upholding the Quaker face to the world.

In England, the Yearly Meeting faced each war, or Militia Bill, as it came along, issuing in substance the same Epistle as the 1660 one, entreating all Friends to be faithful to their Peace Testimony, and also now entreating the

[40] *Christian Practice*, p. 132.

nation to seek a different solution to its problems, the more urgently as the scope of warfare became worldwide. During and after the 1914 War it issued a number of appeals, all of which, alas, after the Second World War and in to-day's threatening situation, are even more urgently apposite . . . " The ultimate choice before the world would appear to lie between fear, with its more complete organisation of the nations for war, and the venture of faith, with its reliance on spiritual and moral forces only " [41] . . . " We may have to learn to give up the whole idea of defending our rights, and to be willing to stand as Jesus stood, defenceless in the midst of a world of possible enemies " [42] . . . " What shall it profit a nation, if it gain the whole world and lose its own soul?" [43] London Yearly Meeting in 1957 added . . . " What do we mean by ' trusting ' those who, we fear, may lack integrity? It is the Light of God in all men, in ourselves as in others, that we must learn to trust, and this we must be ready to go on doing, even though we know that the Light may be hidden in us, and in them, again and again." [44]

Thus Friends have proclaimed their faith.

Other factors following from this, such as the developing attitudes of governments, the press, the public, towards this testimony, and the Society's own extending work, especially in the field of race relations and through Quaker centres abroad, are later discussed against a more detailed historical background;[45] but there is also the essential supporting record of individuals discovering, then standing by, their conviction, not in the committee rooms of the Society but in unfriendly isolation during wartime. It is they finally who make up the Society. Here are two instances of what can then happen.

[41] *Christian Practice*, p. 143.
[42] *London Yearly Meeting Epistle*, 1916.
[43] *Christian Practice*, p. 136.
[44] *The Friend*, 7th June, 1957.
[45] See below, pp. 233, 249–61.

Thomas Lurting was a sailor for Cromwell, a boatswain's mate on a frigate chasing Spanish men-of-war, and a doughty fighter. There were already one or two Quakers in the crew, by 1657, and he used to beat them when they met in silent worship rather than attend the ship's church service. But suddenly he too, under the stress of battle, became dissatisfied with the official practice, and found himself, though with reluctance, turning to the despised Quaker mode of seeking God. His first attendance at meeting caused a stir on the ship—" Thomas ", cried the chaplain, " I took you for a very honest man and a good Christian, but am sorry you should be so deluded "; and the captain, himself a Baptist preacher, thumbed away through his Bible, " to prove the Quakers no Christians ".[46]

But so well did Lurting and his Quaker friends conduct themselves during a ship epidemic, and during subsequent engagements, that they won back the captain's respect. Suddenly again, at the height of battle, Lurting felt a new conviction: that his guns were killing other men and that in this he should not take part. He left his post, and when asked why said, himself still puzzled, that he was " under some scruple of conscience on the account of fighting." That night he discussed it with the other Friends, who pondered it together. This was the period during which Quakers individually were feeling towards the Light on this subject, extending the boundaries of their faith, those in the armed forces especially being cut off from the guidance that Fox and the other leaders were daily giving in meetings.

Yet this minute group of Friends serving on a Navy vessel managed to establish their new conviction. Their trial came in the next engagement when, to a man, they refused to fight. When the captain was told he was naturally enraged, and he drew his sword on Lurting; but Lurting stood up to him, unafraid, and the captain let

46 T. Lurting, *The Fighting Sailor turned Peaceable Christian, etc.*, 1710.

him be. The strength of the new persuasion triumphed. The ship afterwards returned to England, and Lurting left it and joined a merchantman. Many similar trials were to follow, for he was repeatedly press-ganged back to the Navy, but he consistently refused to fight. Each captain in turn gave way. " Take him away ", they would say, " he is a Quaker." The first part of the Quaker witness regarding war was becoming known.

Just two centuries later, in the American Civil War, despite, by then, the accumulated evidence of Quaker pacifist conviction, made the more solid by their lead in the freeing of slaves, a far more fiendish attempt was made to change their minds. This happened chiefly in the South, that had little use for abolitionist Friends. A few of these availed themselves of alternative modes of civilian service, a few paid exemption money, a few fled to the woods and hills, to be hunted down; but the majority were conscripted and sent to military establishments, there to be tortured for their obstinacy till, in some cases, they died, or, and this is not so remarkable, suddenly the officers and men accepted them with a kind of joy for what they were and had been willing to endure; or they were finally deposited in Andersonville and other such horror internment camps.

Some of these experiences went on for years. In the second year of his draft Himelius Hockett, after a five day period of being starved, a parade during which deserters were branded with the letter D three inches broad (" This was done in my presence with a hot iron, accompanied by the screams of the unhappy victims "), was sentenced to six months hard labour in one of the military forts, bound with a heavy ball and chain. There, he says, " we were ordered to assist in unloading ordnance cars, and the officers ordered that we should be pierced four inches deep with bayonets if we refused. On declining to do this service, my brother was pierced cruelly with bayonets, while I was hung up by the thumbs almost clear of the ground.

After I had remained in this suffering position for some time, the corporal was told that he had no orders to tie up either of us, but to pierce us with bayonets, and that he had better obey orders. So I was untied and pierced with a bayonet. . . ." [47] The Hocketts were among those who were suddenly "accepted" by the military, and released, and sent home to their wives and children.

Seth Loflin fared worse. When he refused to handle a gun he was kept "without sleep for thirty-six hours, a soldier standing by with a bayonet, to pierce him, should he fall asleep." Next, "they proceeded for three hours each day to buck him down." This old-time army punishment consisted in tying the wrists together then pressing them over the knees, securing the victim by passing a stick above the wrists but under the knees, thus making him peculiarly helpless and abject on the ground, the butt of kicks and so forth. But this failing with Loflin, he was next suspended by his thumbs, for an hour and a half each day for a week. Then he was court-martialled to be shot.

The regiments were drawn up. "Seth Loflin, as calm as any man of the immense number surrounding him, asked time for prayer . . . He prayed, not for himself, but for his enemies, 'Father, forgive them, for they know not what they do.'" Upon this the firing squad refused to fire. The officers also for the moment gave way.

But afterwards the torture continued. He died of it in hospital. An officer wrote to his wife . . . "He died, as he had lived, a true, humble, and devoted Christian; true to his faith and religion." [48]

There have in fact been many Quaker martyrs, though mostly in the early days simply for keeping their meetings for worship open against all attempts to close them—part of the spade work for our English freedoms long since forgotten by the public; and in particular there were those

[47] F. S. Cartland, *Southern Heroes*, 1895, pp. 254–84.
[48] *Southern Heroes*, pp. 211–13.

Friends who died rather than bear arms, a fact to cherish in this later age that tends to skirt round suffering as at some point or another inevitable to any honest stand by a faith. Those martyred men and women gave sinews to the Quaker testimony, that could then develop comprehensively, and speak with a loving authority safe beyond the flesh. One prays it will always be so.

The present sixteenth Query of the Society of Friends reads . . . "Are you faithful in maintaining our testimony against all war as inconsistent with the spirit and teaching of Christ? Do you live in the life and power that takes away the occasion of all wars? Do you seek to take part in the ministry or reconciliation between individuals, groups and nations and in the breaking down of class barriers?" [49] The individual's part varies, but it rests always on the same foundation; and perhaps it can only discover its scope and its continuing strength through the fellowship of a small faithful worshipping group. The end is necessarily in the beginning.

[49] *London Yearly Meeting Advices and Queries*, 1928.

CHAPTER III

THE FOUNDER OF THE MOVEMENT, GEORGE FOX

GEORGE Fox was the founder of Quakerism. He was the leader of the new movement. Although the resultant ingredients, both with regard to the holding of meetings and the type of message preached, had all been there before, were in fact a permanent feature of charismatic Christianity, as against that of the great institutions, Fox gave them new authority: so intense and all-commanding that doubters, seekers, the disillusioned and those simply tired out by the religious combat of the day, as well as many from settled churches, felt gathered into a new fellowship directly quickened by the Lord Jesus Christ.

Fox was the great vessel of this power. Immediately preceding him there had been others working or about to work along the same lines, individuals like Dewsbury in Yorkshire and Anne Hutchinson on Rhode Island, groups like the Westmorland Seekers and those at Ross in Herefordshire who " did often before meet together by ymselves, & would many times sitt in silence, & noe particular person Appointed to speak or Preach Amongst ym, but Each of ym did speak by way of Exortation as had freedom, Soe yt ye Lords power was mightily at worke in theyr hearts & great openings there was Amongst ym ";[1] but nowhere did anyone speak with the compelling certainty and unity of spirit and comprehensive understanding of the young George Fox. He blazed before them as a sign " that Christ was come to teach His people Himself ",[2] that Christ lived eternally in their hearts and had not died at Jerusalem; and they responded and sought the living Spirit, and

[1] *First Publishers of Truth*, p. 124.
[2] *Journal*, p. 90.

found it together experimentally. Fox sparked off that victory.

Afterwards, though other voices added considerably to the movement, giving it this or that inflection, all were necessarily relative to Fox. No one could say that without him, despite the ground being so well prepared, Quakerism would have burst forth with sufficient vigour and unifying spirit to develop and survive as it did. He was the elder brother in the church and acknowledged and loved as such by his colleagues, who called him " our ancient Friend and honourable elder in the church of God ",[3] " a dear and tender father in the effectual Truth ",[4] " the first and chief elder in this age . . . exercising his eldership in the invisible power that had gathered them." [5]

When he first came to London a Friend recorded . . . " Here are in this city many precious Friends, and they begin to know George, though at the first he was strange to them; and one thing they all take notice of, that if George be in the company, all the rest are for the most part silent, which they did much wonder at ":[6] which same Friend later wrote to Fox in time of great persecution . . . " Dear G. let thy prayers be still for us that we may persevere unto the end in our testimony for God." [7] A convert could write to him . . . " my deare life, my liueing Joy, who beegat me into the liueinge life & put life where none was, & turned me towards an endless Kingdome whose Kingdome endures for euer & stablisht me on him yt was bee fore the world was " [8] . . . and a fellow minister, " Deare brother thy owne seed, begoten by the[e], runes out to thee and salutes the[e] in the lord." [9]

---

3 *Letters of Early Friends*, p. 206.
4 *Letters of Early Friends*, p. 229.
5 *Journal*, p. xlvii.
6 *Letters of Early Friends*, p. 31.
7 *Letters of Early Friends*, p. 125.
8 *First Publishers of Truth*, p. 201 n.
9 *Journal of Friends Historical Society*, Vol. 48 (1957), p. 132.

More soberly, William Dewsbury told him . . . " It would be too tedious to mention the names of them that minded their love to thee, through all the countries where I travelled . . . the deep sense of thy labour and travail is fresh upon their spirits; which causeth many prayers to be poured forth before the Lord, if it be his good will and pleasure, to give thee strength of body and liberty, to travel amongst them to their great comfort as in days of old." [10] They all looked on George Fox as the one who had freed the word of God within them.

Since those days many new figures have risen within the Society of Friends, to rediscover and to extend its witness in the life of their times, but none, not even the saintly Woolman, leap out of their immediate context to press equally upon the world to-day with such ringing power as Fox displays. His words, like phrases of great music, lift up the eternal realities that underpin our lives, scattering all lesser pleas. Stark and true they indicate, whatever the form of challenge facing us, however overwhelming it becomes, where lies the strength to overcome it. He is still, in the mid-twentieth century, the best single advocate for the Quaker understanding of humanity, and that despite the blinding inhibitions his day saddled him with, which conditioned his particular route of experience and his further labours of readjustment: his response remains universal. His is the genius of the movement, that Emerson called " the lengthened shadow of a man "; he is the Quaker archetype. " Being dead, he yet speaketh ".[11]

How was he himself formed? How did he become the channel of such concentrated spiritual power—that he could discern a man's condition at a glance, could heal the sick, could raise up faith in other hearts? What price in other respects did he have to pay for this; and how well

[10] E. Smith, *Life of Dewsbury*, p. 237.
[11] *Journal*, p. xlviii.

did he sustain his rôle, or even strengthen it, as his life progressed?

He was born, in 1624, at Fenny Drayton in Leicestershire, one of several children of a fairly prosperous weaver of the place, surrounded by relatives and interested neighbours. He received little formal education, but at an early age was put to work with a shoemaker, who also dealt in wool and cattle, and for some years he led the open-air life of a shepherd. Then, as his inward tension grew, he broke away from these arrangements, and, supplied with money from home, set off across country in search of spiritual counsel, from every chance priest or scholar; till these in turn sickened him, and he withdrew completely into himself, assisted only by his Bible, for the culminating travail that produced the mature George Fox, the preacher who was to shake England.

Clearly this background was not remarkable, and so far the indication is that Fox simply subtracted himself from it in order to find his unique self, alone, within, facing God, as though this had been determined irrespective of time and place. Such an approach, however, never gives the complete story; even mystics have feet of clay. One must sift again more carefully.

Now, the picture given by the opening pages of Fox's *Journal,* and borne out by the later events, is of one or two irreducible tendencies conditioned by home and family. He was sturdy and energetic, proud of his country health, physically above average; at the same time sensitive and retiring, even as a child abstemious and critical of his elders' fun and cautious of committing himself to more than " yea " and " nay ". " I had a gravity and stayedness of mind and spirit not usual in children . . . I knew pureness and righteousness." [12] There is no play, no relaxation, no easy companionship with the others. He presents himself in fact as a rather priggish little Puritan, a solitary, constrained, cen-

[12] *Journal,* p. 1.

sorious, with undertones of pugnacity and anxiety. There is no note of affection, no warmth: his father is referred to as honest, righteous, with a Seed of God in him, and his mother as an upright woman. His brothers are never mentioned; his relatives figure as a potential threat, in particular one cousin, who encourages him to drink and for once let go, by now at the age of nineteen, precipitates the all-night crisis that causes him to break away from home.

Even so, he can't stay long in any one place: he is restless, tormented, the victim of unbearable stress and then despair. He feels lusts and temptations, " the whisperings of Satan in man in the night Season ",[13] which for the next few years attack him unmercifully. He feels " in a measure sensible of Christ's sufferings, and what he went through." [14] He presents a harrowing picture, in fact, of a child's usual out-reaching feelings being held back, driven under, made to afflict him with guilt and anxiety till the whole world is coloured with sin, and none of it can be endured. This frames his horizon; he is eaten up with his own woes. He is a casualty of the Puritan conscience, like scores of thousands of children of his time. He was to find, however, and this was the achievement that singled him out from most of his contemporaries, a large measure of release from it; and that not by compromise, by hypocrisy. He widened the framework, thrust beyond the first conditioning sense of sin.

To begin with, though, he was a victim of his day, the over-serious dread household into which he was born reflecting the world outside, that trembled with cataclysmic events (as our own world is beginning to do). Aggression and guilt were in the air; the pressure on individual conscience was feeling for its limits, fashioning extreme rewards and punishment. Even innocent pleasures were

13 Journal, p. 9.
14 Journal, p. 5.

suspect; it was hardly safe (immortally, so to speak) to laugh or display affection, so quickly could that turn into a wanton frame of mind. Is this what caught the young George, shutting him fearfully into himself? In particular, were his first love feelings towards his mother rendered insecure, damped down, hedged with caution: so that, especially if these were strong, yet had to be suppressed, everything else in turn was suppressed, if these could be the occasion of doubt, then related emotion was equally so, more so as he grew in awareness of its sexual ramifications? This would not be unusual among the Puritan young.

Consider only how at forty-five he married an outstanding mother figure, Margaret Fell (then a widow ten years his senior), not for the procreation of children for he said he judged such things beneath him, not in order to live with her for by then the movement claimed his life: but, symbolically, for " the redemption of all marriages out of the Fall ",[15] to witness " a marriage as it was in the beginning before sin and defilement was ".[16] He seemed intent on recreating a pristine pure relationship, such as a child sees it with his mother before any other attitudes are imbibed. In fact he projected this idealised relationship into all his views on women, encouraging them in the mother rôle, encouraging them in all desexualised activity; and especially, for his mother also came of the stock of martyrs, in all public religious work. His ideal woman remained his mother, conceived of without love stress.

In this light consider the second part of a dream he experienced during his last mental crisis, two years after his marriage . . . "And I went on again and bid them dig again, and Friends said unto me, ' George, thou finds out all things ', and so there they digged, and I went down, and went along the vault; and there sat a woman in white looking at time how it passed away. And there followed

---

[15] *Portfolio* 10, (53).
[16] *Swarthmore Transcripts*, Vol. V, p. 44.

me a woman down in the vault, in which vault was the
treasure; and so she laid her hand on the treasure on my
left hand and then time whisked on apace; but I clapped
my hand upon her and said, 'Touch not the treasure.'
And then time passed not so swift." [17]

On the other hand he never ceased to decry all that
savoured of the flesh, ceaselessly issuing warnings to
Friends: even against marrying "with the world . . . for
if you do, you break the Law of God in your marriages." [18]
"God will shorten your days." [19] He was equally against
the marriage of cousins. It was a pity because this lop-
sided view of the realms of flesh and spirit was a major
cause of Quaker decline, when young Friends in later
decades insisted on marrying as they pleased, and were
disowned; it was hardly part of the redemptive faith that
Fox more than anyone set forth; it was the work of the
suppressed side of his make-up, that teased and constricted
him to the end. In this, moreover, he further reflected a
not uncommon Puritan trait: one that still bedevils the
Anglo-Saxon character.

Returning to the youth in his early twenties, wandering
about the countryside, he was more and more disillusioned
with his elders, especially the priests, because they were
dissemblers, hypocrites, tainted with the world, and so
unable to sustain him in the rigid purity that his inner
tension demanded. He was desperate . . . "when it was
day I wished for night, and when it was night I wished
for day" [20] . . . "and when I myself was in the deep,
under all shut up, I could not believe that I should ever
overcome: my troubles, my sorrows, and my temptations
were so great." [21] He fasted much, and increasingly
shunned all company and "often took my Bible and went

[17] *Journal*, p. 578.
[18] *Swarthmore Transcripts*, Vol. V, p. 43.
[19] *Sundry Ancient Epistles*, pp. 15–16.
[20] *Journal*, p. 9.
[21] *Journal*, p. 12.

and sat in hollow trees and lonesome places till night came on; and frequently in the night walked mournfully about by myself, for I was a man of sorrows in the times of the first workings of the Lord in me." [22] When they tried to let some blood out of him . . . " they could not get one drop of blood from me, either in arms or head, though they endeavoured it, my body being, as it were, dried up with sorrows, grief, and troubles, which were so great upon me that I could have wished I had never been born to see vanity and wickedness, or that I had been born blind. . . ." [23]

He was nearing a crisis. Such stress is not tenable for ever; feeling becomes exhausted, the nerves snap, the customary pattern of thought collapses. Anxiety, solitude, fasting, despair, an exalted sensibility: it has been the well-worn route of such conflicts, thought of as personal or political or religious, all agonising and unbearable, till suddenly a new structure supervenes, energy thrums round a new centre, welling up from the unconscious depth of the personality (or, perhaps better, pouring in from the unknown beyond consciousness) in terms of joy and salvation. The old ego is disintegrated, and sinks for the moment out of sight. The new man can bear to live.

Fox said . . . "And when all my hopes in them and in all men were gone, so that I had nothing outwardly to help me, nor could tell what to do, then, oh then, I heard a voice which said, ' There is one, even Christ Jesus, that can speak to thy condition ', and when I heard it my heart did leap for joy." [24] He had joined the company of mystics.

Actually, by his own account, though this was the critical moment, there had been several preliminary " openings " —" and though my exercises and troubles were very great, yet were they not so continual but that I had some intermissions, and was sometimes brought into such an heavenly

[22] *Journal*, p. 9.
[23] *Journal*, p. 6.
[24] *Journal*, p. 11.

THE FOUNDER OF THE MOVEMENT, GEORGE FOX 97

joy that I thought I had been in Abraham's bosom ";[25] just as also afterwards the drag of temptation continued, but now at a distance, and wilting before the changed personality. "Then did I see my troubles, trials, and temptations more than ever I had done . . . and the Lord opened me that I saw through all these troubles and temptations. My living faith was raised, that I saw all was done by Christ, the life, and my belief was in him . . . all was manifest and seen in the Light . . . the spiritual discerning came into me." [26]

Fox in fact had been saved by this spiritual breakthrough. If there had been no break-through, he would have gone mad, or swung into extreme profligacy, or become a hell-fire Calvanist; equally if the break-through had not reintegrated him on a pure universal level he would never have become an adequate vessel for the redeeming spirit of God. That he did become such we must give thanks to his obsessive personal need for purity (so desperate it was a life-and-death matter), and to his study of the Bible that impregnated his mind with the most profound religious symbols and values; and beyond that, as he called on God, to the grace of God bearing down. The analogy is with Meeting for Worship; and as we noted then such lone flights are subject to peculiar dangers. Fox did not altogether avoid them.

But to start with he simply rejoiced in the peace he was attaining, in the unity of being that replaced conflict . . . " my sorrows and troubles began to wear off and tears of joy dropped from me . . . and I saw into that which was without end, and things which cannot be uttered, and of the greatness and infiniteness of the love of God, which cannot be expressed by words . . . I was very much altered in countenance and person as if my body had been new moulded or changed . . . and a report went abroad of me

[25] *Journal*, p. 10.
[26] *Journal*, p. 14.

that I was a young man that had a discerning spirit; whereupon many came to me from far and near, professors,
priests, and people. And the Lord's power broke forth;
and I had great openings, and prophecies, and spake unto
them of the things of God, and they heard with attention
and silence, and went away, and spread the fame thereof."[27]

Fox had been renewed himself, and the wonder of it
overflowed; he could testify to a saving power; and because
his earlier state of conflict was common in the Puritan
world, his inward victory (without the paraphernalia of
sacraments and priestly texts, a kind of magic discredited
in many eyes besides his own) at once quickened his
audience. Whatever the other factors involved, and discounting those who didn't need this cure, the mere sight
and sound of such overwhelming certitude in the transforming power of God's grace within touched off a new
struggle in others to achieve this same victory. They were
similarly afflicted with guilt and despair, as their searing
accounts of themselves reveal; but Fox brought hope, and
the right words of direction to assist them, and they
renewed their travail, and many came through. They
were Children of Light, Friends in their new-found joy,
and gradually they developed a method of pooling their
resources in meeting for worship, to sustain and aid each
other of varying degrees of darkness towards successive
stages of light. That was the birth of Quakerism, and
Fox's relation to it. In this he was the " original, being
no man's copy ".[28]

He himself went from strength to strength. Gone was
the retiring country lad, who fled the world because it
encouraged the seeming devil within; he now stood up
before all to preach for hours at a time, trumpeting the
note of victory. He challenged priests, scholars, magistrates
—" ' George, what! wilt thou never have done?' . . . and

27 *Journal*, pp. 20–1.
28 *Journal*, p. xliii.

I told him I should have done presently, so after I had done and cleared myself in the Lord's power, all the priests and people stood still for a time." [29]

He never yielded an inch, whether in court or prison or palace, or beset by an angry mob. Clad in his leather suit, his broad hat clamped to his head, on foot and on horseback he pressed on, robust but more than that unvanquishable, spurning ideas of compromise, calling on men to change themselves through the spirit of Christ their inward strength. He had the courage of one who can do no other.

"He is as stiff as a tree and as pure as a bell, for we could never stir him", his gaolers said [30]—at a time when Fox "was so weak with lying about three years in cruel and hard imprisonments, my joints and my body were so stiff and benumbed that I could hardly get on my horse. Neither could I well bend my knees, nor hardly endure fire nor eat warm meat: I had been so long kept from it." [31]

But a man who has overcome a crisis through a complete shift in his personality can never be daunted by persecution —whether he's a Christian facing lions or a Communist rotting in a torture chamber; he feels compressed and compressed like a rubber ball, the old devil all about him, but the tighter he is squeezed the greater the resilience of faith that is called into being. Disintegration may still be possible, but not when attempted like that from without.

Fox indeed had a knack of transferring the contest into his persecutor's heart, as during the fantastic court scene at Lancaster in 1664 . . . "So I looked him [the judge] in the face. And the witness started up in him and made him blush when he looked at me again. For he saw that I saw him." [32] Against a crowd that hustled him at Brig-

29 *Journal*, p. 188.
30 *Journal*, p. 502.
31 *Journal*, p. 510.
32 *Journal*, p. 481.

house, some of them having sworn to kill him, he maintained his bearing though they pushed him down repeatedly; and finally he was able to speak so that " they were all silent and had nothing to say, and the Lord's power came over them all and reached the witness of God in them. . . ." [33] That was his undeviating objective: to reach the witness of God in all people. To swell the note of victory. There lay the keynote of his preaching . . . " Keep your feet upon the top of mountains and sound deep to the witness of God in every man." [34] A constant word in his *Journal* is " a-top "; as he had conquered so others should conquer. Penn wrote of him afterwards . . . " So full of assurance was he that he triumphed over death . . . even to the last, as if death were hardly worth notice. . . ." [35] The formidable evangelist knew only victory.

Of course, his formative mystic experience was not a once-for-all attainment. Although in a *Journal* of seven hundred pages [36] it is the first chapter of twenty-one pages that contains the seed of all that later happens, by way of repetition and amplification and adjustment to each new field encountered, as though that first experience were the peak of what was attainable by Fox, still, within the structure of his changed personality, he was constantly renewing this vitalising contact. Way had been opened, and the stability, perhaps the life, of the new man required it should be used. Temptations continued as a minor prod, to which was added persecution; and above that a sense of belonging to God, of identity with His will, of an increasingly habitual and joyful contact, was strengthened through prayer alone and in meetings. Of his prayer in public Penn wrote . . . "Above all he excelled in prayer. The inwardness and weight of his spirit, the reverence and

33 *Journal*, p. 179.
34 *Epistle* 195 (1660).
35 *Journal*, p. xlviii.
36 CUP, 1952 edition.

solemnity of his address and behaviour, and the fewness and fullness of his words, have often struck even strangers with admiration, as they used to reach others with consolation. The most awful, living, reverent frame I ever felt or beheld, I must say, was his in prayer. . . ." [37] Fox was a channel of life-giving spirit.

This power in him shone through his eyes—" Look at his eyes ", the crowd exclaimed.[38] It lit up his words, " abruptly and brokenly " [39] in the manner of deeply emotive language, and his ability to fathom the condition of others; it extended through his hands, whose touch together with his hypnotic presence, healed the sick. But in this he was simply making visible the cure his words so often touched off in the plagued souls of his time, a time so awash with psychic trouble that physical disorders like lameness, palsy, paralysing fright, inevitably followed: which in some cases could then be induced back to life through the lead of a spirit such as Fox's. As with Jesus such power was no miracle, but a sufficiently strong witnessing to a redeemed pattern of being, that drew people out of their sickness. Here was proof of another solution. They responded.

" I was at a stand in my mind whether I should practise physic ", wrote the young Fox . . . " seeing the nature and virtues of the creatures were so opened to me by the Lord." [40] But he realised a more profound calling. Health, and life, are primarily of the spirit.

Were there limits to this power and vision? In essence it was limitless, reflecting God's spirit, but within his human personality it was hedged and alloyed with subjective factors, the price Fox paid to his environment and to the way, alone and desperate, in which he first won freedom from it. No doubt this freedom was largely real and

[37] *Journal*, p. xliv.
[38] *Journal*, p. 377.
[39] *Journal*, p. xliii.
[40] *Journal*, p. 27.

he knew thereafter an uplifting joy, but evidence points to
other elements still working powerfully within him, that
rode him strangely upon occasion, and induced two major
crises. At the end of his life he could say, " I am clear,
I am fully clear ",[41] and his habits suggest that by then it
was so; but the intermediate passage was stormy. This
great public servant of the Lord still had private devils to
contend with.

It may be that in some of the outstanding mystic encounters, as in more routine conversions, the stresses
involved are permanently resolved, and the old troublesome
emotions are all transformed into constructive energy, or
into an ability to withhold the flow of energy: this may
be so among the subtleties of Hindu non-attachment, or
in the experience of St. Augustine who claimed, " If you
only love God enough, you may safely follow all your
inclinations ";[42] but it was not so with George Fox.

With him the catastrophic feelings, that up to his
moment of release seemed bent on his destruction, afterwards reappeared bedded in the involuntary part of his
personality, doubtless much diluted and fragmentary, but
still active and now insidious, for they took the form of
explosive warnings and denunciations, and diffused anger,
and a virulent turn of language on occasion, that in part
he could feel was justified as a scourge for a sinful world,
but which narrowed his power of discrimination, his ability
to love with simple warmth, and tended to inflate his sense
of his own sanctity.

Quite likely it was this continuing thrust of dark energy
upwards that in part kept him without pause at work, for
ever extending the kingdom of light through the souls of
other people, to neutralise his own devils as well as theirs,
to maintain as he put it " The infinite ocean of light and
love, which flowed over the ocean of darkness ";[43] and

41 *Journal*, p. 759.
42 In *Joann.*, vii, 8.
43 *Journal*, p. 19.

even thus, good deed by deed, to reclaim the hidden side of himself. It must also have assisted his power of discerning mixed-up conditions.

But beside that it forced on him other negative characteristics. For so long as he was compelled to fight a containing action within, however marginal that might be, Fox could never bear to negotiate, to see a different view or need, to paint in anything but black or white. " He that is not with me is against me ": [44] it is an over-narrow compulsive dictum at the best of times, invoking intolerance. Perhaps, in an age of unrest and oppression, it serves as a useful rallying cry, jolts the undecided, heartens the brethren, but it is a dangerous two-edged weapon. Fox, obdurate, hurling invective, pouring out denunciatory pamphlets with the earnestness of a propaganda machine (one of the vices of Puritan times) was not the man to be fortified by it. It hardened his repressed side, the counterpart to his tender vision of the indwelling Light in all men.

Baxter complained . . . " There is scarce a scold heard among us in seven year's time that useth so many railing words . . . as these people will use familiarly in their religious exercises against the faithful servants of Christ." [45] Fox never minced matters. Much can be excused by the necessity of making a dint in Puritan hypocrisy; but was it necessary to slang individuals with the heady fury he sometimes displayed, or to accompany them beyond the grave with thanks to the Lord for His vengeance on them? After listing a dozen people who had died, who had been instrumental in persecuting Friends, he adds . . . " whom the Lord blasted and ruined . . . the Lord had executed his vengeance upon them." [46] Elsewhere he says of his opponents . . . " all such spirits I laid before the Lord and left them to him to deal with them." [47] The assumption is of

[44] *Matt.* 12:30.
[45] *One Sheet Against the Quakers*, p. 4.
[46] *Journal*, p. 505.
[47] *Journal*, p. 180.

Jehovistic wrath evening the score to Fox's satisfaction. That is not his message to the world; but a thrust of emotion he could not control.

Similarly, an intermittent violence pushes into his visions . . . " I got a great hedge stake and chopped it down his throat to his heart and laid him still " [48] . . . " I had a vision of a great mastiff dog, that would have bitten me, but I put one hand above his jaw, and the other below, and tore his jaw to pieces " [49] . . . "As G.F. was in Bandon getting up and dressing himself in the morning, there appeared a very ugly-visaged man, black and dark, and G.F. struck at him in the power of God, and with his horse rode over him, and his horse put his foot on the side of his cheek." [50] Rage, even in the great pacifist, frothed up beneath the surface, and played its part in his total make-up. Perhaps only in his last years did it die away.

On the surface, within the will, Fox always followed the same vigorous asceticism which included, as with the other early Friends, the practice of fasting for quite long periods. Evelyn notes in his diary how . . . " I had the curiosity to visit some Quakers here in prison . . . one of these was said to have fasted twenty days; but another, endeavouring to do the like, perished on the 10th. . . ." [51] The Swarthmore household cheerfully wrote . . . " Friends here are well, and great and marvellous is the work of the Lord in this family, where several have been exercised and yet are in fasting. Bridget Fell fasted twelve days, Isabel hath fasted about seven and is to fast nine, little Mary [ten years old] hath fasted five, and a little maid that is a servant in the house called Mabby hath fasted twenty. . . ." [52]

Fox heartedly approved of this and did as much himself.

[48] *Journal of Friends Historical Society*, Vol. 4 (1907), p. 124.
[49] *Journal*, p. 428.
[50] *Journal*, p. 539.
[51] *The Diary of John Evelyn*, 1908, p. 191.
[52] *Swarthmore MSS*, Vol. 4 (267).

The practice doubtless helped the spirit at certain difficult moments; but it was also part of the restrictive approach, common indeed to the whole of Puritanism, of a man who still feared the free natural life of the flesh and so fulminated against it. Reason here again was with him in attacking the vanity and pride of his day, but his attitude was so all-bludgeoning, extending even to music and pleasures like wrestling and football, that one feels the drive of hidden inhibitions aggressively at work again. However, besides the right-wing Puritans, really obsessed with man's depravity, Fox could be passed off as a mild chirrupping optimist; there were degrees of that kind of neurosis.

But one cannot blink its presence in him : carnal guilt had overwhelmed his youth, had never been resolved either through normal experiences or through a learning of non-attachment; but instead had been shattered and driven under by the sudden blinding presence of light that lifted him towards his Lord. It thus continued in new form, beyond the conscious orbit of his mind, to prick his feelings and warp his judgment. In this he did not transcend his day.

The corollary of such denunciations without sufficient discrimination, and of the tension that in part governed them, was the tendency, shared by other early Friends, for Fox to see himself as infallible, as at all times the mouth-piece of the Lord. This became the cardinal issue in the first years of their group history. In Fox, besides the inhibitory factors shaping the tenor of his speech, there was the positive factor of his guiding revelation coming to him direct, when alone. When all else had been as ashes, Christ had spoken to him, he writes . . . " These things I did not see by the help of men, nor by the letter, though they are written in the letter, but I saw them in the light of the Lord Jesus Christ, and by his immediate Spirit and power. . . ." [53]

[53] *Journal*, p. 34.

This insight was certainly blessed, the pillar of his life and teaching, and of the Society that gathered round him; and possibly in a man of more balanced nature, out of a different environment, it could have been carried with proportionate humility that would keep the human vessel in its place, though possibly mystics are seldom like that; but in Fox it tended perilously to make him feel that he and all who were awakened by him were already perfect, knowing " nothing but pureness, and innocency, and righteousness, being renewed up into the image of God by Christ Jesus, so that I say I was come up to the state of Adam which he was in before he fell." [54] "And some thought I was mad because I stood for purity, perfection, and righteousness." [55]

To be fair to him one must emphasise the inclusion of the word " righteousness ". This marked him off from Ranters, offshoot of the extreme Anabaptists, who were antinomian both in principle and practice. He saw that the Light, if truly from God, must necessarily distinguish between good and evil, must lead man towards right action, to probity, and care of others. This fundamental qualification was always apparent to Fox himself. Questioned by the courts . . . " Had I no sin?"

" Sin?" Said I, " Christ my Saviour hath taken away my sin, and in him there is no sin. . . ."

. . . They said, " If a man steal is it no sin?"

I answered, " All unrighteousness is sin." [56]

He accepted the basic moral proviso but at the same time claimed he himself no longer could transgress it. During his next imprisonment and trial he told them . . . " The saints shall judge the world, the Scripture doth witness, whereof I am one, and I witness the Scripture fulfilled ", and . . . " all teaching which is given forth by Christ is

[54] *Journal*, p. 27.
[55] *Journal*, p. 61.
[56] *Journal*, pp. 51–2.

to bring the saints to perfection, even to the measure, stature, and fullness of Christ, this the Scripture doth witness, and this I do witness to be fulfilled." [57] Quakers, in fact, *were* already perfect: only the rest need watch their step.

Fortunately, it was not long before a second check, equally important, came to the fore: that the test of true revelation was that it brought Friends into unity. This was the start of the corporate guidance that has continued till to-day, the admission that the human vessel can err, does not always distinguish the Light, though faith be very great, but must as a further check submit it to the insight of the prayful group. This at once offset any follies or exaggerated claims of individual Friends; it was a safeguard against human fallibility.

For Fox personally, it was the hardest lesson that he as the leader had to learn; and though events bore it in on him and he greatly matured in wisdom through them, and himself afterwards built up the framework of the corporate system, he did not escape the inner crises that such shifts of ground occasioned. Twice for a time the spiritual flow that sustained his personality was stopped. For him, conditioned by his lone flight to God, it had seemed that each spiritual awakening was an absolute and final state, an extension of his own perfect victory, to be continued till finally the whole of creation was likewise redeemed. It was hard to accept that " saints " could still err, that " victory " could still suffer reverses, that therefore perhaps (and this took time to work into consciousness) his own state too might still be in question. When it came to this, he was laid flat; though again he achieved new victory over it.

But if it had not been for the martyrdom of Nayler, in so many respects his alter ego, he might not in the first place have been jolted enough to begin this slow reappraisal of

57 *Journal*, p. 135.

realities. James Nayler suffered that Fox could better understand himself.

James Nayler was a farmer who had served eight years under Cromwell, in a foot regiment and as a cavalry quartermaster, and had also been much given to current army preaching (what to-day we would think of as a party man further indoctrinating the troops); he had been invalided out in 1651, returning to his farm. It was then, though snug with wife and children, that the Call came to him . . . " I was at the plough ", he afterwards related, " meditating on the things of God, and suddenly I heard a Voice, saying unto me, ' Get thee out from thy kindred and from thy father's house.' And I had a promise given in with it. Whereupon I did exceedingly rejoice, that I had heard the Voice of that God which I had professed from a child, but had never known him. . . ." [58]

He refused to heed, held by natural ties; but so acute a crisis did this cause that he ceased to eat and his life was despaired of. At that point Fox appeared, and tipped the balance, as inevitably he would: he established in Nayler a sense of the permanent indwelling of Christ's Light, a continuous comfort and guide not just an intermittent and distant Voice. Nayler straightway took to the road as one of the company of preaching Friends, without even saying goodbye to his family—like Bunyan's Christian, fingers in ears, who ran off crying " Life ! Life ! Eternal life !" One should note this, for more than in Fox, as later conduct revealed, he remained attached with part of himself to his suppressed sensual nature: which, as his godly mission took hold of him, he tried to exercise through prodigious fasting and finally was driven to offset by the fantasy of identifying himself with Christ. As with Fox the heights of perfection were in part inversions of the feared abysses within.

A brilliant preacher, magnetic, better schooled than his

[58] *Works*, 1716, p. 12.

leader, he reached London by 1654. There his fame soared, many of the great harkening to him, many households offering hospitality; he was thought even by Baxter to be the chief Quaker. A contemporary description records him as . . . " of a melancholy aspect and he wears his hat hanging over his brows, his clothes very plain. He wears a little band close to his collar, without any bandstrings, as doth the other great Quaker, George Fox. He doth strive in his looks and posture to imitate the picture of Our Saviour as it was sent up to Rome in the days of Tiberius Cæsar and he strives to wear his hair as it were with a seam on the crown of his head and so flowing down on each side of it." [59]

The cult of this ecstatic personality, with its messianic overtones, grew till he found himself the prey of the most unstable among Quaker adherents, those who wavered to and fro across the border from Ranters and Millenarists, who like medieval Beghards or the Free Brothers or the Munster Saints considered that their " state of perfection ", heralding Christ's Second Coming, so inspired and preserved them that whatever they did was no more than a sign of some quickening heavenly intention.

As noted, this was an aberration threatening all early Friends, uplifted by their spiritual experience, but was cancelled out in the majority by their continuing moral sense and by the early established practices of fellowship: only to break out here and there in excesses of language or in the urge to run naked on market days crying " Woe " on bewildered fellow citizens. This last, as Nayler himself remarked, and as later did Barclay, was practised against the conscious will, that is, was impelled by repressed emotion. What can one make of Richard Sale, a Quaker constable, who paraded his town in sackcloth, flowers in one hand, stinking weeds in the other, ashes on his head, and saying of himself . . . " My countenance was as fierce

[59] The Quakers' Quaking, 1656, anonymous.

as a lion, which was dreadful unto the wicked; and when the lion roared through the streets, the beasts of the field began to tremble, and many faces gathered paleness."? [60] Such fantasies were clinical.

In London the nub of such elements was a group of married women who reacted very strongly to Nayler: to his brilliant preaching, his Christ-like appearance, his unstable nervous tension. They got their claws into him and would not let him go; and they so mixed religious acclaim with more earthly blandishment, confusing his contrary urges, that he was doubly ensnared and became their puppet. Partly, he egged them on . . . "I reasoned against [the Spirit's] tender reproof, and consulted with another and so let the Creatures into my Affections" [61]: because his flesh desired flattery and the attention of adoring women, and because also, to counteract this, his spirit longed for a witness to absolute perfection. Despite the sly quibbles at his trial, Nayler was ready, indeed required, to be acclaimed the Christ. However passive and fuddled he appeared, gripped by schizophrenic logic, sweating like a bull, paralysed by fasting, he nonetheless hardened in the rôle, shut his ears to other counsel (which never ceased to plead with him), and absorbed the drama to its last drop. He became the classic warning, to Friends, of the perils of an intensive spiritual life without the controlling fellowship of Meetings. He marked the endpoint of their spiritual individualism.

The scene shifted from London to Bristol, to Exeter gaol, then back to Bristol. The leading harpy among the women, his Kali-like disciple, Martha Simmonds (a goat rough and hairey, Burroughs called her), was a printer's wife aged thirty who had already lured him to her London house and now followed him to the West Country. She and her companions made a public display of kneeling before him,

[60] *Swarthmore* MSS, Vol. 4 (211).
[61] *Works*, p. xli.

claiming, when he touched a girl in a swoon, that he had raised this creature from the dead. She spared time to go on to Launceston, where Fox lay imprisoned, to taunt the leader with her destructive power; then raced back to head the chorus in Exeter that was now addressing Nayler as " The only Begotten Son of God . . . fairest of ten thousand . . . dear and precious Son of Zion whose mother is a virgin and whose birth is immortal . . . Thy Name shall be no more James Nayler, but Jesus."

Released from here, in the full flush of fantasy Nayler let this group escort him back to Bristol, arriving, on a wet October day, in a manner that re-enacted Christ's entry into Jerusalem. Every street was lined to watch him, the whole city turned out; though none of the thousand Quakers of the place joined in the spectacle. Only his little troop performed, throwing cloaks before his horse, chanting " Holy, holy, holy Lord God of Israel." Soon he was hauled before the magistrates, where Martha Simmonds, still singing and bowing to him, insisted he was Christ. So from here he was summoned to trial before Parliament. None less now felt able to deal with him.

His defence there, that he had been but a Sign of Christ's immanent Coming, did not reassure the Members: who, after a month of study and debate, condemned him to be pilloried, whipped, branded, his tongue bored through, and finally to be left languishing in prison. This sentence was carried out. Apart from the ferocity of Puritans, whose natural energies were repressed in so many other ways, this verdict reflected their fear lest Quakers might be teaming up with the more militant left-wing amalgam of Fifth Monarchy Men and other such millenarists, ex-Levellers and Diggers, and Ranters and so forth; for there was growing disaffection in the country and Nayler was just the sort of figure round whom revolt could crystallise. One excess could lead to another. Cromwell for once didn't shield the Society; Nayler was to serve as a warning to the nation.

He also served as a warning to Fox, who did nothing to shield him either: indeed, at the moment of his trial, Nayler was the loneliest man in England, despite a few gestures of sympathy. The writing on the wall was clear to all of chiliastic tendency, who considered themselves and their actions inspired beyond reproach. It was the morning after their night before.

For a year previously Fox had been cautioning Nayler, and he actually visited him during his last days in Exeter gaol, but by then Nayler was too far gone, and Fox in turn lost his temper offering Nayler his foot to kiss; and after trial and sentence four further years passed before Fox agreed to see him again. Those were vital years for the leader, during which he slowly digested the lessons of the Nayler affair; and it was only after they had brought him personally to the point of collapse, followed by renewed inner victory, a renewed integration of self, that he could bear to meet Nayler. It cannot be stressed too strongly that for Fox the condition of other Friends, of every single soul who had found joy after his pattern, was an extension of his own being; so that a reverse of this order threatened to overwhelm him personally with darkness.

In part, it was simple rivalry—who was to be the Society's leader. But was such a question ever so simple? Two factors would enter into it, so far as Fox was concerned: the more practical one of the different emphases that he and Nayler would give to the expounding of their faith and the relation these would bear to current realities, and the more intangible one of stability within the Society's soul, that is to say, within himself. He came to grips first with the former.

Here the central point was not so much that Nayler, especially in his writings, had been more radical socially than Fox, but that, once emotionally he had surrendered himself to the Ranters and millenarists, in his Christ-rôle discarding all checks, there was nothing to stop him from leading Quakers towards more militant action. He could become the tool of non-Quaker insurrectionaries. Fox feared much as did Cromwell, and this he could feel in all his bones was not the Quaker witness. He had called on men to change themselves before they could hope to change the world—he had just issued almost his finest words on the subject, towards the end saying . . . " Be patterns, be examples in all countries, places, nations, wherever you come; that your carriage and life may preach among all sorts of people, and to them. Then you will come to walk cheerfully over the world, answering that of God in every one; whereby in them ye may be a blessing, and make the witness of God in them to bless you . . . keep yourself clear of the blood of all men, either by word, or writing, or speaking. . . ." [62]

He now began to follow this up with a succession of epistles, on the one hand that would reassure Cromwell and on the other strengthen Friends in their inward course. " Go not forth ", says the first of these, " to the aggravating part, to strive with it out of the power of God, lest you hurt yourselves, and run into the same nature, out of the life." [63] He then passed for a year into Wales and Scotland, only to return the more urgently to the theme, especially as the imprisonment of Quakers was increasing, the suspicions of the authorities not allayed . . . "And all Friends, meddle not with the powers of the earth; keep out of all such things. . . ." [64] He reiterated this till it was finally embodied in the peace testimony if 1660, thus fixing limits to Quaker social action, and thus resolving the first of the problems brought to the fore through Nayler.

The other problem lay deeper, and it almost looks as if for a time Fox pushed it out of his thoughts. Spiritually he could dismiss his rival as one ensnared by an evil woman

[62] *Journal*, p. 263.
[63] *Journal*, p. 281.
[64] *Journal*, p. 341.

—one doubts that Fox would ever forget Martha Simmonds gloating over him, as he lay helpless in Launceston gaol, but gradually the problem grew. Till now he had borne the state of the Society as the complement to his own inner state; and so long as success attended his efforts and those of his lieutenants, then all was well; but now it was not just that Nayler had tried to usurp this primal position, he had, in defeat, so unsettled the Society that many Friends were continuing uneasy, doubting the Light (that could split Friends in two), doubting Fox and the umbilical relationship ("You have lost the power, you have lost the power", shouted disturbers of London meetings),[65] doubting the value of the whole witness if it wasn't visibly to be led by Christ and produce immediate social justice, and certainly doubting ideas of perfection. Fox could feel his house tumbling down. As the Light flickered throughout the Society, it positively dimmed in him, inevitably disturbing his balance, reducing him to ten weeks of wretchedness in private, at Reading. Is it any wonder that during this time he refused admittance to Nayler, who had recently been released from prison? Nayler had started the rot, and now it was every year more evident that reverses could happen, through the whole community, that "saints" were not finally perfect, and that Fox himself in consequence, to preserve his own inner balance, must reduce his sense of founding-father involvement. For the moment it was all he could do to summon enough faith to sustain his own being. There, but for Nayler, might have gone Fox.

He came through, Fox always came through; but just eight years later, in the first pause of the Restoration attack on Friends, when internal affairs could be thought of again, it so happened that another voice was raised for personal infallibility on issues that could not but harm the group. John Perrot, in his heady attitude, was back where Nayler

65 *Works*, p. xvi.

and Fox had been, in their first glow of saintly perfection; but Fox by now had learned his lesson. He at once set about establishing the system of Monthly and Quarterly Meetings, that would strengthen corporate responsibility and temper individual certainties (that this also conveyed too much power to a select group of Friends in London is not here material, except in that Fox, in swinging over, devolving the burden that in his eyes had largely rested till now on him—and again, as an extension of that, on the other First Publishers—was less and less able to control the pace or the extent of what was happening). He was spurred on also by thought of how best Friends could withstand persecution, and survive. He devotes eighteen pages of his *Journal* to this task of establishing a framework of meetings; and later his remarkable American journey was chiefly for the same purpose. It was, after his first arousing of the Word in other seekers, the second peak of his life's activity—the strengthening of their own deep spiritual resources. Yet, almost as soon as it was finished (with regard, that is, to the British Isles), he succumbed to a second mental illness, a deeper crisis even than before.

It was as if Fox, who . . . " lay at the widow Dry's all that winter, warring with the evil spirits, and could not endure the smell of any flesh meat . . . and lost my hearing and sight . . . and great sufferings I was under at this time beyond words to declare, for I was come into the deep, and the men-eaters were about me and I warred with their spirits " [66] . . . had, in thus withdrawing from the over-extended burden of his involvement with the Society, this time almost fatally disrupted the mechanism of his own stability. For so long, like all leaders, he had given too much, borne too much, but had become attuned to it; suddenly—and his greatness lies in his having learned that he must take this step, must release his children, must strengthen them in their unity and dependence on one

[66] *Journal*, pp. 570-1.

another: suddenly his chief outlet was narrowed, the umbilical cord was cut, and the tension within him thrown out of balance.

It was then, weakened and distraught, that the psychic disorder of the age and fierceness of oppression bit into him (it could not, with a man of his character, have come about the other way round), and he was back, though now subject to the more complex perils of maturity, at the point of his first despairing collapse. His travail, for all his powers of prayer and habit of evoking spiritual forces from beyond consciousness—the word of God released in the heart—was long and dire. He was submerged; losing even sight and hearing, for they were useless to him in the depths. Doesn't that show that his accustomed mechanism was completely out of gear, that a new disposition of energies was needed? A great campaigner can only be brought down from within.

He triumphed at last. He had found again the immutable Principle of God in his being; his personality was reformed with faith a steady flame burning at the centre. He was never more to suffer disorders, and his life settled to a quieter pattern. There was the great open-air experience of America and two short Continental journeys, a last imprisonment during which he began to dictate his *Journal,* and the final years at Swarthmore and in London. It is then at last, bearing his witness among the others in meetings for worship and business, and in his letters to Friends the world over, and in his way of lodging in simple unaffectedness with this or that family that cared for him, that he emerges as a quite lovable character. He is down to ordinary proportions perhaps, the galvanic stress and triumph brought into a more ordinary life-size frame. These are easily his sweetest years.

As he had risen from his sickness he had said . . . " My dear Friends, The Seed is above all . . . and though the waves and storms be high, yet your faith will keep you to swim above them, for they are but for a time, and the Truth is without time . . . so be faithful, and live in that which doth not think the time long." [67] This is his enduring message, whatever the age and the problems it conditions, whatever the personal complications and the lesson which each lifetime must learn—the perpetually repeated throw of existence. Fox drew an unenviable destiny, on the face of things, but transformed it; he bids us all to find God, whichever way opens to us, which way may not be at all like his, so as to put our lives in order and conformity with eternal principles.

" Therefore be still a while from thy own thoughts, searching, seeking, desires and imaginations, and be stayed in the principle of God in thee, to stay thy mind upon God, up to God. . . ." [68]

The Society he founded is for that purpose.

[67] *Journal*, p. 574.
[68] *Journal*, p. 346.

PART II. THE HISTORICAL SETTING

CHAPTER I

QUAKERS AS REVOLUTIONARIES, 1652–1689

(a) The Spread of the Movement

WHEN George Fox in 1652 spoke to the Seeker groups of Westmorland, stirring them to ecstatic awareness of the immediate possible widening of their consciousness—the bliss of God's spirit among them, as against their former scriptural reverie centred round One who had died at Jerusalem—his following, to date only scattered nuclei in the trail of three years of testifying across the valleys and moors of northern England, took on body and eager lieutenants and a consequent high rate of expansion. In Yorkshire he had found at least three leaders of proved spiritual power — William Dewsbury, James Nayler, Richard Farnsworth—and to these were now added, as both journeymen and apprentice preachers, a troop of fervent men and women who, usually two by two, began to work the neighbouring counties so that by 1654 Yorkshire, Westmorland, Cumberland, Durham, and parts of Lancashire and Cheshire had heard the Quaker message and responded through a chain of meetings for worship, with local congregational life of a fairly uniform pattern, linked by these itinerant ministers and their untiring correspondence between visits. The Quaker Judæa, the hill stronghold of the new faith, had been established.

The headquarters of this activity was Swarthmore Hall near Ulverston, the residence, the largest in the district, of Judge Fell, a leading figure in the north country, whose wife Margaret Fell (later as a widow to marry Fox) had as soon as converted become the housekeeper-general of the young movement. Thanks to her husband's largeness of spirit and enquiring turn of mind her protégés were always sure of a welcome, of bed and food, of money with which to pursue their travels and of a certain amount of local cover against the growing spleen of magistrates. The Fell family owned prosperous farms, whose surplus was sold in the local markets or shipped to Bristol, and they sold iron from their country forge; but though from such sources Margaret Fell could afford to support a few first missionaries, the needs of the movement so enormously grew—for dependent families, prisoners, dismissed employees, the replacement of distrained goods, the purchase or printing of pamphlets, the expansion of the work southwards—that she inaugurated a central Fund to which all meetings were asked to contribute: a move powerfully implementing their sense of responsibility for each other.

In a circular letter of 1655 she writes . . . " Truly dear brethren we would not have troubled you at this time, having troubled you before so lately, but that the necessity is so great, the work so large, and the brethren being gone into so many far and remote places . . . so now for the present, dear brethren, offer freely."[1] In her, early Friends had an excellent administrator, one used, like many ladies of the time, to managing estate or trading accounts. Husbands were inclined to be away fighting or settling their affairs in London. She was also the central correspondent for the travelling ministers, who sent her reports which in turn she passed about in her own letters. They addressed her in the ardent style of evangelists . . . " Dear Sister, who art a fruitful branch in the living vine, and a pleasant plant in the garden of God "[2] . . . " Dear Heart, my dear love in the Lord Jesus dearly salutes thee "[3]—language she could reciprocate, as in this letter to Fox . . . " Our dear father in the Lord . . . O thou bread of life . . . O our dear nursing father . . . O our life . . . O thou fountain of eternal life . . . O thou father of eternal felicity. . . ."[4]

1 *Spence MSS*, Vol. 3, (7).
2 *Letters of Early Friends*, p. 25.
3 *Letters of Early Friends*, p. 68.
4 *Spence MSS*, Vol. 3, (24).

Those were apocalyptic days, with hearts overflowing.

After two years of tilling the North and testing out their several gifts the First Publishers of Truth drove south, to rouse the whole nation. At that time the population of about five millions was ninety per cent. south of the Humber, south of the area so far intensively worked by Friends. Their great challenge lay ahead. Till now it had been rather querulously said of them, " The Quakers would not come into any great towns, but lived in the fells like butterflies ";[5] but now they struck at the main centres of population, London, Bristol, Norwich, the two main University towns, and the more economically advanced Home counties. Generally they still worked in pairs, as " Francis Howgill and Edward Burrough to London, John Camm and John Audland to Bristol through the counties, Richard Hubberthorne and George Whitehead towards Norwich, and Thomas Holme into Wales ",[6] to be closely followed by sixty more, all valiant north countrymen, sturdy forthright dalesmen, not unaware of their worth— as one wrote later to Margaret Fell . . . " Truly Friends in the North is rare and precious, very few I find like them "[7]: though to London eyes they appeared "A sort of People Come there yt went by ye name of Plaine north Cuntry Plowmen ".[8] They were quickly the centre of great interest, sympathetic and otherwise.

Edward Burrough, then twenty years of age, was among the most militant of preachers and pamphleteers, delighting, pacifist though he ultimately became, in language of military assault and capture. He was also brave and consistent through adversity (to the point of a fevered death in prison), and otherwise displayed great qualities of mind. He was just the man to tackle London. As Howgill, his colleague there, said . . . " He was of a manly spirit in the

[5] George Fox, *Journal* (Bi-cent. ed.), Vol. 1, p. 413.
[6] *Journal*, p. 174.
[7] *Swarthmore MSS*, Vol. 3, (131).
[8] *First Publishers of Truth*, p. 163.

things of God. He engaged himself often upon the Lord's account singly in great disputes, when there were many opposers . . . In his public ministry he was elegant in speech, and had the tongue of a learned orator . . . his words ministered grace to the hearers, and were forcible and very pleasant, as apples of gold in pictures of silver . . . God made his ministry very effectual to the conversion of many in the city of London." [9]

A year after their arrival, so great was the crowd attending their preaching, premises were hired at the Bull and Mouth, so called from an inn that used part of the building, where a thousand people, standing, could be present. An eye-witness account of Burrough there says . . . " I have beheld him filled with power by the Spirit of the Lord . . . when the room which was very large hath been filled with people, many of whom have been in uproars, contending one with another, some exclaiming against the Quakers, accusing and charging them with heresy, blasphemy, sedition and what not . . . others endeavouring to vindicate them and speaking of them more favourably. In the midst of all which noise and contention, this servant of the Lord hath stood upon a bench, with his Bible in his hand, for he generally carried one about him, speaking to the people with great authority . . . and so suitable to the present debate amongst them that the whole multitude were overcome thereby, and became exceeding calm and attentive, and departed peaceably and with seeming satisfaction." [10]

This is similar to the power that Fox displayed,[11] that was the mark of the early Quaker ministers; and from such gatherings, as we have seen,[12] individuals were reached and became Friends and joined in the worship of retired meetings. The Bull and Mouth was also used for early church business meetings, to deal with records, the poor, and the

9 W. and T. Evans, *Edward Burrough, a Memoir*, 1851, pp. 397–9.
10 W. Crouch, *Posthuma Christiana*, 1712, p. 26.
11 See above, p. 100.
12 Se above, p. 35.

first tentative oversight of members; and Simmonds the printer worked there, whose wife was so to bedevil Nayler; but the retired meetings were in private houses, as " at Sara Sayers, And one other at Humphrey Bates his house, A Gouldsmith, in Tower street "[13] . . . the chief of these being the home of Gerrard Roberts, a merchant, where also the leading ministers met when in town for consultation. His home for some years was the inner sanctum of the London mission, and out of it grew the later headquarters for the whole Society. Funds were then sent there, no longer to Kendal; it became the stepping-off point for appeals to Parliament, for legal consultation, for extra finance; so that gradually, but inevitably, the outlook of the metropolis, and of merchants, overlaid that of the independent small-congregationally-minded dalesmen. Quakerism came to wear a town coat, of sober but good quality.

Side by side with the work in London went the campaign through the rest of England, meeting with strong pockets of resistance in some of the larger county towns, such as Norwich, Maidstone, Winchester, and increasing resistance almost everywhere as local squires and magistrates, Puritan ministers and business men, began to agree that these over-active Quakers with their nation-wide system of communications and ability to draw large excited crowds, usually among the economically-depressed, were becoming a political danger. They showed respect to neither minister nor magistrate; no sort of punishment appeared to deter them. Were they anarchists, or disguised Papists? Rumour was rife. The ruling classes began to take more forcible action.

But still the Quaker message spread, till every county had been fertilised by these dauntless first messengers, who of course everywhere found Seeker groups and other dissatisfied sectaries, and individuals ready for a multitude of reasons to embrace the new revelation. As later in the days

13 *First Publishers of Truth*, p. 166.

of Wesley and Whitfield, people came over in hundreds. Here was an insight that took them further into the nature of their spiritual condition, adrift as they were in the maelstrom of Reformation controversy; it illuminated, and it sustained them. " We have here in Bristol most commonly 3,000 to 4,000 at a meeting The priests and the magistrates of the city begin to rage, but the soldiers keep them down . . . and many captains and great ones of the city are convinced and do believe in us and that we are of God, and all within ten miles of the city round about the people is very much desirous after truth . . . Yea, at any point we come, we can have 400 or 500 or even 1,000." [14]

Burrough and Howgill spared a few weeks from their London preaching to visit Bristol—there was a constant pooling of prophetic gift, of joining in each other's victories, among these first young ardent missionaries—then a year later they again sallied forth to spread the word in Ireland. But there, as also in Scotland, Friends made headway almost only among the garrison troops, or among those English who had been granted land in return for military services; for otherwise the populace was rooted on the one hand in Catholicism and on the other in Presbyterianism. Burrough did not much like Dublin . . . " a bad place, a very refuge for the wicked " . . . nor in general the people of the country . . . " for generally the country is without inhabitant, except bands of murderers and thieves and robbers " [15]: as similarly his colleague Howgill was to report two years later of Scotland . . . " It is a dark and an untoward nation, and little desire after God, and a false-hearted people and a blood-thirsty ".[16] Like comment was passed on the Welsh and on various Continental peoples. In fact, Quakers warmed to such as were ready for them and responded, but were narrow in judgment

[14] R. Barclay, *The Inner Life of the Religious Societies of the Commonwealth*, 1876, p. 309.
[15] *Letters of Early Friends*, p. 265.
[16] *A.R.B. MSS.* (31).

and uncharitable to those of a different inclination; perhaps the general atmosphere of the times, that included them, was too highly-charged for anything less; and perhaps, typical Englishmen, they felt all foreign habits savoured somewhat of the devil.

Still, nothing stopped them from venturing abroad, and some of the most remarkable pages of Quaker history were later to be written in faraway places, from Moscow to the South Sea Islands. Friends early felt that the world was one. In 1656 John Bowron was testing out Amazonia, preaching to the Indians and in turn attending their ceremonies, "which was performed by beating upon hollow trees, and making a great noise with skins, like a sort of drums." [17] In the same year Newfoundland was reached; but, more important than this, a sustained assault was made on the West Indies and the American mainland. First beachheads led to pocket strongholds, led to a chain of settled meetings; and this despite the most ferocious resistance Friends were anywhere to encounter. This work, though again ministering to local Seeker groups and others on the verge of the full Quaker profession, who once the extra spark had been added never hid their belief nor retreated from it however frightful persecution became, was initially and most dramatically established by Friends voyaging from England, and as many as forty such missionaries came over in the first five years. Nothing could deter them. Imprisonment, ears cropped or tongues bored, ultimately the gallows: where one fell, another took his place, and multiplied ten-fold.

Something of the uplifted spirit of these people is conveyed in the log of the *Woodhouse,* that brought the second contingent of Friends to New England in 1657 . . . "A true relation of the voyages undertaken by me Robert Fowler, with my small vessel called the *Woodhouse,* but performed by the Lord, like as He did Noah's Ark, wherein

---

[17] *Piety Promoted*, Phila., 1854, Vol. 1, p. 234.

He shut up a few righteous persons and landed them safe, even at the hill Ararat . . . thus it was all the voyage, the faithful were carried far above storms and tempests, and we saw the Lord leading our vessel as it were a man leading a horse by the head . . . and soon after the middle of the day there was a drawing to meet together before our usual time and it was said to us that we should look abroad in the evening; and as we sat waiting before the Lord, they discovered land . . . the power of the Lord fell much upon us and irresistible word came unto us, 'That the seed in America shall be as the sand of the sea.' It was published in the ears of the brethren, which caused tears to break forth with fulness of joy." [18]

Such faithful servants of the Lord were already safe in Abraham's bosom, no matter what else befell them. One of them a year later, from " the Lion's Den called Boston Prison ", wrote to Margaret Fell that the message was already spread for two hundred miles through the Colonies, and that even nearby in Salem there were " several pretty Friends in their Measures ".[19] However dark the hour, the note was that of ultimate victory.

On the Continent of Europe they fared less well, for one thing because they didn't speak the languages and their ideas were the sort that interpreters grind into the most deadening clichés. In Holland (it was rather a case there of taking coals to Newcastle) from 1655 onwards they gave extra heart to a few Mennonite and Collegiant groups, but were generally suspect because, bringing excitement in their wake, they were thought to be the more insurrectionary type of Anabaptist; and also the Dutch, just defeated in war by England for the sea carrying trade, viewed all free-moving Englishmen rather sharply. Travelling in Germany they fared little better. A few hearts were reached, something was added to the swell of Reformation thought; but

[18] *A.R.B. MSS.* (1).
[19] *Swarthmore MSS.* Vol. 1, (82).

one can only really think of these first sorties to the Continent as a statement of intent, to be followed up more tenaciously by the altogether better established Quakers of a century and a half later.

This equally applied to the Near East and the Catholic domains of the Mediterranean. Fox indefatigably charged his colleagues to spread their gospel among both Papists and heathen Turk, and at one point he was penning epistles to the King of Spain, the Emperor of Austria, the Pope, the Turk, the Emperor of China, Prester John, and finally "all nations under the whole heavens". The aim was high, but the means were not yet adequately there, nor sufficient comprehension of other peoples and ways of thought, to make much entrée for the Quaker word. Still, in 1657, a year of high adventurousness, a young London Friend going by sea from Leghorn penetrated as far as Jerusalem; and a party of six Friends, fitted out and financed as all such missions were from now on through the London business meeting at the centre of which sat Garrard Roberts, circled round the east Mediterranean in an attempt first to reach Jerusalem, and then to reach and convert the Sultan.

One of them, Mary Fisher, the Yorkshire serving maid, did at last reach this potentate, and spoke her mind; and then when asked in turn what she thought of Mohamet, she answered cautiously " that she knew him not, but Christ, the true prophet, the Son of God, who was the Light of the world, and enlightened every man coming into the world, Him she knew. And concerning Mohammed she said that they might judge of him to be true or false according to the words and prophecies he spoke, saying farther, ' If the word that a prophet speaketh come to pass, then shall ye know that the Lord hath sent that prophet; but if it come not to pass, then shall ye know that Lord never sent him.' " [20]

[20] W. Sewel, *History of the Quakers*, Vol. I, pp. 433–35.

The Turks pulled their long beards at this and bowed to her wisdom, and let her go, satisfied; though the English ambassador at Constantinople, where two others of the party were now with her, felt less charitable towards these " people crept in unawares called Quakers ",[21] because they disturbed the English church services and scoffed at his authority; so he shipped them home.

Two more of the original party had by now circled round to Rome, where they were crying out against the Pope. In consequence, one was hanged, and the other, John Perrot, who later was to be such a thorn for Fox, was imprisoned for three years in a mad-house. In that same year other Friends were venturing, though more quietly, to Rome, and to Venice, discussing their views with any who would listen—chief of whom it seemed were the Jews, who were also keen to forge links with England to which country they were just being allowed to return after an absence of three hundred and sixty years. A year later two Quakeresses were taken by the Inquisition while in Malta, and imprisoned there for three and a half years. Finally, in 1661, a new party reached the Near East, en route it had hoped for China, but only, after a few weeks halt, to be shipped back homewards again. That was the end, for the time being, of these brave sorties, due to persecution in England, that clipped Quaker travelling wings.

Thus, it would appear, the results of these particular excursions had been nil; though the effort alone had testified to a universal faith, in the Light in all human beings that could bring them into spiritual unity, even if this had been unnecessarily overlaid with the doctrinal divisions of the time. Friends had rightly set their sights at nothing less than the whole world. Like that, from the start, they had crossed frontiers in order truly to express their faith. That was the enduring gesture.

21 Thurloe, *State Papers*, Vol. 7, p. 287.

(b) The View of the State

In distant Constantinople the English ambassador had not acted against Mary Fisher and her colleagues until they had provoked him " by reason of their disturbances of our Divine exercises and several notorious contempts of me and my authority ";[22] by contrast, in Massachusetts two years earlier, the moment she and another Quakeress had arrived in Boston harbour, they had had their books burned, they had been stripped and scrutinised for witches' marks, then imprisoned, boarded up so that no one could speak to them, till they could be safely shipped away. Why was that? " Why was it that the coming of two women so shook ye, as if a formidable army had invaded your borders?" [23]

In part it was because of Seeker activity twenty years before, that had resulted in Anne Hutchinson and her friends being banished from the Colony, to found their own free-thinking settlement on what was to become Rhode Island, that had made the Boston Presbyterians very sensitive to all separatist teaching as leading to an abyss of error. They knew that in the early 'fifties Seeker groups throughout England had turned Quaker; and already, before any such appeared among them, there had been a spate of anti-Quaker tracts published in the Colony. They were prepared, they would have none of this mystical religion with its enthusiasms and singular customs. Even so, was there more to it than that, even in an age when man's relationship to God was the most debated public issue: were there further considerations, or implications, that made the leaders of Massachusetts ready to exterminate Quakers like lice?

In England also it didn't take long for the authorities to turn against Friends, though here sometimes action was stayed through the sympathy of local citizens or local detachments of soldiers, or through Cromwell's personal

22 Thurloe, *State Papers*, Vol. 7, p. 287.
23 G. Bishop, *New England Judged*, p. 7.

wish to extend liberty of prophesying to all except Anglicans and Roman Catholics. The charge that Quakers were
Papists was repeatedly made, as in the pamphlet endear-
ingly titled " The Quakers Unmasked, and clearly detected
to be but the Spawn of Romish Frogs, Jesuites and Fran-
ciscan Fryers, sent from Rome to seduce the intoxicated
Giddy-headed English Nation " (1654); and in some aspects
Quaker beliefs were ostensibly closer to Catholics than to
Puritans; but even so, and despite the atmosphere of plots
and alarms and bad regicide consciences, this accusation
was primarily a smear, to work on popular nationalist
feeling, and didn't reflect the chief fears of those who led
the attack on Quakerism.

This was always most savage in the provinces, and at any
given moment was a straight riposte on the part of
ministers who found themselves denounced as hirelings,
deceivers, and false prophets, their services interrupted and
their tithes refused; and on the part of magistrates who
found themselves lectured in court by these same disturbers
of the peace, who additionally refused all phrases of respect,
to remove their hats or pay prison fees, or indeed give any
surety for future good conduct. This was scandal added
to blasphemy, and not to be tolerated even in a country
that, by Cromwell's proclamation (1655), was to allow " the
free and uninterrupted passage of the Gospel running
through the midst of us . . . without any interruption from
the powers God hath set over this Commonwealth . . . a
mercy that is the price of much blood, and till of late
years denied to this nation." [24]

Moreover, though Cromwell himself was tender towards
vagaries of individual conscience, constantly mitigating or
reversing sentences of the county justices—a general advice
of 1657 reads . . . " His Highness and Council have received
several addresses on behalf of Quakers imprisoned for not

[24] S. R. Gardener, *History of the Commonwealth and Protectorate*, Vol. vii,
p. 260.

pulling off their hats, and for not finding sureties for good behaviour . . . though his Highness and Council are far from countenancing their mistaken principles or practices, especially in disturbing godly ministers and affronting magistrates, yet as they mostly proceed rather from a spirit of error than a malicious opposition to authority, they are to be pitied and dealt with as persons under a strong delusion, who will rather suffer and perish than do anything contrary to their ungrounded and corrupt principles. Therefore his Highness and Council recommend them to your prudence to discharge such as are in prison in your County . . ." [25]—at the same time, beneath this mercy, reflecting both the expediency in his make-up and his dilemma of conflicting principles, there was the fact that Cromwell maintained and from 1655 extended the body of laws that could be invoked against Quakers. He sharpened the weapon, allowed it to be tested, then withdrew it here and there if there seemed to be no overall danger to the realm. He dare not be too severe, because the country was restive under his rule, the more so the longer it was unconstitutional, and because the army, in whom his power lay, was in the lower ranks sympathetic to Quakers. Then he, too, had spiritual longings, at times ecstatic ones; he certainly esteemed Fox; and he recognised that many Friends, even when they weren't actually ex-soldiers of his New Model Army, were of that same godly generation that had prayed and wrestled and offered their lives for the good of England's soul. They were many of them his kind of people—truer than he to the ideals fought for.

Still, and in part because they made him face contradictions in himself, there were aspects of the Quaker movement, certain voices among it, that he equally distrusted; so that even in his most enlightened moments he was forced to heed repressive counsel, such as that of his

[25] *Calendar of State Papers* (Domestic) 1657–58, p. 156.

son Henry Cromwell . . . " Our most considerable enemy now in our view are the Quakers . . . I think their principles and practices are not very consistent with civil government, much less with the discipline of an army. Some think them to have no design, but I am not of that opinion. Their counterfeited simplicity renders them to me the more dangerous." [26]

To understand the underlying fears both of Cromwell and the county authorities, and equally those of the Boston magistrates, that gave Quaker protests and peculiarities a sinister significance, one must recall the tussles of the previous decade—not the issues or course of the Civil War but the unsolved problems at its conclusion. The Presbyterians, who had controlled Parliament and had led the revolt against an absolute monarchy and a patched-up feudalism, to make way for the expanding capitalist economy in which generally they stood for the big interests, had been thrust aside by Cromwell's Independents, who so to speak were the smaller operators—the lesser gentry, traders, producers, who nonetheless were in the process of becoming the most progressive element economically—who demanded both more religious freedom (the equality of voice in small congregations as against the rigid propaganda machine of nationally controlled pulpits) and more free play in trade and politics. In fact, they were staking their claim too in the new world that was emerging.

In turn, though, Cromwell had felt pressure from the Left, from army rank-and-file and civilian radicals (representing the more hard-pressed artisans, husbandmen, and some yeomen), who aimed at full political democracy, and hence at a further shift of power to the people as a whole, that to him as much as to all men of property, City merchants, enclosure profiteers, and other strata of the bourgeoisie, threatened a social revolution such as had never been intended.

[26] Thurloe, *State Papers,* Vol. 4, p. 508.

These radicals were called Levellers. They were in essence religious sectaries, stirred by the revolution and the Utopia it momentarily promised, and driven, in their working existence by the constant rise in prices and other such factors, especially in London, that depressed them socially, who transposed their spiritual teaching of the equal and responsible participation of all believers in church affairs into the political arena. They became influential at that point through linking up with a kindred wave of disaffection in the army; so that suddenly Cromwell and his generals—the " grandees "—were faced with a sizeable subversion to which for the moment they had to pay heed.

The main points of view were stated in debates of the Army Council at Putney in late 1647. There the Leveller Rainsborough claimed that " the poorest he that is in England hath a life as the greatest he; and, therefore, truly, Sir, I think it's clear, that every man that is to live under a government ought first by his own consent to put himself under that government " . . . to which Cromwell's son-in-law, Ireton, replied for the ruling junta . . . " No person hath a right to an interest or share in the disposing of the affairs of the kingdom, and in determining or choosing those that shall determine what laws we shall be ruled by here . . . that hath not a permanent fixed interest in this kingdom . . . Liberty cannot be provided for in a general sense, if property be preserved." [27]

There lay the heart of their difference: the new Puritan squirearchy felt that the revolution had gone far enough. They had defeated the more conservative forces with the aid of the radical rank-and-file—in battle united through the slogans of an emancipating faith; but now they did not welcome that faith overstepping the bounds of the personal life into the political sphere, to spread the material rewards, the rights and social power, among the people at large. That might lose them all they had won, might

[27] A. S. P. Woodhouse, *Puritanism and Liberty*, 1938, pp. 53, 54, 73.

upset the balance of this new amazing economic machine, with its needs of capital, enclosure, cheap labour, aggressive nationalism, that was just coming into their hands.

So they temporarised; Cromwell strode among his army (who were wearing the sea-green ribbons of the Levellers) telling them they were an Instrument of God, not of the ordinary people; he reunited them behind him to defeat the King in the second civil war; then he allowed the King to be beheaded and a republic to be proclaimed, and he further listened to Leveller demands embodied in a third Agreement of the People—manhood suffrage, annual elections, a disestablished church and the ending of tithes, no military compulsion, no death penalty except for murder or treason, no exemptions under the law [28] : items that later reappearing in the law codes of the Quaker colonisers, Edward Byllinge and William Penn, passed at least in spirit into the Constitution of the United States. In their principles to-day we could call them Jeffersonian, but to Cromwell and his class they menaced the safeguards of the new property republic. Awaiting his moment he imprisoned the chief Levellers, isolated the army mutineers and shot their ringleaders. After May 1649, ultimately, if not Cromwell himself then the forces he represented would have to come to terms with the monarchy again and the Establishment as a whole.

Part of his response to Levellers was conditioned by the presence of voices among them more revolutionary than their leaders. Lilburne, while seeking equality before the law and the extension of the franchise, resolutely defended private property, never said a word against enclosures; Wildman was himself a land speculator; but others, Overton and Walwyn, with their vision of a neighbourly Christianity, wished to see the common land thrown open again; and in several counties there were groups of Level-

---

[28] S. R. Gardener, *Constitutional Documents of the Puritan Revolution*, Oxford, 1899, pp. 359–71.

lers, condemning the tyranny of landholders (which tyranny they pinned on the Norman Conquest), crying out in this wise . . . " Government we see none, but the old tyrannical Norman Government " [29] . . . " Is not all the controversie whose slaves the poor shall be?" [30] Never, they said, if they had the vote, would they elect " lords of Mannors, Im-propriators, and Lawyers, whose Interest is in our oppression and at this day keep us in bondage like Egyptian Task-masters." [31] The Levellers' news-sheet, the Moderate, the New Statesman of its day, at one point described private property as " the greatest cause of most sins against the Heavenly Deity ";[32] and one of the most popular Leveller pamphlets, " Light Shining in Buckinghamshire " (the work of countrymen whose land had been forfeited through enclosures) declared . . . "All men being alike privileged by birth so all men were to enjoy the creatures alike without properties one more than the others." Here lay the root of Cromwells oppression : if he listened at all to Levellers, then these sort of views might sweep the board.

Even further to the left were the True Levellers, or Diggers, a development out of the larger movement, and out of such tracts as the one just quoted, that was confined to rural districts. The most organised instance of this agrarian protest—collectivist as against the individualism of town and army Levellers—took place, for a year, in 1649, as St. George's Hill in Surrey. Led by Gerrard Winstanley, a man who like Vinoba Bhave of to-day's bhoodan movement in India saw in possessiveness regarding land the root of all social evils, who pleaded for the conquering power of love to effect a moral revolution (though his later writings were less pacific), these Diggers set about digging,

[29] *A Declaration of divers of the Inhabitants of the County of Hartford,* 1650, p. 6.
[30] Anon., *Declaration of some Proceedings of Lt.-Col. John Lilburne,* 1648.
[31] *Declaration* (Herts.), p. 7.
[32] *Moderate,* 4th Sept., 1649.

as a gesture, the common land thereabouts and planting it with crops. Thus defying the dominant trend of the times they were giving a lead to a more brotherly ideal . . . " Not only this common or heath should be taken in and manured by the people, but all the commons and waste ground in England, and in the whole world ";[33] and the spirit of their action was embodied in their song " Stand up now, Diggers all ", which ran . . .

"To conquer them by love, come in now, come in now,
    To conquer them by love, come in,
    To conquer them by love, as it does you behove,
    For He is King above, no power is like to love,
    Glory here, diggers all." [34]

Inevitably, denounced by local squire and vicar, and a sitting target for mob spite, they were set upon by the populace, their crops uprooted and their belongings smashed; Cromwell sent a troop of horse, then, deciding they were a minor lunacy, relinquished them to the mercies of the magistrates, who fined them out of existence. They were too isolated to survive and by 1650, as Diggers, had disappeared; but it is interesting that, when attacked, they had suffered this passively and with good cheer, they had refused in court to seek legal assistance, and, when brought before Cromwell's deputy, General Fairfax, they had refused to doff their hats. They had borne themselves, in fact, like early Friends.

This brings us to the advent of Quakers. Cromwell had crushed the Levellers and seen the Diggers dispersed; but he could not imagine by such strokes that the underlying ferment had been allayed; property law was all the time hardening, the dispossessed were being steadily harassed, whipped as vagrants from parish to parish, their enforced idleness branded as sin; the stream of humanist political concepts, of individualistic spiritual insight, was not sud-

[33] G. Winstanley, *True Levellers' Standard Advanced*, p. 41.
[34] G. M. Trevelyn, *England under the Stuarts*, 1947, p. 234.

denly dammed up. Indeed, when in 1653 he tried the experiment of the Nominated Parliament, the rule by one hundred and forty " Saints ", he was trying to find a channel through which this continuing volume of protest and zeal could be moderately, expediently, employed. But again its demands proved too radical—the overhaul of the legal system and the abolition of tithes—and it was dissolved; and when this provoked the more militant sectaries, now calling themselves Fifth Monarchy Men, who had been strongly represented in this assembly, into a run of plots, they were suppressed.

It was in this atmosphere that the Quaker movement arose. Gathering strength at an astonishing speed, ably promoted, nationally organised, it appeared to be sucking in all the remnants of previous radical protest. Lilburne had called his followers " the hobnails, clouted shoes, the private soldiers, the leather and woollen Aprons, and the laborious and industrious people in England ",[35] and now the mass of Friends were being drawn from the same hard-pressed sections of the community, appearing particularly strong among weavers, tailors, shoemakers, carpenters, masons, and husbandmen. They were the same disillusioned decent poor—not quite "the dregs of the common people ",[36] as one critic labelled them, not the lumpen-proletariat, but literate and articulate enough to fashion telling criticism of the current state of affairs.

And they were not hesitating to attack. Armed with some new vision of reality, that blasphemous though it sounded gave a more unshakable self-confidence to them than any purely rational or legalistic plea had provided, they were de-crying the abuses of the law and the church, the iniquities attending on rich and poor, the inadequacies of the government: in fact, echoing and refurbishing the Leveller complaints so lately silenced. And among them

[35] J. Lilburne, *The Upright Man's Vindication*, 1653, p. 15.
[36] E. Pagitt, *Heresiography*, 1661, p. 244.

surely were certain figures, like Anthony Pearson and George Bishop, already active in Leveller circles; and there were new men, such as James Nayler, or Edward Burrough, who sounded even more subversive; and it was known that other malcontents, Ranters, Diggers, Fifth Monarchy Men, were increasingly swelling their ranks. To the authorities, who had learned in that age to probe beneath prophetic idiom, this seemed like the same old headache: the have-nots against those who had managed to line their pockets. This was the genesis of their fear, swollen by every report of tumult attending Quaker meetings, and the underlying cause of imprisonment of Quakers by every little trick the law provided. Here, if only potentially, was a renewed threat of further revolution.

Hence, Henry Cromwell's indictment, or that of a Judge accusing Dewsbury . . . " If thou and Fox had it in your power, you would soon have your hands imbued in blood." [37] A Presbyterian minister wrote . . . "Awhile ago there came to this city of Bristol certain Morice-dancers from the North, by two and two, two and two, with an intent here to exercise some spiritual cheats, or (as may well be suspected) to carry on some levelling design " [38] . . . and a Colonel reported . . . " My captain-lieutenant is much confirmed in his principles of quaking, making all the soldiers his equals, according to the Levellers' strain . . ." [39]

Similarly, over in Boston, it was declared . . . " The prudence of this Court was exercised in making provision to secure Peace and Order against their [Quaker] attempts, whose design (we were well-assured by our own experience as well as by the examples of their Predecessors in Munster) was to undermine and ruin the same." [40] There, logically according to such fears, they were being linked to the most

[37] J. Besse, *Sufferings*, 1753, Vol. 1, p. 522.
[38] R. Farmer, *The Great Mysteries of Godlinesse and Ungodlinesse*, 1655. Dedicated Epistle to John Thurloe, Secretary of State.
[39] Thurloe, *State Papers*, Vol. 6, p. 167.
[40] G. Bishop, *New England Judged*, p. 3.

violent of Anabaptists. Friends, in truth, in that uncertain epoch, were a powerful bogey to the new Puritan Establishment, to its uneasy hypocritical conscience.

But what actually were Quakers preaching to deserve this reputation? We know they were preaching the Light to be directly experienced through prayful meetings: a fellowship dispensing with priests and creeds but requiring a simplicity of life, truthfulness, brotherly affection, and sense of man's equality before God. In a way, proclaiming this as a recipe for all mankind, they were automatically (like any good Christian) condemning conditions that stood in its path; but what specifically were they uttering that caused so much liverish anxiety, as if at a signal from George Fox they would rise and overturn the State?

In brief, some of their language was strong and aimed at the rich and socially powerful . . . " You lustful ones ", cried James Nayler, " which live on the fat of the Earth . . . you are fitted for destruction, your day is coming " [41] . . . " Howl and weep, misery is coming upon you ", cried Fox, " enemies of God, adversaries of righteousness " [42] . . . " Woe, woe, woe, to the oppressors of the Earth, who grind the faces of the poor and rack and stretch out their Rents " [43] . . . for " the earth is the Lord's and the fulness thereof, and . . . he hath given it to the sons of men in general, and not to a few lofty ones which lord it over their brethren." [44] Fox early condemned enclosure—those that set their " nests on high, joyne house to house, field to field till there be no place for the poor " [45]—and later suggested, in his most detailed social blue-print, that church lands be given to the poor, and abbeys and churches (and Whitehall itself!) be used as alms-houses. In this same docu-

[41] J. Nayler, "A Call to Magistrates, Ministers, Lawyers, and People to Repentence", in *Works*, pp. 135–6.
[42] George Fox, Newes Coming Out of the North Sounding Towards the South or a Blast Out of the North Up into the South, 1656.
[43] W. Tomlinson, *Seven Particulars*, 1657 p. 1.
[44] B. Nicholson, *A Blast from the Lord*, 1653, p. 10.
[45] George Fox, *The Vials of the Wrath of God*, 1654, p. 3.

ment, as at all times, he condemned tithes (increasingly, one must note, the income of Puritan officers, gentry, merchants, who had bought or been given church land) and the oppressive power of priests and lawyers, suggesting a minimum of legal structure. All the laws of England, he said, should be contained in a pocket size book that any layman could understand, and thereafter plead his own cause.[46]

·Then his colleagues, turning to the political sphere—the " two lovely twins ", as Bishop called them, of civil and religious liberty, " that cannot be divided, but with the mutual suffering, if not the Dissolution of each other " [47]— proclaimed . . . " We believe that the Executors of the Law ought to be just men, and not given to pride, drunkenness, or any other evil whatsoever, and ought to be chosen every year, or otherwise, by the common consent, of all people, and that no man be stopped of his free choice. And we believe that all Governors and Rulers ought to be accountable to the people, and to the next proceeding Rulers, for all their actions which may be inquired into upon occasion; and that the chiefest of the Rulers be subject under the Law, and punished by it if they be transgressors, as well as the poorest of the people." [48]

In these and many kindred pamphlets there was thus a strong Leveller accent: a plea for equality before the law, and beyond that a special care for the poor, and a hope, as with Winstanley, that church and State land might be used for the benefit of all. But nonetheless there was a fundamental difference, that singled out the Quaker and, as Cromwell at moments realised, made him socially safe and indeed the best hope of draining off the current pressure, and that was the guiding principle of how these changes

[46] George Fox, " To the Parliament of the Commonwealth of England, Fifty-Nine Particulars laid down for Regulating things, 1659.

[47] G. Bishop, Mene Tekel, p. 4.

[48] E. Burrough, A Declaration to all the World of our Faith and what we believe, 1657, pp. 5–6.

were to be effected. However much Fox fulminated it was never with him a preparatory step to revolutionary action. On the contrary, his aim was to change men's hearts, to widen the dimensions of their being so that they would see the world in a new light; certainly, bluntly to upbraid the Protector for the betrayal of sectarian revolutionary hopes, but beyond that simply to try and awaken his latent sense of justice; and meanwhile, till that could be done, to suffer the prevailing state of affairs. Constantly Fox cautioned his followers to seek no other solution; for, on the one hand, it was now plain that power seized by revolutionary means corrupted those who had seized it, and, on the other, the Lord Himself would in any case have the last word. The most decisive action might well be to offer up petitionary prayer. "The want of our prayers to God for thee", Burrough informed Cromwell, " is worse for thee than the secret plotting of all wicked men." [49] To the political side of Cromwell this could only sound reassuring: better this than that Quakers should brandish a thousand muskets.

Yet despite this fundamental principle of working only through the spirit in man, ingrained in Fox, Dewsbury, Pennington, and any others who were basically " changed " (essential, as we have seen with Fox, to the balance of the convert's psyche) and by 1661 embodied in the Peace declaration that stood for the Society of Friends as a whole, there were nonetheless some adherents in that first decade who, passionately aware of social wrongs and of Leveller reforms that would mitigate them, and already schooled, as Cromwellian troopers, in the legitimacy of revolutionary methods, saw the new movement primarily as the latest rallying point for radical action and were themselves constantly tempted to play a strong political rôle. This comes out most clearly in the case of Anthony Pearson, one of the

[49] E. Burrough, " Good Counsel and Advice Rejected ", in *The Memorable Works of a Son of Thunder and Consolation*, 1672, p. 561.

best early Quaker organisers, who helped to run the first
annual gatherings of Friends near Skipton that so alarmed
the authorities, and in the confusion of 1659, following
Oliver Cromwell's death, did all he could to align Friends
with Sir Henry Vane's militant policies; and, to judge by
the lists that were collected at Gerrard Robert's house, not
without a wide response. The French ambassador commented . . . " The Spirit of God, by which they [the
Quakers] are ruled, now permits them to take part in the
affairs of this world, and the Parliament seems inclined to
make use of them." [50]

In sum, one can say that the dominant trend in the
early Quaker movement was to be spiritually active and
thus to awaken men to their social obligations, but that it did
contain a fringe of members who, recalling Leveller agitation, were ready to seize political power if the chance came
to them; and that the authorities were alive to this. Hence,
the grave suspicions of the Nayler pantomime, the dislike
of large Quaker gatherings, of their national organisation
and system of communications, and their quite outstanding
esprit de corps. When they offered to replace each other
in prison, Cromwell was amazed and asked his Council,
" Which of you would do so much for me if I was in the
same condition?" [51]

Yet he personally appreciated the significance of Fox's
principles, so that he only stood for persecution of Quakers
occasionally, selectively, to keep their militant fringe at
bay. It was in the country at large among the new gentry
turned magistrate and member of Parliament, now too
concerned for the *status quo* to feel for the niceties of
Quaker principles, that the real persecuting spirit was ram-
pant: to achieve its apotheosis in Boston, where Whitehall
had least sway of all. These gentlemen were largely attacking an imaginary bogey, we can see now, blown up by their

[50] F. R. G. Guizot, *History of Richard Cromwell and the Restoration of
Charles II*, 1856, Vol. 1, p. 407.
[51] *Journal*, p. 265.

fear for possessions and by their own bad consciences; but to them it was real. To them the Quaker was primarily a continuing undercover revolutionary.

That takes events to the Restoration; after which, for a further decade, the same view of Friends persisted, despite their peaceful declarations. The temper of the authorities, of the new Anglican majority in Parliament, of landlords, of big trading interests, of bishops and turncoat Puritans, was not such as to admit of any analysis. They were too busy revenging the past, or trying to stifle sectarianism in the interest of a new uniformity, or indeed trying to finish off all over-godly men to make way for a more sceptical opportunist generation. All Dissenters were now their pray —not only Quakers by their thousands went to gaol but such respectable Puritan figures as Baxter, Vavasour Powell, Alleyn, and John Bunyan; yet, throughout, it was the Quakers who bore the brunt of this spleen. They were still the most suspect section of the now generally feared Non-conformists; their refusal to bear arms or swear oaths and their pleading of a supra-national liberty of conscience inflamed old notions concerning them. They were not safe to the body politic, not a good security risk; they must be locked up, ruined, shipped to the plantations. At least till 1672, to be a Quaker in England was to be the figure of an outlaw.

The Privy Council, at the heart of government, was more realistic in its assessment, and as the danger of plots faded, and of unrest among former Commonwealth soldiery, it began, as formerly Cromwell had done, to mitigate sentences against Quakers. Even more the King himself, Charles II, easy-going by nature, glad to abet any toleration that could also help Catholics, eager, especially in the American Colonies, to take Puritan magistracy down a peg, began by showing a genial face to Friends. So long as it cost him nothing he helped them.

But this did not last till the end of his reign. Though by

then Quakers, as well as their opponents and the whole temper of ideas involved, had changed materially from twenty years before. Even if old battle cries were sounded, it was for all concerned a more bourgeois affair. Friends were in the process of being revalued and admitted to quasi-respectability. A new epoch was being prepared.

(c) Persecution

Official action against Quakers, once they were felt to be a civil danger, still varied greatly from district to district and from one season to the next, so that for those first intrepid evangelists with their declamations of love and protest, a journey across England was as full of surprises, petty hazards and joyful encounters, harsh applications of the law that triumphantly they turned to the Lord's account, as the close-packed pages of a morality. John Stubbs and William Caton, for example, while working Kent in 1655, survived the edicts of the Dover authorities through the protection of a shoemaker, one Luke Howard, who staunchly refused to turn them out (he later, as a Friend, converted John Lilburne); continuing to Folkestone they were again received with kindness and held successful meetings, even, just outside the town, being allowed to address a troop of soldiers; at Hythe they were slightly bruised by the crowd, but balanced this by converting at Lydd the eminent Baptist pastor, Samuel Fisher; at Ashford and Tenterden the local ministers were noisily out on the warpath against them, but at Cranbrook and Staplehurst they met only with love, and the offer of gold and silver for their work, and silent meetings were established there. By now, alas, their luck was running out, or a severer test of their faith was being set them, for at Maidstone the magistrates, who were noted Presbyterians and men of substance, applied the brutal vagrancy law . . . " had them into a Room, where They were striped naked, & their Necks & Armes put in ye Stocks, & there cruelly whipped with Coards in a bloudy

Manner, in the sight of Many People, which forced Teares from ye tender hearted . . . And when they had thus cruelly proceeded, They fastened Irons vpon Them with great Cloggs of Wood, & put Them in amongst Transgressors." [52]

They were then ordered back to their own northern country, to be passed from constable to constable the length of England as vagrants; but, as before even leaving Kent the constables grew negligent, Stubbs and Caton soon found themselves free, and straightway returned to Maidstone, there to preach publicly again. This time they were not molested. They completed another round of Kent, so that it was "as a greene Feild of Corne growing vp",[53] then prepared without delay for the Continental missions in which they were to be pioneers. Nothing seemed to slacken their pace or dilute their confidence. It is noteworthy that Stubbs had been a soldier, had served under Cromwell in a victorious revolutionary army, yet now was ready to suffer abuse, degradation, savage punishment, and rely only on the power of his gospel to win over his persecutors. This was the significant change, requiring a different courage, bringing a more lasting sense of achievement.

Prison conditions also varied, being rather more or less disgusting. Fox, cast into Doomsdale at Launceston a year later, described it as "a nasty stinking place where they said few people came out alive; where they used to put witches and murderers before their execution; where the prisoners' excrements had not been carried out for scores of years, as it was said. It was all like mire, and in some places at the top of the shoes in water and piss, and never a house of office in the place, nor chimney. The gaoler would not let us cleanse the place, nor let us have beds nor straw to lie on; but at night some friendly people of the town brought us a candle and a little straw, and we

[52] *First Publishers of Truth*, p. 139.
[53] *First Publishers of Truth*, p. 142.

went to burn a little of our straw to take away the stink. The thieves were put over our heads and the head gaoler lay above with the thieves. It seems the smoke went up into the room and the gaoler was in such a rage that he stamped with his foot and stick and took the pots of excrements of the prisoners and poured it down a hole a-top of our heads in Doomsdale, so that we were so bespattered with the excrements that we could not touch ourselves nor one another, that our stink increased upon us. He quenched our straw with it. And he called us hatchet-faced dogs and such names as we never heard in our lives . . . In this manner we stood all night. . . ." [54]

In scores of gaols all over England conditions were as vicious as this, but it did not seem to dishearten Friends. On another occasion, in Carlisle prison, Fox, while being beaten by an irate warder, " was made to sing in the Lord's power . . . I was moved in the everlasting power of the Lord God to sing; and my voice drowned them." [55] A young Quakeress, Ann Audland, thrust all the winter of 1655 into a " close, nasty place, several steps below ground, on the side whereof was a sort of common shore that received much of the mud of the town, that at times did stink sorely; besides frogs and toads did crawl in their room and no place for fire " [56] . . . could still write to their common Mother, Margaret Fell . . . " This is indeed a place of joy, and my soul doth rejoice in the Lord. I continue a prisoner in Banbury, but I witness freedom in the Lord." [57]

Most remarkable of all, perhaps, was the testimony of William Dewsbury, imprisoned for nineteen years at Warwick, four of which he was a close prisoner: he said he " esteemed the bolts and locks put upon me as jewels ",[58]

[54] *Journal*, p. 252.
[55] *Journal*, p. 164.
[56] *Piety Promoted*, Phila., 1854, Vol. 1, p. 321.
[57] W. Caton MSS., Letter dated 1st Jan., 1656.
[58] *Works*, preliminary unnumbered pages.

and he continued throughout to write sage and cheerful counsel to Friends in all their gatherings, and to fellow prisoners, and in the end, coming out and at once attempting to take up his work as before, he murmured only that, as "it hath pleased God to suffer my health to be impaired ",[59] he was forced to halt on his way to meetings, not finding it so easy to walk. He too, we may remember, had been a soldier of Cromwell.

Moreover, perfectly disciplined himself; released from pulls of his ego through a wider identification with his fellows, he required the same of other Friends. To a woman dreading her husband's imprisonment he said . . . "Woman, thy sorrow is great; I sorrow with thee. Now the time is come that those who marry must be as though they married not, and those who have husbands as though they had none, for the Lord calls for all to be offered up." [60] Faced with the onslaught of persecution, Friends, if they were to preserve their faith, their re-integration of self, must stick to that and that alone; all else, in the final analysis, could be a means of self-betrayal. To the Society at large, to any faint-hearted, Fox repeatedly cried . . . "Be valiant . . . for the Lord may try you as he did Job . . . who still kept his integrity in all conditions " [61] . . . "and do not look at time, nor think your sufferings long; but look at Him that hath all time in his hand " [62] . . . "For your rest is in Christ Jesus; therefore rest not in anything else." [63] A counsel of perfection, but still, the essence of survival under trial, and indeed of the spiritual progress round which humanity builds itself up.

When they were not being thrust into underground pits no better than cesspools, the result of particular rage against them, Friends in prison were able to establish a useful

---

[59] E. Smith, *Life of Dewsbury*, p. 251.
[60] *Some Memoirs of the Life of John Roberts* (1746 ed.), p. 10.
[61] *Journal*, p. 311.
[62] *Letters of Early Friends*, p. 242.
[63] *Journal*, p. 560.

routine of study and prayer, writing to their meetings (or to the Government, or the magistrates), instructing and caring for the other prison inmates, often preaching through the bars to a street crowd, and maintaining contacts through their own prison visitors, who brought them food and the materials and machines for spinning and weaving and similar crafts—the beginnings of the prison work that one hundred and fifty years later became famous through the person of Elizabeth Fry. Quakers at the start accumulated a hardy experience of gaols, of being uprooted and spoliated: a deep ineradicable memory that gave nerve to their later service to other such unfortunates.

In Cromwell's England few Friends actually died in gaol. Among the three thousand or so who suffered only about twenty were total casualties: that is, few beside the three hundred who died under the Restoration onslaught, among, it has been estimated,[64] at least fifteen thousand Quakers (about a quarter of the Society then, including women and children, but excluding those already in the Colonies) who suffered that fiercer persecution. But the earlier period did witness some of the more brutal instances —the death of Richard Sale, crushed into a rock space too small for him, that left him bleeding and swollen till he died; the death of James Parnell, not yet twenty, thrust in a hole high off the ground from which he could only descend by a rope, from which one day, benumbed, he fell; and also, over in New England, the most thorough attack on Friends of all.

There, following the feelers put out by Mary Fisher in 1655 and a second Quaker party a year later, the real penetration, into southern Massachusetts from the friendly base of Rhode Island, began in 1657; and in consequence met with a steadily mounting storm of persecution. That winter two Quakers, for speaking forth in Salem following the

<hr/>

[64] W. C. Braithwaite, *The Beginnings of Quakerism*, 1955, p. 464; *The Second Period of Quakerism*, 1921, p. 114.

minister's Sunday morning sermon, were given three hundred and fifty lashes each during nine weeks of imprisonment. By the following summer this form of punishment had been proved inadequate—although an aged Friend, William Brend, had received one hundred and seventeen strokes with a tarred rope in a day, and others were getting smaller doses: for it did nothing to stop the advent of Quakers, on the contrary it was helping to swell their number through its effect on the New England public. The people were growing sympathetic. The authorities, headed by Governor Endicott, clinging to an impasse of fear and repression that to-day, three hundred years later, seems equally to hold the authorities in South Africa, stepped up the punishment. Quakers were now to lose their ears, to be branded, to have their tongues bored; so, that summer the same missionaries, returning from the safety of Rhode Island, each lost an ear.

But once again the crowd was moved. All such sentences were performed in public. A highly respected matron, Catherine Scott, a sister as it happened of that earlier Seeker pioneer, Anne Hutchinson, spoke out in protest, and was promptly whipped. She was warned " if she came hither again there was likely to be a law to hang her " . . . she replied, " If God calls us, woe to us if we come not "; at which Endicott pronounced, " We shall be as ready to take away your lives as you will be to lay them down." [65]

So at last this stark conflict, among a stark people and a stark environment, entered its final compulsive stage. To the death. Was faith that strong? It proved to be, for the following year, 1659, three Friends, banished upon pain of death under the lastest anti-Quaker law, returned, impelled each said to do so for the sake of the work to which they felt called; and with them a group of sympathisers " moved of the Lord to look your bloody laws in the face

[65] *New England Judged*, p. 95.

and to accompany those who should suffer by them." [66]
It is surely clear that Fox or any other of the early English
Friends would have acted likewise. Such was their total
dedication.

Thus, despite public unrest, drums being beaten so that
people could not listen to the last message of the doomed
trio, two of them, the men, were hanged, while the third,
Mary Dyer, was reprieved after her companions were
already lifeless. She would not, however, accept her life so
long as this critical law remained, and she returned once
more to Boston, and was there executed. That year a
fourth martyr, William Leddra of Barbadoes, followed in
their wake; and even as his sentence was being pronounced,
yet another outlawed Quaker appeared unabashed in the
magistrates' court. It struck " a great damp " among them.
That way there could be no end to it.

Fortunately, the restored monarchy in England saw fit
to put a stop to these Puritan excesses, in any case becoming
intolerable to the local common people, and, somewhat
dramatically, sent a Quaker with the royal missive to Endicott, occasioning a momentary reversal of rôles—the
despised Quaker being handed back his hat, and the morose
irate Governor uncovering; but then, until Endicott's death,
a modified form of persecution continued, through the
Cart and Whip Act, that like a dying wasp's sting inflicted
what pain it could on its enemies. To no avail: the Quaker
foothold was reinforced year by year. It necessarily had
the backing of the more liberal qualms in every Puritan;
and, more than Presbyterian caution, it looked towards the
broad American future.

In England, the Restoration was primarily a time of
readjustment, of a mettlesome but chaotic nation trying
to pull its several parts together so that it could surge
forward into the great new world of trade. It easily
panicked, it was very sensitive to threat of any further

66 *New England Judged*, p. 119.

schisms; so that would-be plotters, old soldiers, Papists, Quakers, all sectaries, anyone with a discredited label was liable to find himself imprisoned at the first alarm. Dissenters generally, after 1662, were admitted to be irrevocably separated from the State church: the question therefore was just how and where they could be safely readmitted to the body politic; and for the time being, till this and other dispositions of forces, of gentry and merchants, of bishops and the law, of Parliament, of the King's secret foibles, had been satisfactorily sorted out, they were intermittently persecuted, to keep their pretensions on the leash.

Quakers, being the most obtrusive and inflexible of dissenters, took the brunt of persecution. Where Baptists and others disappeared into woods or replaced their bibles with soup plates at the entrance of a constable, Friends silently stood their ground. It drew comment even from Baxter that " the fanatics called Quakers did greatly relieve the sober people for a time: for they were so resolute, and gloried in their constancy and sufferings, that they assembled openly, at the Bull and Mouth near Aldersgate, and were dragged away daily to the Common Gaol, and yet desisted not, but the rest came the next day nevertheless, so that the Gaol, at Newgate was filled with them. Abundance of them died in prison, and yet they continued their assemblies still! . . . Yes, many turned Quakers, because the Quakers kept their meetings openly, and went to prison for it cheerfully." [67]

Friends were sentenced for refusing oaths and payment of tithes as hitherto, and additionally now under the Conventicle Acts of 1664 and 1670, designed to suppress " seditions Conventicles ", as all religious assemblies were called if not according to the Anglican liturgy. As Baxter noted, the gaols were filled and Friends perished in numbers there. Already in 1662 Burrough, at the age of twenty-

[67] *Reliquiæ Baxterianæ*, p. 436.

eight, had succumbed to the vile conditions in Newgate, where nearly a hundred of his people were cramped into a single room along with felons, in semi-darkness, the floor, inevitably, running with filth and clogged mouldy straw. Clean drinking water was almost unobtainable. As a Friend wrote . . . "They have found out a new way to murder the innocent and others that they account enemies, by thronging them into infected prisons; and so their cruelty executes them in a short time." [68]

After this, for some, there was the sentence of banishment overseas; though, owing to the reluctance of sea captains to comply, few Friends, less than a score out of two hundred and forty such cases, were actually transported. At the height of the Plague (1655) fifty-five of them were taken from Newgate and thrown into the hold of the *Black Eagle,* a ship destined for the colonies, but there half of them quickly perished, to be buried in the marshes below Gravesend; while the remainder, first captured by a Dutch privateer then driven by storms to Bergen harbour, returned by way of Amsterdam to London, where they dutifully informed the authorities of their presence, and prepared to stand trial again. They never sought to evade the law; till the coming of Penn they barely challenged it. The extent of the persecution perhaps overwhelmed them, and also they saw in it the will of God, as in all things, who eventually would lead them through their trials. As Fox afterwards wrote of those days . . . "There was never any persecution that came, but we saw it was for good; and we looked upon it to be good, as from God: and there never were any prisons that I was in, of sufferings, but still it was for the bringing multitudes more out of prison." [69] With such conviction, and all-embracing love, any amount of suffering could be borne.

Threat of transportation failing, the next infliction con-

[68] *Letters of Early Friends,* p. 149.
[69] George Fox, *A Collection of Epistles,* 1698, p. 3.

sisted of heavy fines and distraint of goods, appealing admir-
ably to the greed of the host of informers called into being,
and to the pockets of the local justices (for little went
beyond there to the Crown), but in turn widely disgusting
the populace, who through this more than any other
measure reacted sympathetically towards Quakers. In
London an informer was found to be a Papist and almost
lynched by the mob, which scared his kind there in future;
in Colchester the people stoned two informers who took
refuge in the gaol (a place, in fairness, it must be said, that
had often protected Friends too, when the mob had not
been on their side); other informers were caught through
perjury, others just cold-shouldered. Yet, the impositions
effected were considerable, wholesale pillage following if
the sum was not produced promptly (£10 for being present
at a meeting, £20 for speaking there, £20 from the owner
of the premises); in Bristol, for instance, one of the worst
centres of informing, as late as 1683, two hundred Friends
were liable, under various statutes, for fines totalling
£16,440. A notorious informer, William Thornaby, alone
was the cause, over fourteen months, for fines of £2,000
against Friends. As a contemporary Dutch historian noted,
these scavengers, exercising powers of distraint . . . " took
away what they could find, oxen and cattle . . . merchandise, household stuff, feather beds, blankets, vessels
and raiment, yea, their very meat they spared not "; and
yet, when the goods were auctioned to the public . . . " some
were so honest that they loved not to buy what had been
lost with grief and could only be purchased with shame." [70]
    It was a forlorn dead-end policy, and not only against
English sentiment, but also very much at that point against
the developing commercial needs of the country. Quakers,
despite their fines, becoming every year better set up as
small traders and entrepreneurs, must have known that
time, as well as the Lord, was powerfully on their side.

[70] G. Croese, *History of the Quakers*, 1696, Vol. 2, p. 69.

(d) Towards Toleration

It cannot be stressed too strongly, however, that Quakers, the core in this respect of the entire Nonconformist conscience, brought nearer the advent of toleration, made apparent to all that it must come quickly, through the staunchness with which they upheld their meetings—in essence, their right to meet freely and speak as the spirit moved them. This more than their fortitude in gaol, or their stand against oaths, tithes, or paying fines, even to the loss of their worldly goods, caught the imagination of their day and made the outcome certain. They acted, as later did Gandhi, as all who eschew violence must act, in the one way most likely to pull the oppressor up short: by making his operative tension unbearble, increasingly inhuman, to himself. Tyrannies dissolve from within.

Fox in 1676 noted . . . " the governor of Dover Castle, when the king asked him if he had dispersed all the sectaries' meetings, he said: That he had; ' but the Quakers the devil himself could not: for if he did imprison them, and break them up, they would meet again; and if he should beat them, and knock them down, or kill some of them, all was one; they would meet and not resist again.' " [71]

More fully, Barclay recorded . . . " When they came to break up a meeting, they were forced to take every individual out by force, they not being free to give up their liberty by dissolving at their command: and when they haled out, unless they were kept forth by violence, they presently returned peaceably to their place. Yea, when sometimes the magistrates have pulled down their meeting-houses, they have met the next day openly upon the rubbish . . . so that, when the malice of their opposers stirred them to take shovels and throw the rubbish upon them, there they stood unmoved, being willing, if the Lord should so

---

[71] George Fox, *A Collection of Epistles*, 1698, p. 5.

permit, to have been there buried alive witnessing for Him." [72]

This inevitably wearied the constables. The doors were open, anyone could enter, no opposition was offered; then next day the ruined site or nearby street was seen to serve as well. Beat a drum, as was sometimes tried, to drown any words being spoken, and Friends settled easily into silence. Throw all the men into prison, and the women and children continued the meeting; throw the women after the men, and the children continued alone. A contemporary historian summed it up . . . " Some called this obstinacy, while others called it firmness. But by it they carried their point; for the Government grew weary of dealing with so much perverseness, and so began with letting them alone." [73] Practically speaking, their freedom to meet in their own way was won.

This needed to be enshrined in law; and here again over a period appreciation of Quaker integrity, inoffensive yet fearless, a banner not only for religious zeal but for the common right of citizens, decidedly helped to win the day. The first and most famous instance of this was Bushel's case in 1670, when William Penn and William Meade were tried at the Old Bailey on a charge of causing a riot: that is, of having preached outside the barricaded doors of Gracechurch Street Meeting to a crowd of several hundred people, many of whom had not been Friends but there simply as onlookers. They pleaded Not Guilty, and Penn refused to accept the indictment as legal, challenging the Recorder in charge of the case to show its basis in common law as claimed; and spoke to such effect that he and Meade were ushered out of court, and the jury instructed in their absence. Next it was the jury's turn to offend. They returned, from the Crown's point of view, an unsatisfactory verdict. " Gentlemen ", cried the irate Recorder, " you

[72] *Apology*, Prop. 14, Sect. vi.
[73] G. Burnet, *History of My Own Time* (Airy's ed.), Vol. 1, p. 491.

have not given in your verdict and you had as good say nothing. Therefore go and consider it once more. . . ." They did so, but again returned a verdict that would acquit Penn. " Gentlemen ", pursued the Recorder, now beside himself with rage, " you shall not be dismissed till we have a verdict that the Court will accept, and you shall be locked up without meat, drink, fire, and tobacco. . . ." Penn, back at the bar, called out to fortify them . . . " You are Englishmen; mind your privilege, give not away your right." " Nor will we ever do it ", sturdily replied the jury foreman.[74]

Nor did they. Shut up all night, bullied next day, finally thrown into Newgate and fined for their pains, they still stood firm. Released on a writ of *habeas corpus* they promptly sued the Recorder for illegal imprisonment; and won the case before a bench of twelve judges headed by the Lord Chief Justice; and so established in English and American courts, the rightful independence of the jury. Bushel, the foreman, had nerved his colleagues, but the inspiration for the whole spirited stand had come from William Penn.

Penn for the next two decades was to be the central figure among Friends. Fox had brought the Society into being, the power of his convincement releasing the necessary fervour among his colleagues, and through prayer, counsel, and epistles, incessant travelling and conduct under trial, he had set his mark upon the movement, making it the vehicle for a highly spiritual approach to life, within the group and society at large. Fearing its fragmentation under the Restoration oppression he had begun to link it securely together, through its system of business meetings; but this was already work of consolidation, conservation (that would unfortunately hand the lead to minds of a more conservative type); and by 1670 he could do no more, except significantly in the pioneer settlements of America,

[74] *The People's Ancient and Just Liberties Asserted*, London, 1670.

than, rather more quietly, remind Friends of their central witness.

This, of course, needed to be done, and is the chief thread to this day; but, under the stress of persecution, it began to give ground to some extent to a more purely worldly alignment of energies, based on law and reason, that had always been present in the Society, embedded there by Leveller thought, but that now supremely under Penn's lead came to the fore and concentrated on winning civil rights for Quakers. In fact it can be said that Penn, pre-eminently a champion of such liberties—those fundamental laws of England that he urged so strongly in the Bushel case—found in the Society of Friends the best vehicle, ready-fashioned, fearless, incorruptible, for the common cause that inspired his genius. Here was a group that would stand till death. He threw in his lot with them.

As a result of success in the Bushel case, the Society began to contest the law, thus reversing its earlier other-worldly attitude to lawyers. Fox himself was saved by a brilliant lawyer, Thomas Corbett, in 1675, who was then appointed standing counsel to Friends; the Meeting for Sufferings was set up " to endeavour for relief by the Law of the Land to stop the destroyer ";[75] advice was sent out and reports collected, listed, and presented to Parliament, the King, his judges, the whole populace, until every breach of fundamental law with regard to Quakers had been dinned into the nation's consciousness. The Society became an effective machine for legal, and so for political, reform; and the lead in this trend was given by Penn, supported by like-minded Friends, who were thus heirs to the Leveller tradition but without its violence and in a changed social context. It was no step at all for them to lobby members of Parliament assiduously, and from 1677 to 1679 to canvas actively for the emerging Whig party : steps that helped, ten years later, to give them the Toleration Act.

[75] *London Yearly Meeting Minutes,* 1675, Vol. 1, p. 25.

Penn himself, in 1682, lost patience with the snail-like pace at which reform in England comes about, battling then as always with the final venom of the older order, and, much encouraged by the King, by then eager to be rid of Quakers who he was beginning to see as so many Whigs, founded the Colony of Pennsylvania. This was to be the model State, a haven for oppressed citizens both of England and the Continent, that by its example might also help the cause of toleration at home. Penn had already assisted in drawing up constitutions for Carolina and New Jersey; he had listened to Locke and other such thinkers, he had read widely, he had absorbed such documents as the Agreement of the People, and he had been a practising Friend for years and himself tasted persecution. He was equipped therefore, and eager, to embody the quintessence of such study and experience in his constitution for Pennsylvania. His code of laws proved to be the most advanced of its day, a veritable trustee of future American liberties; though in bringing it into service Penn was not so much an original thinker as a practical engineer.

Certainly, the rush of Nonconformist emigrants to the American Colonies, and especially to those run by the Quakers, and the tales that came back of freedom and plenty, worked for toleration in England. Mercantile and financial interests, the great bedrock of Whig expansion, realised that trade would suffer, might considerably go to Holland and then lie between there and America, if a more rational atmosphere, the equal at least of these other places, were not quickly established. Toleration was underwritten by the requirements of trade.

In this, Friends, who had improved their position in almost every branch of commerce, and were pioneering in some manufactures, were both powerful movers and, in this purely worldly sense, considerable beneficiaries. In fact, it was not just religious liberty that came to them with the new century, offering the Society a place in English life, nor just a greatly strengthened position as individuals before the law, but also a much wider and secure prospect economically.

Which, as the decades passed, was to prove of most interest to them?

CHAPTER II

QUAKERS AS BOURGEOISIE

(a) Prosperity

THE first Quakers, transformed by their religious experience, and the unity and fellowship it brought among them, quickly found its power extending through their secular affairs. Life they intensely realised, was one. Step by step this conviction helped them to iron out inconsistencies of behaviour, or to hearken to the counsel of their leaders that at points took them far beyond the prejudices of their day, or to chide those of their brethren as yet less open to the redeeming power of Holy Spirit. As most of them were artisans and small traders, and yeomen with a growing interest in textile manufacture, already by occupation on the wave rising towards an enhanced material future, the conduct of their business was a primary sphere for consideration. Here unquestionably their guiding intuition of truth must prevail.

As early as the Balby gathering of 1656 they had decided " that all Friends that have callings and trades, do labour in the thing that is good, in faithfulness and uprightness; and keep to their yea and nay in all their communications : and that all who are indebted to the world, endeavour to discharge the same, that nothing they may owe to any man but love to one another " [1] . . . to be reinforced five years later by Fox in his most noted pronouncement on the subject . . . " Keep out of debts : owe to no man anything but love. Go not beyond your estates, lest ye bring yourselves to trouble, and cumber, and a snare; keep low and down in all things ye act . . . do rightly, justly, truly, holily, equally to all people in all things . . . and therefore, keeping your word, your day, and keeping your just

[1] *Letters of Early Friends*, p. 281.

measure, your first weight, that keeps down the oppression
. . . there the blessing is doubled. . . ." [2]

This clear-cut prudent advice, stressing honesty and
moderation, was added to equally urgent counsel against
idleness, waste, indulgence in pleasures, or disbursement of
capital on worldly possessions: all at this stage being
primarily corollaries to the use of one's life, alone in thought
or face to face with one's fellows, as a vehicle for the Lord's
power. All to facilitate that end.

Puritans generally, as also Catholics, advocated likewise;
in principle a religious approach to life was the cornerstone
of Christendom; but especially Quakers, in their early days,
carried principle into practice, were more self-disciplined,
more uniformly honest than their contemporaries. Their
lives, within and without, were one.

And this, it came about, served their pockets.

Fox, who missed little, noted . . . "But at the first convincement, when Friends could not put off their hats to
people nor say ' you ' to a particular, but ' thee ' and ' thou ';
and could not bow nor use the world's salutations, nor
fashions, nor customs, many Friends, being tradesmen of
several sorts lost their custom at the first; for the people
would not trade with them nor trust them, and for a time
Friends that were tradesmen could hardly get enough
money, to buy bread. But afterwards people came to see
Friends' honesty and truthfulness and ' yea ' and ' nay ' at
a word in their dealing, and their lives and conversations
did preach and reach to the witness of God in all people,
and they knew and saw that, for conscience sake towards
God, they would not cozen and cheat them, and at last
that they might send any child and be as well used as themselves, at any of their shops."

He continues . . . "So then things altered so that all the
enquiry was, where was a draper or shopkeeper or tailor
or shoemaker or any other tradesman that was a Quaker;

2 *Epistle* 200 (1661).

insomuch that Friends had double the trade, beyond any
of their neighbours. And if there was any trading they had
it, insomuch that then the cry of all the professors and
others was ' If we let these people alone they will take the
trading of the nation out of our hands.' " [3]

" For conscience sake towards God " was the determining
factor for the Quakers themselves, but it proved the foundation of their credit. They could be trusted. Even an
Anglican commended them . . . " We commend the
Quakers because they are at a word in all their dealings." [4]
It was the start of fixed retail prices. Other traders might
follow the precepts of Baxter's "A Christian Directory "
or Steele's " The Tradesman's Calling " (or such worthy
manuals as " The Weaver's Pocket-Book : or, weaving
spiritualised ", " The Young Man's Guide Through the
Wilderness ", " The Spiritual Merchant ", " How to Walk
with God in Our Callings ", and suchlike current clerical
outpourings), and achieve high standards of thrift and
diligence; their energies, as with Friends, largely excluded
from civil office and professions and thus channelled into
commerce. Yet Quakers, through their absolute integrity,
outmatched all in trading reputation. Their word was the
best coin in the land.

Other factors that helped to consolidate this position were
that Friends were the most free both from worldly tastes
and from stultifying doctrines, their outlook was empirical,
to the point, practical; as the most persecuted group they
were on their metal to re-establish themselves in the eyes
of the nation; they were the most closely-knit community,
with a sense of responsibility for each other; they forged,
as we shall see, the strongest trade links with America
through their co-religionists there; they were abandoning
agricultural occupations because they would not pay tithes,

---

[3] *Journal*, p. 169.
[4] The Morning Exercise at Cripplegate, St. Giles in the Fields and in
Southwark : being divers sermons preached A.D. 1659–89. *Sermon X*, Vol. I,
p. 208.

and this, with other civil limitations, further pointed to opportunities in business, opportunities that were soon identified with the desirable austerities of a godly calling; and then among them men were appearing whose ideas were more openly in step with the realities of growing wealth and the sense of status this promoted. Penn, echoing Locke, told them . . . "Solomon praises Diligence very highly, First it is the Way to Wealth: The Diligent Hand makes Rich . . . Secondly, it prefers Men . . . Seest thou a Man diligent in his Business he shall stand before Kings. Thirdly, it preserves an Estate . . . There is no living upon the Principal, you must be diligent to preserve what you have, whether it be Acquisition or Inheritance; else it will consume. . . ." [5]

The conduct praised is as before, but from a substantial shift in viewpoint.

Fox before he died grew anxious. He had preached . . . "I warn and charge you from the Lord not to make any of the world's jewels your God" [6] . . . "Let him that buys, or sells, or possesses, or uses this world, be, as if he did not." [7] What was happening? Were Friends, prospering almost as a by-product of their single-minded dedication to Truth, starting to prize this new estate before their old prophetic calling? What did they now most mean by " calling "? Fox died before fully learning the answer.

In retrospect, the answer is clear. For a season, a rather lengthy season, Quakers, that is the increasingly predominant middle-class trading element in the Society, headed by an inter-related group of merchant-manufacturing-banking families, who represented Friends to the world, who began running the Society itself like one of their counting houses, giving it its sedate conformist air, did in fact lose the Quaker thread handed to them by their

[5] *Works*, 1726, Vol. I, p. 908.   [6] *Epistle* 169 (1658).
[7] *Epistle* 200 (1661).

fathers, the tentative way into the darkness to the meeting place of God and man, with centuries of other men's prayer behind it, of blissful communion or partial failure and now through the gathered Quaker group given a new small area of experiment: because they became over-involved in making money, and more than that in maintaining the attitudes and status their prosperity conferred on them. Not all Friends were in business, but the growing majority were, and it consumed them; it veiled, except in certain individuals, the pressing insights that were waiting to be realised within their meetings for worship—that most delicate of instruments, that became clumsy in their hands.

Admittedly, the business "calling" would seem to them desirable, apart from anything else in that it offered at that time the widest opportunity for practising integrity in dealings with other men, and for practising self-control and simplicity, and for extending at least patriarchal benevolence to workmen, apprentices, the deserving poor, and beyond to other unfortunates. The motives could be most laudable. Yet, once embroiled in the arithmetic of trade these worthy Friends, totting up their ledgers, increasingly compromised their values. Their pronunciamentos might be the same, but the echoes rang less clearly. The fixed price, through astute combination, was not always the just price; self-control too easily became massive capital accumulation, simplicity while averse to a gay cloth did not bar the more expensive materials; and benevolence, that after-thought of the rich, was a poor substitute for the earlier social radicalism. No wonder historians in general lose interest in Friends after 1700—except perhaps for Elizabeth Fry at Newgate, John Woolman or Joseph Sturge pleading the cause of slaves, perhaps Bright washing his hands of the idiocy of the Crimean War, and a just noticeable diffused influence, stemming from some Quaker grandparent, among the higher echelons of contemporary Anglo-American society. Little wonder that ordinary folk tend to be sceptical of Quaker piety, and that already by the eighteenth century this was being loudly voiced.

For Friends were not just prospering, they were proceeding to become a very rich community; it was as if all their pioneering zeal, awakening the nation to the Light within, had switched with the greatest ease to the new mundane target; from being the shock troops of the Spirit they were becoming the shock troops of commerce. Unkinder critics said of them that they pursued riches " with a step as steady as time, and with an appetite as keen as death." [8] However unsought, and unexpected, the first rolling in of wealth might have been, once this trend was under way it soon was no longer treated with any profound sense of balance or religious understanding (despite exclamations of alarm from certain individual Friends), it was seized with both hands. An acquisitive spirit was now held by the world to be inseparable from Quakerism. What a change from the world's view of Friends at the time of the Restoration! Of course some comment was scurrilous smoke, but beneath there was plenty of fire.

Already by 1700 the Gracechurch Street Meeting, in the heart of commercial London, was noted as being composed of " the Richest Trading Men in London " [9]: in fact, the Barclays, Gurneys, Hoares, Lloyds, Hanburys, Osgoods, Dimsdales. In Philadelphia this predominance was even more pronounced. An English doctor visiting there in 1744 reported that " the Quakers are the richest and the people of greatest interest in the government ", adding that whereas Catholics and Anglicans, Methodists, or Presbyterians would engage in general conversation together, Quakers sat there talking " only about selling of flour and the low price it bore." [10] Anthony Benezet, who along with Woolman led the opposition to the American Quaker holding of slaves, remarked in 1757 " one would think,

[8] T. Clarkson, *A Portraiture of Quakerism*, 1807, Vol. 3, p. 253.
[9] C. Leslie, *The Snake in the Grass*, 1698, p. 362.
[10] *Gentleman's Progress* (ed. C. Bridenhaugh), pp. 20–22.

by the general conduct of even the better sort of Friends in matters of property, that some of our Saviour's positive injunctions to his followers had no meaning." [11] In England too, from concerned Friends, there might be intermittent voicing of anxiety, a gentle censure of this "hastening to be rich", but it tended towards the end of the century to peter out, to be deflected into the insidious lush bypaths of Evangelical conservatism. The original Quaker vision was so clouded, the Society as a whole so compromised, that few of its members for the time being could step outside the skin this gave them.

Quaker apologists actually tend to designate this period as one of retreat from the world: as if, with the spiritual voice being low, one can ignore the activities of hands and feet. In fact, Quakers were never so active, but as it happens, as entrepreneurs. "The more important chapters in the early history of the iron industry might have been written almost without passing beyond the bounds of the Society of Friends." [12] The Spencer group in Yorkshire, the Rawlinsons in the north-west, the Lloyds in Wales and Birmingham, and greatest of all the Darbys at Coalbrookdale in Shropshire, were laying the foundations of the heavy industry that a century later was to make Britain the workshop of the world. Abraham Darby, around 1713, discovered the use of coke-smelting for casting iron into domestic pots and pans, and into engineering parts that later facilitated the development of the steam engine. His process, with ingrown business caution, was kept secret for a quarter of a century, an important pillar of subsequent wealth. The firm pioneered foundry practice and the use of iron railroads, and the building of single span bridges; and one of the partners, Richard Reynolds, built up their Melingriffith Forge into the largest tin-plate works in the world. The process of making tin-plates had been

[11] G. S. Brookes, *Friend Anthony Benezet*, Phila., 1937, p. 224.
[12] T. S. Ashton, *Iron and Steel in the Industrial Revolution*, 1924, p. 213.

largely promoted in Wales to this point by another Quaker family, the Hanburys, also ironmasters, though later to marry into banking and brewing and the cloth, tobacco, and slave trades with America, and even later into pharmacy where their name, in "Allen and Hanburys", appears to this day. The families, of course, with which they intermarried were all Quaker.

Other basic industries in which Friends were prominent were the mining and smelting of lead and silver: from 1692 for two centuries the London, or Quaker Lead Company was paramount in this field. In 1704 when Sir Isaac Newton, appointed Master of the Mint, was charged to redeem the silver coinage, it was from the Quaker Lead Company that he took the new silver ingots, of such pure standard the resulting coinage was known as " Quaker shillings ", a service that continued for thirty years. The Company had mines and smelting works throughout the British Isles, and were important promoters of canals and roads, the means of transport being then, as now, in a shocking state in the country.

In Wales, several families of Friends pioneered in copper smelting; and at Bristol, William Champion was the first man to make zinc in England. With the Champion family another linkage of Quaker interests appears. They were dealers and general warehousemen for most of the Quaker ironmasters, receiving large consignments of pig and bar iron from Northern and Midland forges, relaying these to local nail and wire makers and to the tin-plate mills. They also owned a company for the manufacture of brass (" probably the most up-to-date and efficient works in the country "),[13] had interests in copper, then added zinc, and then in 1768 partnered William Cookworthy, also a Friend, to manufacture the first porcelain in Britain. They married into iron, and banking, through the Lloyd family.

[13] H. Hamilton, *The English Brass and Copper Industries to* 1800, 1926, p. 156.

Metals however were not the only plank in the Quaker rise to capitalist pre-eminence—though, one notes in Pennsylvania, Friends who prospered in trades of various sorts, such as shipping or brewing or textiles, afterwards liked to secure their money in the basic iron industry; they near-monopolised it there as in England. But besides this, firstly, there were textiles. In this industry Friends could not be pioneers, but a number among them soon rose to the then commanding position of middlemen, buying the wool and giving it out to be spun (by other Friends on the domestic system), taking the yarn and giving it to weavers, to dyers, and so to the Quaker cloth merchant. Friends dealt with each other because there was absolute trust, and shared memory of persecution, and the backing of their highly organised Society that encouraged loans and combination among them and was perfectly willing to handle debts, excessive prices, shoddy goods, incipient law suits and so forth under the heading of sins against the Lord; also, meeting together for worship and at Monthly and Quarterly Meetings, Friends in business (increasingly the same as those appointed as spiritual mentors) could discuss prices and wages and supplies, and order everything to their common satisfaction. This factor, of belonging to a closely-knit sect, almost an extended family group, was, along with their willingness to save and accumulate capital, the key to their rapid growth in prosperity; and the reason why, once they were established, they took steps to ensure that the Society continued to serve this useful function, even if in its vital inner life it meant standing still while doing so.

Regarding textiles, in the north of England the chief Quaker families were the Peases and the Backhouses, both in their stride by the early eighteenth century. They soon intermarried, then further linked with the Hustler family of Bradford, wool staplers and combers. Together this clan developed canals, including the Leeds and Liverpool Canal, and in the next century pioneered railways: their Stockton and Darlington Railway (the Quaker Line) initiated the railway era in Britain, it was they who sponsored George Stephenson, whom they partnered in his Newcastle factory for the manufacture of steam engines. They were concerned in the York, Newcastle and Berwick Railway, and the York and North Midland Railway. Further, together with the Richardson family, they were related to the Rawlinson group of ironmasters, and so later to the Consett Iron Company; and then, one might now say inevitably, their funds and first-rate credit were turned into banking (there were both Pease and Backhouse banks), and soon here a marriage with the Gurneys. Business arrangements and marriage of children proceeded conveniently side by side; in that close highly-geared community of like-minded people it was even unavoidable.

In West Country textiles the chief Quaker families were the Weres and the Foxes, linked with the Crewdsons, cloth merchants of Kendal, and then, again through marriage, extending into iron and steel and shipping; and directly, on the basis of their credit, into banking. This thus becomes a regular pattern, and it only requires mention of the Gurneys, almost the greatest house of them all, rooted in East Anglia and in the interlocking stages of the textile trade, and thereafter suitably linked with other leading Quaker families, to have run the network around the country.

Gurney's bank, built up on the credit afforded to their subsidiary associates and on their dominance of the stock position in the local textile market, gradually absorbed their neighbour country banks till, according to the 1838 Circular to Bankers, they " may now be described as exercising an influence and a power inferior to that of no banking establishment in Great Britain, that of the Bank of England alone excepted." In 1825 Samuel Gurney earned the title of the Banker's banker by lending when even the Bank of

England was refusing loans. Together with Nathan Roths-
child he launched the Alliance Assurance Company, and
with John Overend and Thomas Richardson he launched
Overend and Gurney, that by 1850 was counted the greatest
discount house in the world. By marriage the Gurneys
were linked to the Barclays, and were themselves absorbed
by the latter's bank in 1896.

Most of these Quaker banks were established in the third
quarter of the eighteenth century, some out of iron, some
out of textiles, showing once again how these entrepreneur
families maintained the pace of economic development;
here lay their most concentrated efforts; and one which
brought logical rewards. Sampson Lloyd, Birmingham
ironmaster, found that his bank produced a profit of
£10,000 in its first six years, far more than iron could show,
so he sent his son into Lombard Street, to build up a branch
that through subsequent amalgamations, became one of the
Big Five in banking. In finance, the Quaker drive was
prodigious during this so-called century of retreat.

Two of the great Quaker banking families, the Hoares
and the Barclays, had been active as merchant-bankers
from the start of the century. They both married with
other banking families, including the Gurneys, forging a
chain of credit through the Quaker business world; and
with them one plunges to the heart of the Quaker merchant power in London, which, fostering the Anglo-
American trade and extensive land investment in the
Colonies, secured both enormous worldly influence, and,
through control of Meeting for Sufferings, the key position
in the Society of Friends, at least throughout the eighteenth
century. Theirs became the governing mentality, in Quaker
discipline, meetings, homes, all of it shaped by the daily
needs and mechanism of trade. They were by no means
unique among Friends, they were simply, this caucus of
great London merchants, at the apex of the Quaker business
community; and thus best placed and most ready to give

expression to its requirements, veiled in suitable piety, of course, in which doubtless they honestly believed—but alas, producing words and conduct that became more sterile with each decade.

The leading family group were the Barclays, cloth and linen merchants, bill brokers, agents for the Logans and Pembertons of Philadelphia, big investors in Colonial enterprise, members of the Royal African Company with its interests in shipping and slaves, friends of the nobility that effectively ran the country and of the royal family. They were linked by marriage to the Hanburys and the Osgoods, the leading tobacco merchants of the time, with vast plantations in Virginia and Maryland (who were again linked to the Beaufroys, with similar interests), who were bankers and London business agents for the Proprietors of Maryland, Virginia, and South Carolina, and who promoted the Ohio Company to ensure the westward expansion of British investments (so largely their own) at the expense of the French. Through the vital middle years of the eighteenth century (as regards Britain's relation with America) the active figures were David Barclay, John and Capell Hanbury, Mark Beaufroy, Daniel Mildred (in the fur trade), Peter Collinson (in the silk trade), Richard Partridge (their chief Colonial and Parliamentary agent), Robert Plumstead (an important shipper), Joseph Hoare, Sampson Lloyd, Henry Gouldney, Andrew Pitt, and a few other merchants and bankers. Some Friends, such as Thomas Hyam, were also trading east, to the Baltic, but the main interest was towards America. Up till the Revolutionary War the Atlantic trade was largely Quaker.

Their prime concern was to safeguard this trade, and therefore the position of Friends in the Colonies who were building it up at that end. Theirs was an inter-Atlantic fraternity, certainly closer than any seen since. Each Colony had its correspondent in London (parallel to the Government's Colonial agents), whose job was to learn of any adverse measures intended by the Colonial authorities, to report this to Meeting for Sufferings (after 1748 to a sub-committee for Parliamentary and Colonial affairs), and thereafter see that the issue was settled satisfactorily in the British courts or settled by appeal to Parliament or sometimes directly to the Crown. This worked most successfully, sometimes with the judicious help of bribes. Friends were known for their prior intelligence concerning American affairs; no other group had such a liaison.

In turn, at the time of the Seven Years War, that vital moment in British Imperial history, this same central group of London Quakers, partly because they did not want French Catholic interests to triumph and partly because there was a danger (constitutionally, very slight) of fresh civil disabilities being placed on Pennsylvania Friends, induced their fellows in Philadelphia to withdraw from political office: thus ensuring a government there that would stand up to the French, and later help win the American campaign, save the Ohio land investments, and open up new export markets. The Hanburys had for some years past urged a strong policy on the British Government, and at the crucial moment Peter Collinson reaffirmed this merchant view to Lord Grenville; while Robert Plumstead, for one, in his letters of March 12th and 18th, 1756 to his merchant associates in Philadelphia, Abel James and Benjamin Shoemaker, put the issues in such a way that the London view would be followed there. The prime concern was to keep the trade.

In return for this signal co-operation on the part of the Philadelphian Quaker merchant-politicians, nine years later English Friends—that is, the Hanburys, the Barclays, the Mildreds, the Reeves and Cootes of Bristol— organised strong pressure for the repeal of the trade-inhibiting Stamp Act. Finally, when war threatened between Britain and the American Colonies, they did all they could through close contact with Benjamin Franklin to help avert it, and then to persuade their American colleagues to stay loyal to the mother country. Apart from any pacifist principles the Society as a whole might be invoking, this élite of London merchants was concerned to safeguard their commerce. Even then, when American independence was achieved, and for a time over there Philadelphian Quakers were discredited on account of their English loyalties, the old relationship did not cease. London Friends, of a conservative temper, though this began to take new forms, continued well into the next century as advisers and re-inspirers of American Quaker Orthodoxy: that is to say, of the older established merchant and property-owning families. The kindred interests stuck together—to the detriment of American Quakerism as a whole.

As a footnote to the above one must add, in view of the excellent news-service prevailing in the Society, that when in 1785 Pitt, the English Prime Minister, to relieve the almost unbearable economic distress in Ireland, partly consequent on the loss of the American market, proposed a free trade area embracing both islands, Friends again, to wit, principally Richard Reynolds, and William Gibbons of Bristol, seemed unable to stop themselves from putting their business interests first. Didn't any Irish Friends (active in all their country's trades and industries) beg for a hearing or point out the tragedy that would follow any worsening of the already near-starvation level of their satellite country's life? The facts, in view of Quaker professions, are remarkable: for the two above-mentioned Friends headed the protectionist outcry and led the formation of the United Chamber of the Manufacturers of Great Britain. This became one of the chief factors pushing the Irish to desperation, and precipitating the risings and repression of eleven years later, one of the bloodiest chapters in British Colonial history.

Friends could not really plead ignorance. Charitable, progressive, godly, when it didn't hurt them economically, out of the surplus of swollen prosperity, they seemed unable, in that ungainly commercially-ridden epoch, regularly to put first things first in the way their Meetings should have led them to do. They were too bound up in the logic of business. Their rise in the world, however, merited by diligence and good faith, had cost them their eternal vision. They were, as one of their own critics noted, " as salt which hath lost its savour." [14]

But they waxed fat. That underlies their conduct in every sphere, their growing caution and uniformity, their lessening appeal to their contemporaries; and so it can be seen as the starting point for the necessary reaction, the breaking out from bonds, which took various forms according to the insight of such different individuals as a John Woolman or a William Savery. These Friends, and their increasing following, reacted against the dominant trend, and, through family visits and Meetings,, stirred their Society to a re-examination of itself. The Quaker thread could never be entirely lost.

(b) Caution

In the eighteenth century Englishmen were still being hanged and transported for offences, some of them pitiably small, against property, or for standing in the way of the ever-encroaching rights of property over those of the landless, often the summarily ousted labourer, and over those of the new types of wage earners, first in cottages then in factories, who had only the work of their hands to live by, who had no other stake in the ownership and responsibilities, the great developing social venture, of the commerce and industries in which they were involved. Protest and riots there were in plenty, and the spread of an inturned violence and despair, all proceeding in the shadow of the militia, the harsh-faced courts, the gallows or the transports. The two nations, that Disraeli later noted, were

[14] G. Crosfield, *Memoir of Samuel Fothergill*, p. 256.

being allowed to appear and harden, and the consequent deep psychological tensions that still plague and paralyse Englishmen, so loyal in their self-deceptions, to-day.

In all this Friends chose to " walk wisely and circum-spectly towards all men, in the peaceable spirit of Christ Jesus, giving no offence nor occasions to those in outward government, nor way to any controversies, heats or dis-tractions of this world, about the kingdom thereof. But pray for the good of all; and submit all to that Divine power and wisdom which rules over the kingdom of men. That, as the Lord's hidden ones, that are always quiet in the land, as those prudent ones and wise in heart, who know when and where to keep silent, you may all approve your hearts to God. . . ." [15]

That is to say, they did not, like their fathers, grand-fathers, or great-grandfathers of Cromwell's day, speak out on the national stage against the abuses of a system that put property before people (except very gradually, and first to their own members, with regard to the overseas slave trade), they were no longer the prophets of the common man, extending their insight of a spiritual fellowship into any comprehensive call to arrest, or even consider, the social and economic cleavages increasing with each decade; they were doing nothing to change or stir the hearts of their rulers, to whom, indeed, they were very quick to send repeated assurances of loyalty. No Quakers of these quiet generations found themselves hanged or transported; as a Society, they no longer caused alarm to any section of the Establishment. So their radical lead slipped away to the Academies of the Rational Dissenters, to working men's Societies and Unions, to Owen and the Chartists. A visiting monarch, Frederick of Prussia, wished that he had Friends as his subjects. Naturally. Which upholder of the new capitalist order would not?

Up till the middle of the century they did continue with

[15] *London Yearly Meeting Epistle*, 1689.

public gatherings, called Circular Yearly Meetings, in all
parts of the country, for the spreading of their purely
religious insights; but in these their new inhibitions showed
them up. Their old cry of Christ within, fostering a
socially radical outlook, had naturally found a wide appeal;
but now their social note was muted and, the more respectable they became, the more conformist grew their theology,
so that they were already abasing man before an all-power-
ful immutable Judge, an inert cramping relationship out
of tune with their earlier approach. Their public ministry
dried up, paralysed from within by this crossing of opposed
attitudes; they were stuck halfway between early Friends
and the Wesleyans who on every side were offering with
cathartic bliss the once-for-all leap to salvation—provided
of course that converts led orderly, obedient lives in the
service of their employer's "calling". The public found
Friends half-hearted, offering neither the down-to-earth
spirit-in-man challenge of their fathers, with its co-operative
social overtones, nor the up-to-the-heavens release of Wesley. Quaker public meetings faded out. Friends became
even quieter.

Behind this trend, the prime influence regulating their
conduct in society at large, was their continuing success
in trade. In the first place it had been their integrity, and
their self-disciplined austerity, their internal links and loyalties, and so forth, that had brought a disproportionate
amount of the nation's commerce and wealth to them;
but then increasingly it was the trade itself, the social status
and the economic outlook it conditioned, that shaped
Quaker developments. Till nearly the middle of the nineteenth century, till the introduction of legal protection for
joint stock companies, the governing factor of business life
was the shortage of capital (as with under-developed countries to-day), and therefore the business man's need to
ensure that his credit was good, in order to expand or even
to stay in business. Quaker credit was very good, people

trusted money with them, were ready to share in their enterprises, were eager to be employed by them. In all these ways Friends stood for security.

Not unnaturally therefore there arose, especially among their leading traders, desire that this reputation should not falter, should not be blemished by any member who might lack economic zeal. Gradually, the thought processes, the regulations, the very atmosphere of the Society veered in the same direction: to maintain this irreproachable front, good for any sum. Caution became the dominant key.

Bristol's Men's Meeting when asked by Meeting for Sufferings in 1721 for an account of the work of the First Publishers of Truth in their city, replied . . . "As we do not perfectly know the reason of your desiring these accounts, so we doubt not but you will think it necessary to act with caution in a thing of this nature as may give no occasion either to the Government in general, under who we enjoy so many favours, or the magistrates of this city in particular." [16] Caution even with regard to history! These became the days when Quaker Elders, gingerly propelling their thoughts through every possible periphrase, thought it wiser to refer to the Devil as " the great enemy of mankind " and " the Prince of the power of the air." A Friend asked about the health of his wife, replied . . . " Thank thee, I think I may safely say that she is much as she sometimes is." Another Friend, giving advice to a young business trainee, warned . . . " Keep thy Business to thy self . . . Endeavour to know what Prices other People give for Goods, but Say nothing of what thou gives thy self . . . If thou finds out a Place where they Sell cheap, keep it to thy self . . . it will increase Business." [17] The trader's sly taciturnity and the worshipper's growing anxiety over getting a single word out of a place met in a mode of respectable caution.

[16] *First Publishers of Truth,* p. 11.
[17] Letter dated 22nd June, 1743, in Reynell Letter Book, Coates-Reynell Papers (MSS in Hist. Soc. of Pennsylvania).

Dress was another area of personality soon brought under control, the earlier feelings for simplicity reduced to a uniform requirement. This meant, in moments of popular distress, as during the riots of 1800 due to the high price of corn, that Quaker merchants, distinguishable a mile off, got rolled in the mud by the crowd; but equally this same appearance was the badge of a man you could leave your money with, a warrant of dependability. It kept up Friends' *esprit de corps,* it made the transmission of the Discipline easier, curbing any flightly impulse—except among the richest families, where " gay " or " wet " Friends, if they didn't eventually resign their membership, became something of an exception, due in part to a counter-requirement at that level of business and society not to seem too strange, too outré, to their non-Quaker associates. At more modest levels, however, the strict Quaker garb was prescribed, without heed of the damage to spontaneity, a danger Margaret Fox had foreseen in 1698 . . . " It's a dangerous thing to lead young Friends much into the observation of outward things, which may be easily done; for they can soon get into an outward garb to be all alike outwardly, but this will not make them true Christians. It's the Spirit that gives life." [18] "A silly, poor Gospel ", she added two years later, " this narrowness and strictness entering in . . . in so much that poor Friends is mangled in their minds." [19]

But alas none of this was to count, for another hundred and fifty years, against the dominant trading ethic. The Spirit had to suffer. The creative impulse, the free-flowing birth of insight, as necessary to worship as to every facet of developed human life, went undercover, managed best it could within the external regulations. A passionate cellist who joined Friends could no longer play his cello, felt it wrong to give it away, could not bear to destroy it: so he buried it. There is the symbol of what took place, a by-

[18] *Works,* p. 535.
[19] *Port.* 25, (66).

product of business caution, of the long hard road to sufficiency in the realm of capital and credit.

Of course, there was also the internal need, as between the leading Quaker combines and small Quaker tradesmen, as between the employers and their workmen and servants, of maintaining what marks of equality they could, of re-emphasising their religious fellowship, of keeping up morale; though in terms of wealth, responsibility, social status, freedom of action, they were in reality worlds apart. The ironmaster buying up a tin-plate mill or marrying his daughter into shipping or brewing, or discussing in the intervals of Quarterly Meeting some aspects of the national price structure with a banker who had just hurried in from dealings for a Colonial Governor : such a man, such men, were daily conditioned by very different pressures from those of the workpeople they employed, or those of neighbour artisans. Likeness of dress restored some balance, as did the undying Friends' practice of sage rebuke and godly counsel from any one member to another. In Meetings sobriety and tongue-tied awe provided the same safe canopy for all : formally, they were still a highly-unified group. But, the more considerable this formal edifice the less the exploratory function of worship, drawing Light into every corner of their lives, their best chance of rediscovering a more balanced set of values, could operate. Impossible conditions were being applied by their now extra-mural, though ostensibly sanctified, over-riding secular interests.

Worship, vitalising fellowship, suffered; but the outward marks of membership were kept up, and doubtless helped the workers to work their long hours with better heart, to foster their own secular ambitions, and to accept the Society's stringent regulations—for instance, the certificates of " clearness " required, as to character, debts, general abilities, before a member was allowed to remove from one Monthly Meeting to another. The business machinery was wonderfully complete, underwritten by stern needs. More over, even at the other end, the most successful capitalists among Friends, with their primary responsibilities to their credit-trusting public, must have found, from somewhere within their conscience, something reassuring in their continuance even of the externals of Quaker practice: these somehow did keep them from becoming irremediably committed to material ambitions. Tradition, if finally only its shell, kept them open to small promptings that they could never entirely do without and be at ease; and, it also provided a ready-to-hand safety line if religious need was more deeply stirred. They never let quite everything go.

For instance, in Philadelphia for the first half of the eighteenth century the richer Quaker merchant-barons unabashedly pursued success, high station, worldly grandeur, to the detriment of their spiritual machinery. There of course there had been no Establishment, Anglican or Puritan, occupying the front seats, nor legal barrier to Quaker advance. They therefore filled the vacuum. Some, coming from Massachussetts or Rhode Island, were already men of substance; others, traders, artisans, even indentured servants, within a decade or two had established themselves with a sound business, a town house, a country estate, a seat on the council or in the Colonial Assembly. They sorted themselves into a hierarchy based on degree of wealth, based also on Barclay's words (that anti-Levelling tendency of this second more respectable generation of Friends) . . . "such as God calls in low degree, to be content with their Condition, not envying those Brethren, who have greater abundance, knowing they have received abundance as to the inward Man " [20] . . . a notion that turned sharper through the voice of a leading merchant spokesman, Isaac Norris, who condemned any radical tendencies that had shipped across among the Brethren as being " perni-

[20] *Apology,* Prop. XV, Sect. 2.

cious to the growth and freedom of trade" [21]: thus pointing the division that existed at the start between his sort of city-merchant interest and that of the poorer sort of Friend (the "mobbish" people as Logan, Penn's right-hand man called them) and also of the simpler rural Quakers, who, settling the Pennsylvanian hinderland, kept at least in principle closer to the earlier Leveller ideals. Here in fact lay the seed of the later schism in American Quakerdom.

Norris himself, the arch-example of these go-getting merchants had arrived in 1691 with a hundred pounds to his name and died in 1735 leaving, in stock, business buildings, goodwill, and land, an estate that was valued in tens of thousands, that thirty years later his son had increased to a value of over sixty thousand pounds. Both these men were politicians and served as Speaker of the Legislative Assembly, which together with their fellow Quaker merchants they controlled till 1756, the year in which this group withdrew, as we have seen, for largely tactical reasons, into the main bastion of its trade. They equally dominated the Philadelphia municipality; indeed, as with the Lord Mayor of London, one had to be wealthy to become the Mayor, and so it was largely Quaker grandees, Norrises, Shippens, Prestons, Morrises, Hills, Shoemakers, and so on, who occupied the office.

They intermarried, and with other rich Quakers throughout America and back in Britain; and gradually stepped up their style of living, with fine architecture, fine plantations, silver plate and epicurean fare—a dinner that a visiting Congregationalist noted, with some surprise, in his diary included . . . "ducks, hams, chicken, beef, pig, tarts, creams, custards, jellies, fools, trifles, floating islands, beer, porter, punch, wine . . .";[22] and then, besides the very best stuffs, and even occasionally their portraits in oils to supplement the three standard prints of Quaker homes, the one

<hr/>

[21] *Penn-Logan Correspondence*, 1870, Vol. 2, pp. 223–4.
[22] *The Works of John Adams* (ed. C. F. Adams), Vol. 2, p. 369.

of William Penn making treaty with the Indians, the one of a slave ship in mid-Atlantic, and the one of a meeting house or school, they added, that crowning necessity of the social register, a fine array of four-wheeled carriages. Old Norris sent to England for his coach, debating whether or not to put his coat of arms on it; a few years later he wrote for liveries "Strong and Cheap, Either of a Dark Gray or Sad Coullour . . . or any Grave Coullour thou likes." [23] Sombre hues were still maintained, like the sombre taste in entertainment, but could not conceal the underlying appetite for ever-increasing worldly substance, for all the perquisites of social power. In fact, the élite of this Quaker community, like their fellows in London, became so very well established that they let go a good deal of their caution; some of them, continuing along these lines, even dispensed with being Quaker. That was not an uncommon route out of the Society. Three generations, Emerson considered, were required to turn a radical Friend into a Tory churchgoer.

However, for those who remained, for whom being a Friend in the final analysis was not only more useful or congenial or a family habit but did pose, if less clearly after decades of business preoccupations, a profound spiritual involvement, that could best be explored through corporate prayer, there was bound to come a moment of self-questioning, a dissatisfaction with merely formal observance, and then an attempted fresh start.

In Pennsylvania this was touched off by the 1756 withdrawal from politics, the realisation by the Quaker merchants, who had carried all before them for fifty years, that Imperial interests were striking out and they had best pull in their horns, and that numerically in their own Colony they could no longer claim the same authority: facts that thrust caution on them, a re-emphasis of Quaker sobriety

[23] *Norris Letter Book*, 1716–30, p. 224. (Norris Papers, MSS in Hist. Soc. of Pennsylvania).

and inoffensive piety in union with all their less well-to-do members who had been more cautious all along. Even though after the Seven Years War some of them resumed their worldly stance, it was never to the same extent or for long; and the final lesson of the Revolutionary War, from 1777 onwards, when they were reviled by their compatriots, imprisoned, fined, two of them hanged, for their warm though spectator sympathy for the British, worked decisively on them. Orthodoxy became the mode: a highly-disciplined group piety, restraint in every field, even business, a binding caution that indeed ultimately succumbed to Evangelical fervour, but only after it had realised that by that date (the eighteen twenties) Evangelicalism was socially the least radical force to choose from. This then was the conservative approach to the successive situations it met with. It gripped tighter to the formal observance of strict Quaker life. It marked time.

If this was not profound self-questioning, it did at least make way, by its very inadequacy, for more vital currents of reassessment, that had started with the witness of John Woolman, and to a less extent, of Anthony Benezet, winning Friends from their addiction to slave-holding. These true Quaker prophets had shown up property-love at its most vulnerable point; and after Woolman had spoken to the 1758 Yearly Meeting of Philadelphia a concerned self-questioning began, that opened up in many young hearts a need for a more inspiring Quaker life than the business-orientated local leadership of their Society offered.

For some this was to plunge them more profoundly into the interior way of prayer, into an ascetic dependence on God, stripped of surrounding worldly ambition and its compromise morality; till their mysticism, though one-sided, world-denying, over-quietistic, gave the spiritual peace they sought. Not only in Pennsylvania, but throughout the American Colonies and Britain, where like situations were developing, or had developed, within the Quaker fold, a number of such extreme-minded Friends appeared, typical of whom was Job Scott (born in Rhode Island, 1751), who said of the prevailing business interest . . . " I have seen the progress of this spirit with sorrow, and mourned over some who have been grievously entangled and ensnared in it—Oh! thou traveller Sion-ward, flee, flee, flee for thy life, from all these allurements." [24]

Actually for a time the preaching of Scott, and of Sarah Grubb in England, pure and beautiful though it revealed their own inner paths to be, tended among the Society at large, with its vital group-worship technique rigidly controlled by the conservative hierarchy, rather to increase the prevailing caution and awestruck muteness. It did not offer to the majority the much needed path of release.

This came through the second development of the widely felt desire among younger Friends for a more inspiring Quaker life: which was the swing to Evangelicalism, to a lyrical outpouring of soul, to an emotional rebirth from on high. In Philadelphia since 1740 there had been a sustained Wesleyan campaign, but it was only towards the end of the century, with the dry formalism of Quaker leadership and the over-intensity of the extreme Quietists leaving an unsatisfied limbo in many young Quaker hearts, that these were finally captured by Evangelical persuasions —by now, of course, also available from more socially-acceptable Anglican sources. There was at once a resurgence of ministry, a new fluttering of religious zeal, an outpouring of public testimony to the work of Christ Jesus in the heart. Weighty Friends at first disapproved, but had themselves so little to offer; they had buried the true Quaker technique, so they could not counter this one. Eventually, they succumbed to it, too; then made of it a means of Discipline, a new piece of bigotry.

A similar process unrolled in England, though it was from the United States that William Savery, David Sands,

[24] *Journal*, London, 1787, pp. 78–79.

Stephen Grellet came to intensify the gospel call. Theirs were among the most impassioned voices calling for spiritual rededication; their exhortations offered release from a constricted habit of mind, and the appeal of that was irresistible.

Even if eventually it was to prove over-biased for the corporate Quaker exercise, and all too soon to find itself gathered into the armoury of conservative Friends, it was not without first having brought new hope and self-confidence into many a Quaker life, a new sense of energy and of commitment to service in the world. It marked the second turning point in the Society's history. Even if inordinate concern for business was not to be broken down so easily, at least the climate of feeling began to change, and at its key point, in meeting for worship. Friends became freer to respond to their inspirational openings. The century of abysmal caution was over.

(c) Missions

Throughout all this time, since the days of Fox, itinerant ministry had neved ceased within the bounds of the Society of Friends, though consonant with the prevailing temper it had become toned down except in the promulgation of uniform Elder-inspired rules of behaviour, appearance, and largely negative thoughts, and also, in the interests of Quaker trade, in the performing of various merchants' commissions, gathering of useful information and so forth, while on circuit. Sometimes Ministers did manage to be more than official mouthpieces, and sounded deep, like early Quaker converts, into the heart of meetings with the recounting of their spiritual travail, but as often as not they said never a word. The century waited for a new impulse.

This came with the Evangelicals, men and women from outside the Society who had been reached by Wesley (like Mary Dudley) or by the corresponding Anglican fervour (like Rebecca Jones), or were of a deep and troubled sensibility open to the currents of the day, who joined Friends and at once began to press the Society to their way of thinking and feeling. The over-neglected ground was theirs, there was a wide young audience ready to respond to them, they touched a nucleus of birthright members who in turn preached in the same tenor. Ministry became influential again, became oracular, prophetic. Elders found themselves swept along on a flood of spontaneous palpitating feeling. Faith (without asking too closely in what) throbbed like a passion. This was new.

These Ministers were all great travellers. Their aim was firstly to regenerate Friends, to infuse this smug trading body with a more active sense of sin, till each of their hearers should go away gasping with his need for pardon and a deeper faith. They preached Christ crucified, the all-atoning sacrifice for all men at all times; they worked up climacteric tension, with the horror and despair of hell on every side, then led their audience through to redemption. In the greater intimacy of family visits they didn't hesitate, with a growing psychic fluency concomitant with their highly-strung condition, to nail down individual states, to expose them (as the early Calvanists had done), and to put forth the saving call to the particular member of the family being scrutinised, detailing what should be done.

These occasions were called " opportunities ", they were times of " deep wading ", of " openings ": as for the Ministers themselves was almost every minute of their own lives. They never relaxed, they were a First Aid Squad always on the go, their orders, without which they couldn't move, received directly, specifically, from God. They leaned on their Saviour with a passionate yearning, for ever re-enacting, through an ever wider audience, the moment of their first recognition of Him; for them this should be the universal pattern, they did not take kindly to other methods, and they inevitably sought out, beyond Quakerdom, the most distressed, the most abandoned of human beings, as those most likely to respond to their miracle. This led to some useful work (when followed up by more practical associates), but it was, emotionally at least, an extension of their primarily subjective rather feminine need for continual Divine reassurance.

Thus, sustained citizen endeavour or examination of root social forces was not their forte. They were heart stirrers. They warred on doubt, indifference, habit—whether in the depths of vice or virtue; they raised the temperature, and brought warm feelings of love, and compassion to fruit in their trail. None of this could last at such a pitch for very long or provide a broad enough basis, for Quakers or any-one else in society, to tackle the complicated material and spiritual problems besetting them; but it gave a boost when that was badly needed. It started countless individuals on lives of service for their fellows, on lives now more im-pelled to be aware of humanity's suffering and deprivation (one might also say that the French Revolution and fear of anything similar in Britain was waking up the middle-class conscience), it brought challenge emotionally and for many a sense of a more worthwhile existence, and for others a badly needed opiate; and it primarily, among Friends, gave a Cause, a rallying cry, a new grouping of emotions, with which to break forth from the shell of recent generations. It was a ferment, and, amongst other things, it quickly carried members of the Society to every corner of the earth. In this too the Ministers led. The whole world became their parish.

Among the most interesting of these new men was Stephen Grellet. Etienne de Grellet du Mabillier, born 1773 into a minor though wealthy strata of the French nobility, Catholic, exiled by the French Revolution, had at the age of twenty-two found refuge in America. There his unusual childhood sensitivity and an intermediate period

of doubt in which he had felt "There is no God" [25] were
carried further, as invariably occurred with these apostles,
through stages of critical despair and sense of sin, to sudden
bountiful revelation of his Saviour: as it so happened, in
a Friends' Meeting, where acquaintances had taken him.
"I was favoured to find *in* me, what I had so long, and
with so many tears, sought for *without* me . . . I felt the
Lord's power in such a manner, that my inner man was
prostrated before my blessed Redeemer. A secret joy filled
me, in that I found Him after whom my soul had
longed." [26]

Later in the day a visiting English Friend, already
powerful in the ministry and skilful in the divining of
"states", Deborah Darby (of the Coalbrookdale family),
spoke to Grellet, clarifying his experience still further to
him, so that the Divine visitation was ineradicably im-
pressed on his being. "O what sweetness did I then feel!"
he concludes, in a passage that points to the theme of all
his future exhortation to others . . . "I was like one intro-
duced into a new world; the creation and all things around
me bore a different aspect,—my heart glowed with love
to all. The awfulness of that day of God's visitation can
never cease to be remembered with peculiar interest and
gratitude, as long as I have the use of my mental faculties.
I have been as one plucked from the burning—rescued from
the brink of a horrible pit. O how can the extent of the
Lord's love, mercy, pity, and tender compassion be
fathomed!" [27]

In another Meeting, struggling in the silence, his experience, his theme, matured in him—and typifies the
Evangelical impulse catching at extremes of language—
"Great was the awfulness and the reverence that came
upon me. It was succeeded by such a view, and sense of

[25] *Memoirs,* (ed., B. Seebohm). London, 1870, p. 10.
[26] *Memoirs,* p. 14.
[27] *Memoirs,* p. 15.

my sinful life that I was like one crushed under the mill-
stones. My misery was great; my cry was not unlike that
of Isiah, ' Woe is me, for I am undone!' The nearer I was
then favoured to approach Him 'who dwelleth in the
light', the more I saw my uncleanness and my wretchedness. But how can I set forth the fulness of heavenly joy
that filled me when the hope was again raised that there
was One, even He whom I had pierced, Jesus Christ the
Redeemer, that was able to save me? I saw Him to be the
Lamb of God that taketh away the sins of the world; who
was delivered for our offences, and raised again for our
justification; who is our propitiatory sacrifice, our advocate
with the Father, our intercessor with God. I felt faith in
his atoning blood quickening my soul, giving me to believe
that it was He who could wash me from my many pollu-
tions, and deliver me from death and destruction, which I
felt to be my just desert, for my many sins and transgres-
sions. On my earnest petition being put up to Him, the
language was proclaimed, ' Thy sins are forgiven; thy
iniquities are pardoned.' Floods of tears of joy and gratitude gave vent to the fulness of my heart!

    " Then I thought I heard again a sweet language saying,
' Proclaim unto others what the Lord has done for thy
soul '. . . ." 28

Thus, Grellet found his vocation, performed the feat
that, like the ascent of a mountain, for the rest of his days
he would demonstrate to others; here was the formula
through which all his energies, compressed, like a torrent
would pour, the nutshell of all his activities. He now
joined Friends, was recorded a Minister (after the " deep
baptisms " of spirit that preceded the first utterances in
Meeting of these minutely God-guided souls), and thereafter began travelling in the ministry. For nine years he
was confined to America, but then began, what he had
long envisaged, the central mission of his life, to Europe,

28 *Memoirs*, p. 17.

in a series of four journeys spread over the next twenty-six years. France, Europe, from which he had been driven by the upheaval of revolution and war, continued the scene of social conflict and distress. The answer, he necessarily felt for that continent, for its lowest wretches and highest potentates (the symbolical figures his mind fixed on), must be the same redeeming impulse as had transformed his own condition. Humbly, but unswervingly along his groove, his expenses paid by himself, his wife left to mind the home, he set forth.

The first journey in 1807 was largely a reconnoitre, a re-establishing of contact with ancestral ties and a feeling-out of the old environment in terms of his new allegiance. His second journey, 1810–14, when he covered twenty-six thousand miles, plunged him straight to the heart of his work. This, apart from ministering to Friends, was to preach the saving grace of Christ to the poor, the depressed working class, prisoners of war, and, in London, to the thieves, pickpockets, and whores who abounded in the vicinity of (to-day's) Westminster Meeting House. To suit their convenience he appointed the Meeting at seven o'clock in the evening, so to speak their social hour, being assisted, so commanding was his zeal, by sedate Friends who for over a century had attempted little of this sort of thing. " O, it was a solemn time ", he records, " the Lord's power was over us . . . I have seldom known such brokeness, and so general, as it was that evening." He preached against sin and outlined fearfully the consequences of dying in sin, and preached Christ the Saviour of sinners. (He did not of course preach the need for better housing and working conditions). After he had done the awestruck silence was broken only by sobs and sighs. " What a display of the Lord's power and mercy!" he comments, himself having relived his personal ecstacy.[29]

<hr />

[29] *Memoirs*, p. 95.

After this he visited Newgate and all the other prisons of London, and the poor houses, and other quarters where meetings for " the vicious and degraded portions of the community " could be held. It was in his character to keep on the move, to pitch his tent just long enough to make his appeal, to give his performance, and then to be off to fresh halls, new encounters, keeping the stimulus frothing at the brim. Besides not delving very seriously into environmental factors he did not stay to work with any one case or group of unfortunates. His was the rôle of star performer, already booked for the next engagement.

Did this really help anyone? Without question, yes, if they felt he cared for them, this stranger descending out of the blue, bringing his other-worldly balm into their present hopelessness; his, they would see (only seeing him once and thus missing the element of exhibitionism), had been a gesture of disinterested love; it would reaffirm their self-respect, from an unexpected quarter. More important, was Grellet's knack, shared by other such star Ministers, of selecting just the right associate to follow up the start he had made. In this case it was Elizabeth Fry whom he (with William Forster) persuaded to carry on, more plod-dingly, at Newgate.

He himself passed on to the Continent, travelling into Italy; but then, suddenly, at the Lord's command, veering north through Switzerland and Germany, where for the most part he had pious meetings with people of similar gospel interests. For the preacher, a relatively quiet season; though, for the diarist, one full sparkle. Grellet was always a great observer. One of his little asides, for instance, a delight throughout his journal, notes . . . " Mentone, a very beautiful little town at the foot of the Alps, whose summits are covered with perpetual snow . . . the heat of the weather would be unbearable, were it not that the air is very pleasantly tempered by the ice and snow above.

The orange trees are abundant in that valley . . . they are continually blossoming and bearing fruit." [30]

Very different from his journey in Tennessee, thirteen years before, when "encamping during the night, which we did several times, we kept up a good fire to protect us from the panthers, bears, and wolves. The latter were numerous. Sometimes it seemed as if a hundred of them were howling at once round about us ";[31] and different too, in its familiarity, from his excursion six years later through Russia when at one point he "set off early in the morning of the Sixth Month for Baktchiserai. The country is beautiful, rich and fertile, and well cultivated; there are very fine vineyards, and lofty trees on the high ground. This town is very ancient: it was the capital of old Tartary, where their Khans used to reside." [32]

But for Stephen Grellet, whatever changes of geography his eye noted, however scholarly or sensitive his note-making, he was basically being confronted by the single unredeemed world, the ground waiting for his plough: that was the unifying factor in his travels. Like early Friends in this respect, his scope was universal.

Returning home and engaging in business, with some need to recoup his funds, he was soon enough in pocket to be off again. Barely a year had gone by before he was in Haiti, invited by the mulatto President to preach in the Catholic cathedral there, and to circulate through the market places and drawing rooms of the island, which he found, through the ebullience of the Haitians, in religion as in everything else, sympathetic. But this was a skirmish. The greater challenge of Europe was ever-present to him. In 1817 he recrossed the Atlantic, picked William Allen, a highly practical Friend, as the Lord's appointed companion for him, and struck east through Scandinavia to Russia. They spent four months in St. Petersburg, in 1819.

As usual, no matter where he was, Grellet made straight

30 *Memoirs*, p. 115.   31 *Memoirs*, p. 38.   32 *Memoirs*, p. 226.

for the prisons; and between them he and Allen conducted a searching enough survey to persuade the authorities to make some improvements. He records . . . " 10th of Second Month, 1819. We have been several times with Count Miloradevitch, the Military Governor of several provinces. He has kindly made way for our admission to several prisons. He inquired what we had observed amiss, that might be remedied. We told him that much might be done, but that there were certain things that should be attended to immediately. We remarked upon the great impropriety of confining men and women indiscriminately in the same apartments, and the demoralising effect it must have; the soldiers on guard, being placed inside the wards, adding to, rather than diminishing the evil. We represented the great filthiness of the prisons, which are full of the most disgusting vermin, and do not appear to have been cleaned for years. We suggested that as they have several large prisons, totally distinct, they might easily confine the women in some, and the men in others; taking care to make an entire separation between the older offenders and the young prisoners, and those confined for small offences; and to keep out of doors the soldiers on guard. To this the Governor replied, 'All this *can* be done.' On our being with him to-day, he said: *'All these things have been done.'* The prisoners have been furnished with brooms, brushes, water, lime, etc. etc.; they have themselves thoroughly cleansed their prisons, and care has been taken that daily attention shall be paid to cleanliness henceforth. The Governor seems disposed to have many other improvements made. Thus with gratitude to the Lord, we see a little fruit resulting from our painful labours among these sufferers. We have also succeeded in having many released, who had been in prison for months because their passports were irregular, or they had come to the city without them." [33]

[33] *Memoirs,* p. 197.

Indeed, it was really extraordinary for a foreigner to have made even the least dint in the monolithic Russian system of repression and indifference, though this was a period there of quasi-liberalism, of esoteric plans and ideals and quarter-grasped opportunities, of Princesses who were Anglo-maniacs and Princes who studied humanist philosophy, at the summit of which ruled Alexander, that most enigmatic schizophrenic of Tsars. Stephen Grellet and William Allen had already met the Tsar in London, in 1814, in days when he was full of the Holy Alliance and his mission as the Christian leader of Europe, and when he seemed to have felt among Friends something akin to the mystical flame lit within himself after the burning of Moscow—in any case, those had been fervent days; and now again clearly his patronage opened all doors for the visitors in Russia, and gave their requests weight.

He himself saw them twice privately. He had just been away, himself a restless traveller, but their attention to the prisons had been reported, and he expressed approval and his determination to see such work continued. At the second meeting there was discussion of the Bible and of prayer, and he told them of his own spiritual difficulties, perhaps finding in them, simple Quakers, in a world that for him was wracked with insecurity (and the burden of a parricide's conscience), two men, two gurus, with whom he could feel towards a moment's prayful peace.

He suggested they should wait on the Lord in silent meditation together, in the hope that " He condescend to give us a manifestation of his Divine Life and presence." This they did, and Grellet notes . . . " The Lord was present during a solemn silence that came over us . . . and after a while, in the love of Christ, I felt constrained to impart a few words to the dear Emperor for his encouragement; that he may hold fast in the ways of the Lord unto the end, fully relying on the efficacy of his Divine grace to preserve him from all evil, and to strengthen him for every good

work. He was bathed in tears; then dear Allen, on bended
knees, supplicated the Lord on his behalf, and that of his
people. The Emperor, who had kneeled by him, continued
some time thus prostrated after William had ceased utterance. Our separation was solemn."[34]

Alas, the Tsar, for all his good intentions, the various
poses in which he liked to see himself, was at that point
turning increasingly despotic. The next year, 1820, was
decisive, in his Polish domains and in Russia itself. He
might toy with Quaker prison reforms, but over against
these there were the brutal " military colonies " throughout
the provinces; he might agree with Grellet that schools
required better Scriptural texts, but his whole educational
policy was shifting to reaction; and even if his conscience
was touched by their visit, and their undoubted faith in the
good in him, this was quickly caught in the toils of vanity
and dissimulation. One is even bound to ask if their whole
impact, high-keyed, effervescent, serving to strengthen his
Imperial conviction of being the recipient of God's commands, did not settle him further in his purblind path.
Such private ecstasies are bad for kings.

But Grellet throughout his travels, apart from ministering
to the sick and imprisoned, seemed drawn for the greater
part of his time to pious talk and prayer with such highly-
placed persons—the Princes, Ministers, Cardinals, Kings,
that fill his pages like an ambassador's memoirs. He no
doubt, a scion of nobility, felt at home with them, they
were gracious, civilised, well-informed, linguistically able,
persons, as he says, of " superior minds ", and of course
in responsible positions, the key men for social welfare;
responding to his exalted tones, murmuring their own
piety, they afforded him the most gratifying proof of his
Saviour's power over the world; and, it was in their style
of living to dispense a ready, and " problem-solving "

[34] *Memoirs*, p. 204.

charity. The Evangelist's liking for quick returns was agreeably served in these circles.

In Russia he kept very largely to them, so far as private contacts went, as also in Italy, Austria, Spain. In that latter country, after meeting the royal family (this was his fourth European journey, 1831–33), he was shown by a fellow traveller in the Valencia-bound coach a copy of the *Madrid Gazette,* with the King's Order to all provincial Governors and authorities to afford civility and free entrance to the two travelling Quakers. (William Allen was again with him.) This was evangelism in the grand style. In Rome he was treated like an eminent sightseer, like a present day American Senator, and finally conducted before the Pope, with whom he had most loving discourse. In Constantinople he dined with the Ambassador; one wonders if they thought of Mary Fisher. In fact, Stephen Grellet, for all the tens of thousands of miles he covered, kept to a relatively narrow groove, a select audience, a carefully chosen pitch: the one that most readily released in him his dominant emotion. All other factors, social, religious, in whatever, sphere, were kept static, were not required to play any part. His was the individualist's bliss, not the labour of the concerned group.

Within the Society of Friends, this was to prove serious. Grellet was then the foremost Quaker Evangelical in America, the one who most swayed Friends in this direction, the first to oppose Elias Hicks and the country radicals as anti-Christian. He was also of considerable influence in England, in the formative years of the next generation. His pattern of behaviour brought needed release, but ultimately was to prove reactionary. The highly personal emotional boost, however much a tonic in 1800, however picturesque and newly adventurous, was not a broad enough basis for Quakerism, for the responsible corporate exercise in worship, nor for a responsible social analysis. As is seen by Grellet's own record, this sort of religion was

socially framed by the *status quo*. Over the next half
century, especially in the States, its effects impeded the
Society as a whole from rediscovering its true centre.

The other great traveller in those days from within the
leaven of Evangelical ministry permeating Friends was
Daniel Wheeler. If Grellet was something of a Byron,
Wheeler was more of a Robinson Crusoe, a practical man
strongly pulled to discourse with God in solitary places,
and concerned for such, especially sailors, whose life took
them beyond the haven of organised society. Like most
missionaries he had a terrific sense of man's frailty before
the Universe; his journal shows none of Grellet's gift for
neat civilised observation, it is with primal forces like the
sea he is concerned and where his writing gathers power
. . . "As the day advanced, the wind and sea increased,
and the fog was so dense close down to the horizon, that
there seemed but little prospect of discovering the land, at
a sufficient distance to prevent our running directly upon
it. As the afternoon wore away, the danger hourly increased: but at this juncture, the Everlasting Arm of
strength, in wonted mercy and compassion, was signally
displayed for our preservation, and in such a manner as
wholly to exclude the slightest pretence of mortal man's
having the least share in it. The mist cleared suddenly
away; and though but for a short interval, yet it was sufficient to discover a lofty rocky island, about half a mile
distant, standing nearly perpendicularly out of the sea, far
above the mast-head of the *Henry Freeling*. We soon
perceived that this was the island called Inaccessible. . . ." [35]

And again, as the South Atlantic storm rose about them
. . . " Towards evening the wind and sea increased in such
a dreadful manner, that the horrors of the scene cannot be
faithfully described. It blew a perfect hurricane; and
although we had only sufficient storm canvass set to keep
the vessel's head to the sea, yet she seemed in danger of

[35] *Memoirs* (abridged), London, 1852, p. 137.

being torn to pieces with the intense pressure, against which she had to struggle for some hours together. The captain was much alarmed and said, ' If she gets through this, she will get through anything.' The agitated waters broke in upon us on every side, like cascades, frequently loading the deck with their weight: the whole frame of the vessel trembled and shook with the strain in an unusual manner. This hurricane at length became a steady gale of wind, but very heavy." [36]

Finally, Wheeler reached his goal, the faraway Pacific islands . . . "The stupendous mountains, however steep and rugged, were clothed in the richest and fullest manner, with every kind of fruit and forest-tree which flourish in these tropical climates, where perpetual summer reigns; their luxuriance only now and then interrupted by falls of water hurrying down the steep declivities in beautiful cascades to the vales beneath: but the noise of these numerous cateracts is at once overpowered and lost in the roar of the mighty Pacific, whose waves incessantly thunder in endless succession upon the shores and reefs of Tahiti." [37]

But how had a Quaker got to Tahiti? This was the furthest point yet. The sequence of events is that Daniel Wheeler, at the age of forty-five, a careful business man of Sheffield (though he had been a sailor in his youth), after some years of perplexing anguish had begun to take part in Quaker ministry. This hurdle crossed he had straightway felt a Call to the Lord's service overseas: though in the first place tied to a practical project of land reclamation in Russia. For fourteen years he had lived near St. Petersburg, responsible, as an employee of the Tsar, for developing fifteen farms on three thousand acres of reclaimed land, and for draining a further three thousand acres ready for use. He had been visited there by Stephen Grellet and had known the wayward Tsar well.

But suddenly in 1832 he had felt the Call to go even further

[36] *Memoirs*, p. 145–6.   [87] *Memoirs*, p. 175.

afield, and this time without attendant purpose, only, as he told Friends in London, to visit the inhabitants of the South Sea Islands, and of New South Wales, in gospel love, and to turn them " from darkness to light, and from the power of Satan unto God ",[38] and to affirm solidarity with other church missions.

This was approved by London Friends. The money was provided, a post-office packet, the *Henry Freeling,* of 101 tons, was fitted out with supplies and crew, and the intrepid Minister, this time wholly surrendered to the Call, eventually arrived in Tahiti, just six years after Captain Cook, and eighteen years after William Ellis of the London Missionary Society. The gospel was already being vigorously preached, and the Tahitians togged up like respectable British, and it was necessary for Wheeler from the start to dispel any fear that, as a Quaker, his views might prove discordant.

Doctrinally, however, there was little fear of that, through the all-embracing flood of Evangelical submission; and he was a man of great personal humility and openness towards others, and moreover, he disarmed suspicion by avowing to the missionaries that " I was waiting as at the posts of wisdom's gate, not knowing to what I might next have to turn my hand." [39] He mostly wished to declare his loving heart, and for this they gladly co-operated, and left him free to speak in their assemblies. He was actually a valuable recruit to their work, to the dissemination of Bibles and Testaments and suitable tracts (including Wilberforce's " Practical View ", that most reactionary treatise on the social order, with its emphasis on " pie in the sky "), and he united with them in condemning the traders and liquor-smuggling sailors for their debauching of the islanders. It was soon especially towards the sailors that his concern developed, and firstly for them that he advertised a Friends Meeting on his own ship. It was well attended, and also

38 *Memoirs,* p. 111.   89 *Memoirs,* p. 160.

by the missionaries, and thereafter periods of silence were arranged in the mission services so that he could speak, if he wished, out of his accustomed background. It was certainly a time of loving hearts, and the Tahitians (the most genial and inclusive of people) equally expressed their fondness of him. Among all the knights errant who were to visit their island—Robert Louis Stevenson, Rupert Brooke, Gaugin, Josuah Slocum—Daniel Wheeler was very likely, in his simple disinterestedness, in his very vagueness, the closest to their own taste.

For the next eighteen months he cruised the Pacific, north to Honolulu, south to Raratonga, finishing by way of New Zealand. An extract from his *Memoirs* shows him arriving at Vavau, in the Friendly Islands, for a mission service . . . "About ten o'clock A.M. we landed . . . we were soon met by the principal chief, Daniel Afu, and several of his people, who welcomed us to their neighbourhood; and after spending a short time at the chief's house, the meeting was assembled by the sound of heavy strokes upon a hollow piece of wood, a sort of native drum, which may be heard at a great distance. The people were soon collected, and after John Thomas had opened the meeting in the usual way, and read one of my certificates, all became silent. I had largely to declare amongst them the unsearchable riches of Christ ', the beloved Son of God, and Saviour of men; whom all men are commanded to hear : whose Holy Spirit speaketh in every heart, to bring us to repentance and amendment of life in the fear of God. To this heavenly Teacher I was concerned to turn them, and to exhort them in the love of the gospel to ' believe in the power of His Holy Spirit in their hearts, and wait for it there ': we were favoured with a solemnity, which nothing short of this irresistible power can produce. Many of the people came to us in a loving manner, when the meeting broke up, and hung about while we remained in the neighbourhood.

"After meeting we partook of some refreshment at the chief's house, in true native style upon the floor on mats, with the milk of the cocoa-nut as a beverage, and the pulpy shoots of the banana bruised between the fingers, to answer the purpose of washing the hands; some native cloth from the dress of the chiefess served for a towel: this was found a very needful and agreeable part of the entertainment, having had literally to tear the food to pieces with our fingers. When our repast was finished, we took leave of the chief and his family and others present, and returned to the sea-side, and were safely paddled back again to the sandy bay near Neiafu. . . ." [40]

So went the gospel work, the fulfilling of the imperious inner command to visit the most far-off places, the most isolated or abandoned (or seemingly secure) of human beings, to instil in them the need and the hope of Christian salvation after the pattern that had already transfigured the Minister's own heart: work that, through these men and their successors, carried the name of Quaker to every corner of the earth, though not with much teaching of the distinctive Quaker exercise; that galvanised the Society with its enthusiasms, though only to lend authority subsequently to the more conservative forces, social and theological, among Friends, and so help precipitate divisions. It was a brave individual witness to passionately-held beliefs, but essentially it had not sprung out of the Quaker scheme of worship. The attempt to fit that worship to it necessarily caused decades of disturbance.

One can say of it, it was essentially romantic, in an age of essentially romantic individualism.

(d) Philanthropy

In the wake of the Evangelical revival, intertwined with qualms and fears brought to the surface by the French Revolution, there was a steady growth of philanthropy on

[40] *Memoirs*, p. 269.

the part of the well-to-do for the poor, for slaves, for all
manner of sufferers who happened to catch the imagination.
So immense were the problems revealed as this work
gathered pace, so many the openings for personal effort,
that it developed into the standard outlet for the nineteenth
century middle-class conscience, harnessed of course to the
progress of society as then constituted, as well as to the
satisfaction accruing from the rescue of souls.

This philanthropy sprang to life as the stirring of compassion, of Christian mission in a few pioneers, not to mention their revolt against the materialism that rode them too,
and it settled into drawn-out efforts, first to abolish the
worst abuses, such as slavery and the slave trade, and then,
improving conditions here and there, as in the teaching
of children or the use of prisons, to aid the grossly under-
privileged to fit themselves better to society. It nearly
always faced Tory opposition and a good deal of general
indifference, and it couldn't by its nature perfectly distinguish between primary and secondary social targets; so
its advances came by fits and starts, relapsing at times into
temporary palliatives of the soup kitchen variety. But it
did gather up the threads of social conscience largely latent
since Cromwell's day, and by its example sufficiently captured the outlook of the British people to make a reformist
approach to their problems, even into this century when the
economy that bred it is falling apart, so far prevail.

In all this some Quakers were very much to the fore.
Caught by the new tenor of feeling, that swamped the
differences between churches and banded Evangelicals
together, they joined in the work going forward and
brought it much of its practical success. They had the
wealth, they had the connections, but most of all they had
the experience within the walls of their own Society of
tackling wrongs and disabilities. They had just ended their
own involvement in slavery and the slave trade; and, a
level up from this, they had for more than a century investi-

gated, case by case, their own poor, caring for the sick, the aged, the imprisoned, training the children, apprenticing the unskilled, gradually improving the social condition of the whole membership. In this they had been helped by a trade expansion that could use all willing hands (for which one must credit their entrepreneurs), and after 1737 by the rules of membership that enabled them to disown anyone not willing enough to be so used—thereby constantly sifting the ranks and maintaining a first rate labour corps; but the fact remains that besides their contemporaries and for England as a whole they had been shining examples of enlightened community-mindedness.

For the country had been neglecting its poor except to victimise them further, parish by parish, workhouse by workhouse, reducing them by the time of the Napoleonic Wars to a mass of helots not dissimilar from black South Africans to-day. They were a race apart, semi-starved, driven from the land, corralled for the factories, their children indentured to manufacturers or employed in the darkness of mines, generally without other instruction; the charity schools and hospitals were glaringly inadequate, the prisons squalid; while the rest of the nation groaned, it was said because of this self-defeating policy, under the burden of taxes for paupers.

By contrast the Society of Friends, while paying its share to public funds, had not been calling on them itself, nor had it left its members in want, nor, though dynamically capitalist in outlook, had it allowed its working poor or children to be treated merely as hands; rather, despite the blinkers on its outlook during the eighteenth century it had throughout its meetings retained some sense of what was due to all, in line with early Quaker thought, which quickened again towards 1800.

For instance, Quaker employers had attended to the education of their apprentices; they had pioneered, in tentative fashion, with welfare schemes for their factories.

Following the initiative of John Bellers there had been experiments with workhouses where progressively for the children working hours were decreased and hours of study lengthened (till in 1811 Clerkenwell workhouse became a full-time charity school); while for the old and the sick there had been free provision of medicines and comforts, and the constant visiting of women Friends. Each Monthly Meeting was responsible for its indigent, its orphans and widows, and for schooling, though it could seek assistance from a central London fund, in turn replenished from legacies and from levies on the richer meetings. One must not exaggerate the depths of concern, for there was always an eye to the commercial return in this provision for needy Friends, and despite all a good deal of indifference—as in the reception by the Society of John Bellers's more progressive schemes, in 1696, for the investing of capital in community enterprise (similar to the present kibbutzim in Israel) rather than in private trading ventures, or in the sphere of education where until the founding of Ackworth School in 1777, under the lead of Dr Fothergill, very much less was done for poor children than for those whose parents could pay fat fees.

Possibly, the best single work of that century was the opening of the York Retreat in 1796, again through the lead of an individual Friend, William Tuke, overcoming the caution of his fellow Quakers. There for the first time the insane, instead of being chained like criminals or exhibited for entertainment money, were carefully diagnosed and lovingly treated to effect where possible a cure. This, moreover, was a good example of the way in which experience gained within the Society could later be used for the country as a whole; for in 1815 a Parliamentary commission, set up on the new tide of social feeling to study the subject and bring improvement, looked to the York Retreat as its model; though it took a further thirty years for the Quaker methods to become nationally accepted.

Thus, in a number of directions there was a Quaker tradition of welfare activity on which those Friends could draw who, at the beginning of the nineteenth century, felt called to a broad humanitarianism. And, as they ventured forth, and found it necessary to appeal to Parliament or whoever had power to further their projects, in fact to think in terms of the nation's responsibilities and of rights that should apply to all citizens, and not just those of the " peculiar " and " separate " Society of Friends, they could draw courage too from the thought that this was how their founders had acted. Fox, Burrough, Nayler, Penn, and then other Friends such as Thomas Lettsom and John Bellers, had surveyed the national scene as a whole, relating whatever problem they were dealing with, such as poverty or terms of employment, to the principles they believed should regulate the entire social organism. Theirs had been a unitive vision, and they had declaimed this without whittling it down in their various addresses to Parliament. Evangelical Friends never quite attained such a degree of consistency, due to their consciousness of belonging to the prosperous sanctified élite that across a wide gulf was dispensing charity, but they moved half-way back towards it, as they were pulled further into the public arena; and this in turn enabled more advanced social attitudes on the part of their children and grandchildren towards the opening of the twentieth century. The right direction was setting in.

The most considerable piece of philanthropy to which these awakening Friends applied themselves was undoubtedly the abolition of slavery throughout the British dominion. Here pressure was being felt from American Friends, who by 1780 had largely cleared themselves of their long drawn out involvment in the business, due, as we have seen, to the patient efforts of John Woolman: whose writings had moreover stirred John Wesley, so that by that year the Methodist Conference had also condemned slavery. Anti-slavery sentiment was gathering from many quarters, from Rationalists and Evangelicals, from political economists and European emigrants, and although the British Parliamentary lead was in fact taken by Wilberforce, Clarkson, and T. Fowell Buxton, none of them then actually Quaker, they each, through his marriage or philanthropic interests, was closely linked to Friends. Quakers largely manned the committee of the first Abolitionist Society formed in 1787; already in 1783 London Yearly Meeting had sent the first petition on the subject to Parliament—thereby surprising the politicians, who had imagined that this ultra-respectable body was by now completely quiescent. From then, till 1838, certain Friends such as William Allen, the Forsters, the Gurneys, Luke Howard, James Cropper, Joseph Sturge, devoted themselves to Abolition, giving their time, their money, their increasing involvement in public lectures and pamphleteering for the Cause; and behind them gradually was marshalled their Society. This work on behalf of slaves, and then on behalf of freedmen, awoke Friends to their public obligations more than any other activity.

But other activities were all the time being added, started often by the same individuals, who worked in concert (as closely as their fathers for the sake of trade), giving yet a new twist to the sense of "calling" in the Society of Friends. Evangelically aroused, they had tremendous energy, and tremendous disquiet if they were not applying it. "Indulged the flesh too much this morning by lying in bed till eight o'clock. Oh, my lightness and chaffiness! Lord, strengthen me to oppose it, for, of myself, I can do nothing",[41] wrote William Allen, scientist, lecturer, and business man; for a spell, financial adviser to Queen Victoria's father, travel companion to Stephen Grellet, and also, as if that were not enough, an active Abolitionist, editor of *The Philanthropist,* fellow worker with Peter Bedford (a Friend, founder of the Bedford Institute) for the

[41] *Life,* Vol. I, p. 4.

juvenile delinquents of Spitalfields (earning Friends the name of " Friends of Thieves "), and also there, with other rich Friends, for the provision of cheap food supplies in the years of near famine.

He partnered Robert Owen in the New Lanark cotton mills, to try out better labour conditions. (This, however, was a very canny enterprise, making, in four years, a profit of £160,000, paying five per cent on capital, raising the investment value by fifty per cent: showing that model employers, as Quakers increasingly strived to be, though they were willing to reduce working hours from seventeen to ten per day, and to educate the workers' children rather than to sweat them — admittedly not inconsiderable advances, as their success encouraged others to follow— were in fact operating from an olympian vantage point, pocketing the increased profits, and the worker's touching gratitude, as their just and holy reward. Which in turn made them a little self-righteous, a little exclusive, inclined to deprecate the wider labour struggle for Trade Union and political rights, and to oppose State interference with their rôle: an illuminating example of benevolent impulse, consequent pleasure, and self-interest bound together.) Owen and Allen later fell out over the education of the workers' children. Owen favoured dancing, music, and drill; Allen, who had watched thousands of pauper children suddenly learning to read and write through Joseph Lancaster's system of schooling, which he himself had propped up financially and where the Bible was the only text book, naturally again sought pride of place for the Bible. In any case, for an Evangelical, the place of Scripture in life was paramount.

Apart from his work for the London Peace Society, which requires later mention, and his prison committee work and that for the abolition of capital punishment, William Allen finally gave himself, from 1832 till his death in 1843, to his farm school at Lindfield in Sussex. His idea was, through donations of allotments and then the teaching of husbandry, to train labourers to support themselves, rather than to subsist on poor relief or drift to the industrial slums or emigrate. He saw the scheme developing through a number of agricultural colonies, with a place for crafts-men and technical administrators. The idea was very much his best, owing perhaps something to John Bellers, and it gained momentary notoriety, but not the sustained support it deserved. Like so many of these philanthropic ventures it waxed with the vitality of its founder, and waned when he disappeared.

But the impulse, the example of such men as Allen, was there to encourage younger Friends; and from then on-wards, until to-day, there has been a steady pressure within the Society seeking humanitarian outlets, though gradually of course both the nature of this and the framework through which it sought expression has changed. To-day's Quaker work teams function, so to speak, at ground level; but the recognition, the backing, the sudden mustering of energy both within the Society and in government quarters that attends them and wings them towards their objectives, owes a great deal to the solid reputation of the nineteenth century Quaker philanthropists. The zeal plus the eminent respectability of those not-so-distant benefactors has made its impress on the national mind.

A name that all cherish from among them is that of Elizabeth Fry. A tender, modest, practical woman, already mother of nine children, she started, in 1817 through her Association for the Improvement of Women Prisoners at Newgate, to bring to those unfortunates the constant personal sympathy and attention, and the ability to win their co-operation for sewing and knitting groups and for hygiene and reading instruction for their children, that made detention bearable for the milder cases, and reform possible for the more vicious ones. Now at last the ecstatic ministrations of Grellet, Savery, Deborah Darby were turned into systematic service, that had led by 1836 to prison visiting throughout Britain, and the provision of female warders for women, and to the beginnings of something similar on the Continent, all this being linked to a broad scheme for penal change. Prisons then were as bad as during the Restoration years, equally over-crowded and filthy, the supervision still being arbitrary, classification non-existent, they being used as detention pens till fines were paid or a trial held. Punishment as such was more by hanging or transportation. It was with the idea that a term of imprisonment should be the only sentence imposed, and that during that term the prisoner should be helped, in fit surroundings, each by category, to remodel himself or herself for society, that Elizabeth Fry carried through her sensibly limited but determined demonstration of what could be achieved. She had been drawn in through compassion; but then her head continued with the organisation of all that might lead to penal reform. Many of her conclusions became law, though some not till a century later.

Surrounding her were her family—Gurneys, Hoares, Frys—the great Quaker bankers of the day; and beside them the old familiar figures of William Allen, Peter Bedford, the Forsters, her relatives the Buxtons, and a host of enlightened and Evangelical enthusiasts, who, founding a Society for every good Cause, now founded one for the Improvement of Prison Discipline and for the Reformation of Juvenile Offenders: so that investigations were started systematically, appeals launched, reports prepared, very much in the modern manner. It was the forerunner of the Howard League. This was work that went beyond the mitigation of evil conditions, and increasingly led Friends to look for their root causes. But not just yet, not searchingly, not so long as their outlook was imbued with the Evangelical formula. That deflected attention from sociological enquiry.

It was also work based on what had gone before, principally the recommendations of John Howard in 1777, which by now were even more overdue as the authorities had much praised him and then done little else, and somewhat on the writings of John Bellers in 1699, who even in those days had called for an end to capital punishment and for the use of prisons primarily for the reform of criminals. He had urged study of the formative factors, to give understanding of the prisoner; then provision of work so that the man could earn and learn a craft; and then, if he was still unassimilable by society (and even marriage, to be arranged for him, did not do the trick!) he was to be deported to make a fresh start in an unfamiliar environment.[42] Bellers had taken into account the wider social factors, the responsibility of all citizens for their poor and for their criminals, and his suggestions were rational and devoid of humbug, and also devoid of pious maxims. Later philanthropic Friends, feeling back towards the Society's earliest witness, in this as in their other concerns, though they achieved much nonetheless never reached quite the same clarity of view. They made concession to their time, to their own social standing, to the tracts that they relied on to do part of the job for them. They became tangled up in the fashionable highly emotive language being used by fellow workers in the field. Each generation tends to do this, to become ensnared by its own idiom.

Turning to America, to trace there the development of a similar philanthropic outlook among Quakers towards society at large, we find, for instance, that in Pennsylvania Penn had inaugurated a relatively humane penal system, but after his death it was much rescinded, undefended during the openly acquisitive period, so that by 1776, the Philadelphia Society for Assisting Distressed Prisoners, founded in that year, discovered it was not unusual for prisoners to die of starvation, that gaol fees were both

[42] *Essays about the Poor, Manufacturers, Trade, Plantations, and Immorality,* London, 1699, p. 17.

general and arbitrary and that prisoners were often detained beyond their term for non-payment of these.

Benjamin Franklin, astonished at the reputation of Quakers in France, in particular at Voltaire's description in his *Traité sur la Tolerance* (1763) . . . " the very name of Philadelphia, which reminds them constantly that all men are brothers, is the example and shame of peoples who do not yet know tolerance " . . . could only comment . . . " While we sit for our picture to that able painter, 'tis no small advantage to us that he views us at a favourable distance." [43] This, indeed, is much the case with those who down avenues of history see eighteenth century Pennsylvania as a Holy Experiment. It was more of a liberal bourgeois one, with its radicals safe in the countryside and its constitution safe in the archives, and the day-to-day pace being set by the city merchants. Anyone not in line with them, as in England, tended to forfeit regard. Hence the deterioration in the gaols, as in so many other respects.

But by the last quarter of the century, after Woolman and the great decision to liberate their own slaves (not in itself an act of philanthropy but rather one of painful re-adjustment by individual members to the guiding Quaker light), and also following the political uncertainties of the Independence War, the social thinking of Philadelphia Friends (and Philadelphia has always been for American Friends the key centre) became generally more sensitive. So that of a sudden it became possible for the Wistar family (also suddenly concerned for the Indians), for Isaac Parrish, Dr Jones, Caleb Lownes (who devised the Penitentiary system) to join freely with Anglicans and others to humanise the penal code, to put up better prisons, to open a House of Refuge for juvenile offenders. They studied Howard's reports, lately published, and acted on these more swiftly than in England; so that again, as with Abolition, once aroused and now additionally sustained by an Evan-

<hr>

[43] E. Phillips, *The Good Quaker in French Legend*, Phila., 1932, p. 63.

gelican sense of mission is was to be the Americans who gave a lead (William Savery and Stephen Grellet carrying the precious pollen of urgency) to their fellows across the Atlantic. The American Quaker conscience for a time was quicker off the mark.

Then, in turn, ideas flowed back from England. Elizabeth Fry's prison visiting resulted, in 1823, in a Philadelphian Ladies' Committee for the same work, that led, thirty years later there, to the Howard Institution for discharged female prisoners. Philadelphia's example, as usual, was followed by Friends throughout the States: as witness the labours of Sarah Smith, later in the century as matron of the Indiana State penitentiary.

But this, though a fruitful beginning, was not philanthropy on a big scale. The main potential field for American Friends was being approached with renewed difficulty: that is to say, the continuing institution of slavery throughout the South and South-West, closely linked with the interests of Northern shippers and cotton manufacturers, was not rousing the full chorus of emotion to be expected from pious bystanders, themselves in the clear and philanthropically-inclined. Half the Society, the Hicksites, were active, following the lead of Elias Hicks; they were responding to the call of Benjamin Lundy, Lloyd Garrison and others who were running Abolitionist papers, that aimed to engage all Quakers in the agitation against slavery; of the twenty-one Friends who were delegates to the National Anti-Slavery convention of 1833 in Philadelphia, all but one were Hicksites; and they were prominent in the work of the Underground Railways, helping slaves north to Canada. But, against them, the sedate overentrenched Establishment of Orthodox Friends, especially on the eastern seaboard, were anxious to tone down such activity.

For instance, in 1837 at Newport in Rhode Isand, still the main base for the slave ships that, flying the stars-and-stripes, were immune from British search at sea, the Yearly Meeting denied the use of its meeting houses to Abolitionist lecturers. It was this degree of local appeasement that outraged Whittier, and about which Joseph Sturge, there in 1841, commented . . . "It is about as bad as the worst description we have had of it can make it as far as the leading influences of the society are concerned . . . They referred a proposition from one of their own Quarterly meetings, as well as the London Anti-Slavery epistle, with scarsely any discussion, to a committee who are nominated, I believe, almost without exception from those who were against any Anti-Slavery action. Indeed, in this meeting it is admitted that an active abolitionist is, by an understanding of the ruling influences, generally omitted on meeting appointments." [44]

He found it much the same in New York, Baltimore, and Philadelphia, with Grellet and others pleading the snags of working along with non-Quakers in the cause of Abolition—rather specious in view of the penal work already thus undertaken: but then work for prisons was less controversial. West, in Indiana, this growing disagreement as to what Friends should do, between those who favoured doing nothing . . . "lest if we overact the part called for at our hands, we injure the righteous cause, and suffer loss ourselves " [45] . . .and the Hicksites grouped round Levi Coffin and his most famous Underground station (that by itself saved 3,000 slaves), led to a physical separation of meetings. Hardly the assured impeccable pose required from a philanthropic body.

But leaving aside, till the next chapter, further mention of schism among Friends, and the reasons for the lukewarm attitude of the Orthodox group towards active Abolitionism, one can note that, partly due to Whittier and Sturge tackling individuals as Woolman had done, there

[44] *Memoirs,* 1864, p. 237.
[45] Minutes of Indiana Yearly Meeting, 1841.

came about by the time of the Civil War a sufficiently common viewpoint on this issue to make possible, from 1862 onwards, the first really big essay in American Quaker philanthropy. This was lavished on the emancipated negroes; who, by the end of the war, numbered at least three million souls.

Now Friends, whether Hicksite or Orthodox, operating in complementary areas, swept into action raising funds and distributing bundles of clothing; backed by Government grants and gifts of land they built cabins for the coloured refugees, supplied seeds, tools, the use of horses, and co-operative stores where day-to-day needs could be purchased at cost price. The freedmen were not only destitute, they were uneducated, unused to running their own lives. The longterm requirement was therefore education, and Friends, in the decade 1865–75, turned increasingly to the setting up of schools, primary and also technical, to counter this deficiency. One of these was at Little Rock, Arkansas. Gradually, most of this work was handed over to the regular State agencies.

Another field entered into from 1869, for a decade by Orthodox Friends, and for rather longer by the Hicksites, was the care of American Indians under the general authority of the State, the government feeling that the bearing of Quakers, and their relatively clean record here, was that most likely to pacify the Indians. Schools were opened, the Bible taught, and some farm training given. The rights of Indians were in detail protected, though their overall position as a subject people was by now circumscribed.

A less demarcated field that caught the enthusiasm (and so was to hold it rather longer) of Orthodox Friends, though not at all of the Hicksites, was that of Foreign Mission work. Following the lead of Eli and Sybil Jones, fervent footloose evangelists, first to Africa and then in 1867 to the Near East, young Orthodox Quakers, fresh from the excitement of their crash programme for negroes, shot forth, Bibles in hand but with little other training, to evangelise the rest of the world. New Englanders went to Syria, New Yorkers to Mexico; those from Ohio to China and India, from Iowa to Jamaica, from Philadelphia to Japan; and there were several joint missions. Much of the organisation was vague, the work capricious, and knowledge of the cultures they were penetrating nil. But they brought funds, made a start with schools, and generally expressed the mood of the times which demanded this sort of outlet. Returning home they were fêted like heroes, their stories heard by hushed gatherings.

For this great philanthropic wave, as with the earlier one in England, was, at least among Orthodox Quakers, carried forward by Evangelical zeal that, as the century progressed, became ever more intense. Constricted, put on the defensive by the Hicksite separation, and then by subsequent separations, bottled up by conservative fear of any radical social analysis or consequent activity, it burst forth heightened by the horror and hysteria of a civil war to spend itself first on one and then another group of unfortunates, whose souls it could also feel called to save. Increasingly it lost its Quakers moorings, to float off among the heady fevers of revivalist meetings, cheered and adroitly steered by pastors, who were only too ready to shoulder the tasks that should have been the slow work of the group. Being well-off it could afford to do this; it was bolstered up by the expansionist phase of a continent-wide industrialism, and also by the perennial American need to escape across prairies away from the reality of the rest of the world. As education improved and then contact with other points of view within the Society, a realignment had to be attempted: which even till to-day has not proved easy, although it is in train. The Quaker thread, once lost, requires, unless by a sudden understanding, the most painful and slow sifting of assumptions until it can be found again, and this necessarily is a group exercise, based on the silence of meetings.

Meanwhile, by the end of the nineteenth century, most of the other American churches, especially Episcopalians and Congregationalists in the industrial area of New England, had begun to challenge the doctrines underlying the free enterprise social order. Being more theological than Friends, with a tradition of controlling the world from the pulpit, they were perhaps better placed to do this; but even Baptists and Unitarians were speaking up for the more obvious needs of depressed unorganised workers. Quakers once again seemed restrained by caution. It took a Hicksite, Jane Addams, by her Bellers-like approach at Hull House, Chicago, which developed locally into pioneer work for labour legislation and trade unionism in sweat-shops employing women, and also into municipal services, to remind the Society (in America) that at its very beginning it had joined its worshipping life to a concern for social justice.

This was more profound than philanthropy, though, as a liberating step towards renewal of this first standpoint, philanthropy finds its proper place in Quaker history.

(e) Schism

The separations within American Quakerism during the nineteenth century are usually represented as a tragedy. This is to take a simplified view. At the time no doubt they weakened the part the Society could play in the world, confused other people's view of it and invited ridicule; and certainly if the opposing factions could have clung to the framework of Quaker practice, within which ultimately to reconcile through the transcending experience of Meeting for Worship their antagonistic attitudes, and the relative inadequacy of all their words, then the most signal triumph for the method itself would have been manifested. But this is to overlook the degree to which Quaker practice—egalitarian, open, creative, building up the "sense of the meeting"—had already been undermined by the wealthy

Establishment of the Society, that, whatever transpired in public meetings, took its own decisions in private, in the closed sessions of Elders and Ministers who were its nominees. The liberal rank and file felt that the Quaker framework, a thing of the spirit, had already been abandoned, and that they must first set this up again. The fault most certainly was equally theirs for letting affairs reach this point, for the gradual erosion of materialistic decades, but once the situation was recognised (for them suddenly a desperate one, so ecclesiastical was the new framework becoming, with their mildest of queries labelled a heresy) they had to take a stand against it: which meant, as the other party would not listen, would no longer even accept their vocabulary, their traditional Quaker terms of reference (as similarly between to-day's delegate at international conferences who can't agree on each other's agenda), they felt it wiser to draw apart for a time.

In the long run, weren't they well advised? It gave liberty to both parties to try out their convictions to the full, to discover what these led to, and still call themselves Quaker; and then finally, as passions waned, and rigid viewpoints began to look absurd (as in a broken marriage when the other partner is no longer there to listen), and wider social forces began to modify their tangle of assumptions, it was suddenly not so difficult for their descendents to draw together again (the shared name of Quaker, and much else, providing a strong attraction), and now with less misunderstanding, and with chastening humility. This has been the trend in the last forty years. Say that it has taken a century to come about, and that it may well take half as long again: the lessons meanwhile it has taught the Society should give American Quakerism, in the infinitely more difficult period ahead, a toughness and a tension it would otherwise have lacked. Moreover, by this course, the total membership has been more or less preserved.

In England, by contrast, there was no overt split, though

something of the same conflict was there. The countrywide predominance of the main families, closely knit in such a close social scene, the way in which for a century they had been disciplining their membership, the fact that by then they were mostly townsmen, devout, industrious, and as they prospered beginning to educate themselves better, the fact, moreover, that as Dissenters they still belonged to that part of the nation most likely to be modified by new liberal views: all these factors helped to keep them, though often much tried by each other, from physically dividing. By the way in which London Yearly Meeting stolidly backed the Orthodox party through each separation in America, often without hearing the evidence, one would have imagined it to be equally diehard socially, disregardful of Quaker practice, Evangelical to a man: and yet . . . already by 1860 there were counter-trends of conciliation, trailers of a more reasoned attitude appearing on the home scene, suggesting that in fact from within it was bearing round in a new direction. All this seemed to happen without any need for front page drama.

But actually what occasioned the transition, apart from the more immediate pressure of wider social forces in such a relatively small nation as Britain, and the sensitivity of some Friends to these, was the stunning decline in membership. At a time (1815–71) when England doubled her population, the English Society of Friends reached its low point of fourteen thousand members. Here then was the other side to its smooth handling of oppositional tendencies. Those who did not toe the line with respect to its hieratic laws, or disliked the official orthodox theology, were all the time being disowned, or were resigning. There was no Hicksite group for them to join, to shelter in until the Society as a whole could liberalise itself again. They disappeared into the crowd. A few at a later date rejoined, as the Discipline was progressively relaxed, but most were lost to Quaker meetings. In the long run, set against the

American development, has this really been the triumph for forbearance and compromise that is usually supposed? The equivalent of a Hicksite group might have served English Friends better.

Most important, though, is that over in America, during that century of conformist theology and social conservatism mixed together, the essential thread of Quaker practice, democratic, responsible, a labour of slow inward transformation accepted as the task of the group, was kept going by a body of Friends more resolutely than anywhere else: indeed, it was the staunchness of those liberal Hicksites that, once the truth about them penetrated the blanket of censorship and false reporting, did much to encourage the liberal element among Friends in England to gird itself and hold the Society from bowing too low before the Evangelical altar.

This was not a question of individual temperament, because clearly for some the release obtained through an Evangelical pattern of belief was valid and could well contribute to the constructive tension of a Friend's Meeting: it was a question of the framework of that meeting itself, the ground out of which worship should spring—was it to be renewal of insight through the creative experience of the group together, the mystic reality, or was it to be an ordained service accepting the ruling letter of Scripture and the saving act of the Crucifixion, the logical form for which, as ultimately among American Orthodox Friends, was a congregation being moulded by a pastor? Only the first of these was Quakerism, as the Hicksites the most firmly of all maintained. Their contribution has yet to find its full place in Quaker perspective.

They were so called after Elias Hicks, not because he engineered the decisive moves of these liberal elements but because he was the outstanding liberal, the great Quaker commoner, of that time in America. He was country born, married, with eleven children, full of domestic and country well-being, with a sense of the growth and renewal of life coming silently from within; he was a plain Friend, a bit of a perfectionist like Fox, earnest to the point of being over-critical of minor levities; he had a commanding prophetic oratorical power—like Daniel Webster, people said. He was illogical in that, a critic of doctrine arrived at in the abstract, he later ventured some of his own; but it was not for this he was attended to; he was feared, he was followed because he stood for an open, receptive frame of mind, for the guiding experience of Inner Light, and for a social viewpoint that condemned slavery and, as with his teacher Woolman, critically examined the material interests and prejudices of wealthy city Friends.

As they, in the decade to 1820, became more reactionary, and seized, not on the emotional release, but on the tenets of Evangelicalism to enforce a stricter more static Discipline, that would place both interpretation and initiative securely with the Elders and Ministers, Elias Hicks spoke out vehemently against this. So great an issue was now at stake, so great the interest and feeling roused, that meeting houses were crowded to hear him—became disorderly, the conservatives said, as once the English authorities had said of Penn's preaching outside Gracechurch Street Meeting. Indeed, the radical-Leveller tradition was once more being condemned by those in places of worldly power.

Walt Whitman, himself inspired by the sonorous rhythms of Hicks' declamations, said . . . " Elias was of tall and most shapely form, with black eyes that blazed at times like meteors . . . he had an inner, apparently inexhaustible fund of volcanic passion, a tenderness blended with a curious remorseless firmness as of some surgeon operating on a belov'd patient." [46] He moved his listeners profoundly, so much so that some of them wished to silence him all together.

This was a very real issue for the rank and file who were

[46] *Complete Poetry and Prose,* New York, 1948, Vol. 2, pp. 400, 468–87.

opposing the priestly tendencies of their Establishment. The threat to silence any dissident had repeatedly been carried out through disownment. Over all still loomed the case of Hannah Barnard, disowned in 1801 because she had queried Scripture where it offended her conscience and her reason, for instance in the passage where Jehovah commands the Israelites to make war on others, or in the matter of the virgin birth: she pleading, as Fox had pleaded, the discerning power of her own spiritual experience, her opponents standing, as Baxter had stood, on the letter of Scripture as literal fact and the sole basis of faith. Elias Hicks had agreed with her; and just as then she had been silenced by a battery of Evangelical opposition headed by David Sands, now new church doctors—William Forster, Thomas Shillitoe, Elizabeth Robson, Anna Braithwaite, George and Ann Jones—came over from England to toughen the Establishment's view that Hicks and those like him ought to be silenced.

Hicks at this time was over seventy, the most considerable figure among American Friends, not excepting Stephen Grellet, yet it didn't stop Elizabeth Robson from calling him "that poor deluded old man"[47] or Ann Jones, the most raucous of them all, from branding him an "openly avowed" infidel whose teachings were "diabolical and luciferian and damnable."[48] At one meeting she spoke so vigorously that the local elders had to tell her that her conduct was "inconsistent with gospel order . . . calculated to sow discord among brethren, and produce disorder in the church."[49] She promptly returned to repeat her views. There was no lack of opinion on either side, and an unfortunate gathering of bitterness. Hicks said of the English visitors that they "spread themselves over the continent, and where ever they went they separated husbands and

[47] *Elizabeth Robson MSS.*
[48] *The Christian Inquirer,* New York, 1828, New Series III, pp. 38–9.
[49] S. M. Janney, *History of Friends,* Phila., 1867, Vol. 4, pp. 247–50.

wives, parents and children, brothers and sisters, and the nearest and dearest of friends." [50] They certainly added to the ferment, with a metropolitan arrogance as if this continent were still their domain, such as one hesitates to imagine them employing in their own home meetings (as one always hears said of the British abroad: "They are so much nicer in England"): yet, even without them, the conflict was there and could hardly at that stage have been differently resolved.

The first peak of the crisis was reached in 1827, in Philadelphia Yearly Meeting, where John Comly, the Assistant Clerk, led the liberals into separation. It was now evident that Orthodox Friends, though a minority of the Yearly Meeting (8,000 against 18,000) intended to use their control of committees (due to their strategic position in the cities, their social standing and close support for each other, and great zeal for running affairs) to disown all active liberal voices, to institute theological tests to comb out further heresy, and to block all attempts to change the membership of key committees such as their Meeting for Sufferings. Eldership, they ruled, was a lifetime appointment; and on a Monthly Meeting querying this, it found itself promptly dissolved. The situation had reached an impasse. At the Yearly Meeting the liberals tried to get a new Clerk elected to represent the majority feeling, as the one last chance of reform from within, but could obtain no agreement. Separation ensued.

The scene was repeated in other Yearly Meetings, with mounting boisterousness and even violence. At New York, Thomas Shillitoe intervened, objecting to the presence of Friends from Philadelphia who were not of the Orthodox party, and so, he argued, had been "disowned". All Orthodox present sided with him, all liberals refused to accept the point; thus there came about another local split, again with the liberals (or Hicksites, as they were now

50 E. Hicks, *Memoirs*, Phila., 1851, p. 106.

more colourfully being called) in a majority of twelve, to six, thousand.

At Mount Pleasant in Ohio, Orthodox Friends even guarded the doors to keep the Hicksites out, but these entering in turn created such a disturbance that the meeting lost its head, thinking the building was caving in, and there was a stampede for doors and windows. The Clerk had a rib broken, his table was smashed, and several Friends were trampled on. Dust and riot filled the room. But, the controversy continued anon, the Orthodox party appealing to the courts, with an eye to holding the Meeting's property. Though, in this and other instances, the Hicksites were by no means well-behaved, the Orthodox Friends, steeled by their aggressive theology, tended to be just that much more provocative, unyielding, sweeping in judgment, and capable of unfair practice. They held, with authoritarians everywhere, that the end justified the means.

The division in Ohio was roughly equal. In Baltimore, the next separation, nearly all declared themselves Hicksite, in Indiana, nearly all proved Orthodox. The other American Yearly Meetings (New England, North Carolina, and Virginia, at that date) did not divide but supported the Orthodox party and disavowed the Hicksites, as did also Dublin and London Yearly Meetings. In total, therefore, the Hicksites were in a decided minority. Very likely if there had been in those days truer information about them spread through the rest of the Society, and then free expression, so to speak, from the floor, they would have received wider backing. But this was not encouraged to happen; and in any case in these other areas there were good local reasons why a sufficiency of leading Friends—through economic link with the governing order, or through fear of radical immigrants, through isolationist tendencies, or through emotional preference for Evangelical absolutes—should try to minimise the liberal influence. But they were laying up further trouble for themselves: the problem was not one that could be banished thus externally, it continued in their own hearts. Each true Meeting for Worship would to some extent raise it: which explains a little why subsequently they fell away from the Quaker method.

For this was only the first round. That is to say, though from now on the Hicksites moved out of the arena of dissension, to continue their lives as Friends and citizens in internal tranquillity and at a steady pace of liberal development, from that time until to-day, by contrast the Orthodox faction splintered first to left then to right, wrestling with their distorted situation.

In 1843, as already noted, we find them again dividing in Indiana over Anti-Slavery activities—always, at that time, the touchstone of the Establishment's interests in society, explaining its unwillingness to offend ruling class sentiment, its fear of being thought socially unsound. This specific division took fourteen years to heal, with the conservatives gradually coming round, in keeping with feeling in the North generally.

During the same period as this, due to the influence of Joseph John Gurney, who had replaced Thomas Shillitoe as the leading British visitor to American Orthodox Quaker circles, the ecclesiastical trend further hardened through the meetings, causing a new upsurge of protest, and more separations. Gurney, a younger brother of Elizabeth Fry, stood for the extreme right wing of Evangelical Quakerism and had already been instrumental in swaying London Yearly Meeting officially to his standpoint, through his writings backed by his social position and activities in committee. He had upheld Isaac Crewdson, a Friend who in a booklet, "A Beacon to the Society of Friends " (1835), had decried Inner Light as a delusive notion and in its place put Scripture as the sole authority for Christian belief— as we can see now, the recurring issue. Crewdson, with three hundred supporters, shortly afterwards had left the Society, to join Plymouth Brethren; but Gurney had remained and more than any other man was to hammer Evangelical doctrine into the thought processes and speech of English and then American Friends, giving the best cover so far to their social conservatism, and enormously increasing the difficulty for succeeding Quaker generations (so soon to be encountering a world that prompted a renewed empirical approach) of knowing or being able to say exactly what they stood for.

Even Shillitoe, himself committed to Evangelical views, on his deathbed wrote that Gurney was " an Episcopalian, not a Quaker . . . He has spread a linsey woolsey garment over our members; but in a future day it will be stripped off; it will be too short for them . . . This is my dying testimony, and I must sign it." [51] Like Grellet, though more cerebrally, Gurney dwelt much on the depravity of man, naturally subject to the dominion of Satan, and on the atoning sacrifice of Jesus that, for those who believed, brought personal salvation. " In consequence of His propitiary sacrifice and through faith in Him alone, we obtain everlasting life." [52] He willed this formula on himself, on Friends, sealing up, as with all doctrinarians, the abyss of unsolved problems surrounding him. It finally sent him to preach in America for the space of three years.

There he proved too much of a cardinal even for Orthodox circles. They seem to have felt he was just that much too rich, too polished and well-connected, too obviously the *eminence grise* of their still rather narrow Quaker world; though paradoxically he went down well in the rustic Middle West. The opposition to his influence collected round John Wilbur, an ancient Friend (it is remarkable how old all these protagonists were: perhaps in itself a partial excuse for the teenage fling of the later Revivalism) within New England Yearly Meeting. Wilbur, through this specific protest, voiced a renewed mood of perplexity and resent-

[51] W. Hodgson, *Society of Friends in the Nineteenth Century*, Vol. 1, pp. 312–3.
[52] *Biblical Notes*, 1833, p. 352.

ment at trends within the Orthodox Establishment: as well
he might, for when his own Monthly Meeting stood by
him, it was irregularly dissolved and its members attached
to a " safe " Monthly Meeting that was willing to carry
out the edicts of the ruling group in the Yearly Meeting—
Gurneyites, as now additionally they called themselves.
Wilbur was cast out without a scruple.

The same occurred in another Monthly Meeting, and in
consequence first the Quarterly Meeting then the Yearly
Meeting divided into factions. Wilbur was conservative
enough in his own way, as regards formal Quaker customs
(his followers, having missed the main liberal movement of
fifteen years before, were never to find the impetus to re-
fashion these for modern times, and so stayed, honest back-
woodsmen, on the fringe of the Orthodox settlement,
gradually diminishing in number), but he was not conservative to the degree or in the sense called for by
Gurneyism, that would also, in order to play socially safe,
constrict the guidance of Inner Light.

From now on divisions multiplied. Gurneyites and Wil-
burites parted company in the other Yearly Meetings,
except in Philadelphia that solved the problem by cutting
its lines of communication with the rest of the Society, and
in London, where, without any attempt to hear both sides
of the story, the verdict went to the right wing faction.
This was logical, for Gurney had been their man, but
short-sighted if their wish was also to hold the Society, from
this point on, as far as possible together. For they were
continuing to support an amalgam of interests and ideas,
an old régime, whose creative energies were spent, whose
pronouncements would inevitably go more rigid—as in the
1878 Minute from Ohio . . . " We repudiate the so-called
doctrine of the inner light, or the gift of a portion of the
Holy Spirit in the soul of every man, as dangerous, unsound, and unscriptural " [53]—and then would crumble

[53] Ohio Yearly Meeting of Ministers and Elders, 1878.

before some new-fangled but forceful movement. Which is just what happened, in the decades following the Civil War when an intense backwash of guilt mingled with escapist longings swept across the States, working up a Revivalist fever, that in its course affected Friends, and brought pastoralism into the Society. There were no habits of mind left to resist it, in the Gurney-conditioned faction, just as a century before there had been no barrier to the onslaught of the first Evangelicalism. As soon as Quaker practice falters, the tending of the inward fires, with all that that implies, then the soul of the Society is amongst those most easy to capture.

An English Friend, Walter Robson, present at the first of the Revivalist separations (the inevitable next crop), in Western Yearly Meeting of 1877, begged for more charity for those who were being forced out, who clung to Quaker custom rather than the new hot gospel techniques, but was at once reprimanded . . . " J. H. Douglas, D. B. Updegraff, and a few other ' progressive ' leaders were very severe, telling me I was ' encouraging a spirit they wanted to crush ', and that all *they* did was by Divine command, and therefore must be right. The word ' crush ' explains much of the spirit of Separation in the U.S.A.".[54] The new incipient pastors, like nationalist leaders in old colonial territories, brooked no interference, nor compromise. The same year they drove a wedge through Iowa Yearly Meeting, similarly in 1880 in Kansas, in 1884 in Canada, and in 1904 in North Carolina. In all these Yearly Meetings they captured the majority of the members. Soon the Orthodox citadel was to be completely theirs.

This marked the endpoint of ecclesiasticism among American Friends. Finally it had become not only inevitable but healthy in that it gave the right forms and nomenclature to those social and organisational tendencies that had ridden undercover for too long. It must have brought

[54] *The British Friend*, October, 1913, p. 287.

a great deal of relief. It also made possible the sort of reappraisal that would lead to real Quaker development.

This has been the work of this century: the slow process, after tearing apart, of patiently stitching together again. Many factors have contributed to this.

(f) Development

In England during the nineteenth century there was a similar thickening of Evangelical arteries. The first liberating impulse, inwardly to God and as the mainspring of reawakened social concern, while still newly penetrating the upper reaches of society, in the main grew sluggish, its charity silting up with a piety that limited the further free flow of thought and spirit. It became bogged down in its doctrines, that were a useful aid to the bourgeois order in an era of almost continuous stress, encouraging its adherents to frown on those who ran ahead waving banners of a more rational enquiry or of a more radical social activity or even of more profound involvement in the spiritual potentialities of man. Because this became the chief attitude of almost all churches, the mass of English people, excepting those who swung back to a still more ritualistic context, and despite the degree to which the crowd and its leaders were schooled by fundamentalist moral passion, gradually lost faith in organised religion, a trend that was afterwards never reversed but much accelerated by the two world wars.

The Society of Friends was inevitably caught in this bourgeois situation, its powers of discriminating insight more than ever battened under by the system of ideas to which it had succumbed, which, as the first emotional release and philanthropic zeal somewhat fell away, seemed to press more than ever down with the mantle of respectability. There were those, up till 1860 at least, who feared it might never recover.

Fortunately other forces were at work. Friends could never be entirely unresponsive to the merits of successive Radical appeals (at no point more advanced than the

Levellers' programme of 1649), even when accompanied by alarming agitation; and, moreover, their own charitable ventures had accustomed a sufficiency of their number to a new public rôle, exciting in itself and with its own logic, making sure that the next generation would want to do the same or go one better. The older William Forster was a business man, an Evangelical preacher, a philanthropist; his son, William Edward, stepped on from this into the established channels of public service (though he first found it necessary to leave the Society) and in 1870 as Minister of Education put through the Education Act initiating the system of compulsory national schools. Old Edward Pease was the acme of Quaker Evangelical conservatism, pioneering in big business and sifting his charities with provincial caution; his son Joseph, despite the doubts and protests of the entire clan, became the first Friend to enter Parliament, in 1833, where later both his sons were to follow him. Shortly after him appeared John Bright, to give the star performance in that field; while in the neighbouring sphere of public meetings pamphleteering, petitions, informed pressure groups, Joseph Sturge took over from William Allen and the Abolitionists, and, going just a few steps further, more than any other Friend of that time set the tone of ensuing Quaker citizen activity.

This trend, of course assisted by improved Friends' secondary schooling, and all through the century given more scope by legislation transferring power from the gentry to the urban middle classes—such as the Reform Bill of 1832, the Municipal Reform Act of 1835, the repeal of the Corn Laws, 1846 (this being the first piece of the Free Trade and capitalist Company legislation of the next fifteen years), and the Universities Test Act of 1871—that bestowed on Friends, among others, a still more developed sense of inescapable public involvement, in turn was bound to influence them as regards their own Society, to set enquiry going there, to modify the structure of authority, and so

suddenly to clear the floor for a re-examination of their faith
and current mode of worship.

This, in embryo, was the saving development, the
involvement in liberal public activity, as citizens and
committee men and national spokesmen, with conflicting
loyalties and arguments to deal with, an obligation set
before them most effectively by Sturge and Bright: that,
though radically speaking, did not take them very far from
their comfortable bourgeois centre, did fashion a more
rational mood, a more open way of looking at themselves
in relation to the world, that, loosening them up and by-
passing entrenched Evangelical clichés, also freed the
spontaneous spiritual life within their meetings, that slowly
began to function again on a democratic basis. They not
only survived, but began to show a new capacity for growth.

Joseph Sturge, archetypal to this embryonic Quaker
renaissance, proved his metal in 1835, when the Evangelical front against slavery was congratulating itself on
victory: when in fact the freedmen throughout the West
Indies were still being exploited through the Apprentice-
ship clause of Emancipation, that had enabled the planters
to pocket twenty million pounds compensation yet effectively carry on as before. It was one of those lauded half
measures of reform that are actually a step backwards.
Sturge raised the cry against it, but meeting with little
interest among the satiated reformers, set off for the West
Indies to investigate. Affairs there were worse than
reported, with the taste for punishment stepped up—in
Jamaica alone he noted . . . " During the first two years,
apprentices were punished (by the special magistrates in
Jamaica) to an extent, in the aggregate, of a quarter of a
million lashes, and 50,000 other punishments, by the tread-
mill, chain-gang, solitary confinement, and mulcts of
time." [55] The most trivial complaints, such as " imper-
tinence ", were seized on by magistrates to place the negroes

[55] M. Richard, *Memoirs of Joseph Sturge*, 1864, p. 158.

once again at the disposal of planters, who now irresponsibly victimised them. It was this phase, of four years, that afterwards so embittered memories, even to this day.

Sturge, returning home, published his finding, still to meet with coolness from pious Abolitionists, who made it clear that continuing ardour was no longer political. He was obliged, through a series of public meetings, to raise understanding anew and form his own organisation. He stumped the country and got support from active radical circles, in any case eager to shake the Government. He won his case in 1838. Lord Brougham, his ally in Parliament, commented, " Joseph Sturge won the game off his own bat." [56]

Such was the character of the man: dedicated, scrupulous in the extreme, modest, untiringly like Bright concerned to bring the moral law into the life of the nation as a whole. Eight years later when the Evangelicals, now promoting a world convention, shirked the issue of American slavery, Sturge (who after all had been first inspired by the preaching of the Evangelical William Forster) squarely put it before them, to their annoyance. As his friend and co-worker Whittier wrote to him then, " I see your Evangelical Alliance has shipwrecked itself on the slavery question . . . When will men learn that there *can* be ' no compromise ' between right and wrong?" [57] It was this sort of public stand, fearlessly showing up hypocrisy no matter where it lay, that was Sturge's great contribution to Friends, bound as a consequence to stir up thinking within the Society itself, and break through the layers of humbug there.

His chief service in the public sphere was his work for international relations. The Peace Society in England had been formed by William Allen in 1816, together with a small Evangelical group most of whom were Friends, to propagate the principle that war, like slavery, was anti-Christian. Following their Abolitionist technique, they

[56] *Memoirs*, p. 180.   [57] *Memoirs*, p. 382.

had printed pamphlets and composed petitions, calling for a reduction in armaments, an International Court of Law, a general recourse to arbitration rather than to war. Their arguments were based not simply on the testimony of Quakerism, but were also culled from a succession of writings running back through the seventeenth century—the ideas of Grotius, Sully, Erasmus, from whom Penn had liberally borrowed—to the Middle Ages, the Romans, the Book of Micah. If they had searched the writings of ancient China they would have found material there. There has scarcely been a time when man has not sought some alternative to war.

But the nineteenth century Peace Societies, started off by the one in London and later to spread through Europe and America, formed the first coherent movement organised to this end—not unnaturally after the long night of the Napoleonic wars. Friends played a big part in this, and no one more than Joseph Sturge. By 1827 the first enthusiasm was seen to be lagging slightly, as always with Evangelical enterprise, but in that year he formed the Birmingham branch, with a rather broader basis of support bringing radicals in and Free Traders, who could agree together that peace was good both for political reform and the pursuit of trade, and from that time the momentum of the Peace crusade gathered. There was a first general Peace Convention in 1843, and further such international congresses, in Brussels, Paris, London, Frankfort from 1848 to 1854. From these, petitions were sent to governments, calling especially for an agreed system of arbitration. An impact was undoubtedly made, firstly on the Press (that swung from sneers and scepticism to a more reasoned interest), then on the public that gained some understanding of its own moral responsibility, and finally on statesmen who began to realise that war, if it became unpopular, could not so easily be invoked as an instrument of policy. The mass conscience was being stirred.

Sturge was at the very centre of this movement until his death in 1859; his moral integrity put its stamp on the quality of the appeals advanced; he was a Friend who, like Woolman, could kindle the Light in other men. In a practical way this led him to try mediating personally between Denmark and the Duchies of Schleswig-Holstein in 1851, a move that was leading to arbitration before the Great Powers intervened; and again in 1854, on the eve of the Crimean War, to visit the Tsar Nicholas in Moscow, to temper that ruler's obstinately blind designs on Turkey with some thought of the human toll in warfare, a move again that might have had effect (such moments are potential turning points in history) if someone of equal spiritual stature could have attended both on Palmerston (who though not at that moment in office was leading the bellicose outcry in Britain) and on the British Ambassador at the Porte. Sturge had to content himself, after the war, by visiting Finland (whose coast had been lambasted by the British fleet) to see what was needed in the way of relief: nine thousand pounds were in consequence raised, for replacement of seed, fishing nets, and the like; and, continuing the long-term endeavour, to influence the statesmen in Paris to introduce a clause advocating future arbitration into the Peace Treaty. This in fact, for the first time in European history, was accomplished (Protocol No 23): a small advance, but the sort on which much of to-day's such work is built.

His attempts to bring humanitarian concern into foreign affairs, to seek justice through process of law rather than explosions of violence, based for him on a lively sense of Christian obligation, was to a lesser extent complemented by his alliance with the Chartists at home. Here, like Bright and most of his middle class contemporaries, he was limited by belief in a free enterprise economy, in which all must strive to improve themselves, although the vast difference of position, already established between the owners of property or capital and the dispossessed labouring poor (in 1839, 1842, and 1848, the peak years of Chartist protest, brought almost to starvation level) was by this system all the time increasing. He never showed any interest, as Owen had shown, in co-operative alternatives to capitalism, nor in re-emerging State paternalism, ushered in by Shaftesbury, in the matter of wages and working conditions; but, for a short time when the leading cry, equally from the working class, was for manhood suffrage as the most feasible first step towards subsequent social reform, he did give strong support to that. Possibly, to some extent this political emphasis, as with the repeal of the Corn Laws, was a red herring designed to hold the workers' attention while the middle classes consolidated their economic position; but in fact, except by revolution, which Sturge, as a Friend, abhored, the working class was bound at that time to seek redress through Act of Parliament, which meant patiently playing on the middle class conscience. Sturge assisted them to that end.

He said (as an alderman of Birmingham resisting an oppressive Police measure in 1839, following Chartist riots there) . . . "He felt that he would not be obeying the injunctions of his Divine Master, 'to love his neighbours as himself', if he did not use any little influence which he might possess to prevent encroachments upon the liberties of his country, though they might not affect him personally; and it was also his duty to advocate the rights of the poorest individual in the community to all the religious, civil, and political privileges of the wealthiest in the land"[58] . . . for, as he wrote to an American friend, "Our unenfranchised countrymen are politically much in the same position as your slaves."[59] In 1841 he wrote to Cobden . . . "I have been driven to the conclusion, that it is not only hopeless to expect justice for the labouring population from the representatives of the present constituencies, but that the

[58] *Memoirs*, p. 265.   [59] *Memoirs*, p. 296.

infatuated policy which now guides our rulers will be persisted in until they plunge millions into want and misery, if not bring them into a premature grave. I, therefore, think the time has arrived when every friend of humanity, of whatever class, sect, or party, should endeavour to obtain and secure for the people a just and permanent control over their own affairs." [60] This for a banker and a corn merchant was quite an enlightened stand, and for a member of the Society of Friends at the time it marked a big advance in social commitment, way on from that of the Philanthropic élite; one only has to think of Stephen Grellet, or of Joseph John Gurney, to see the difference. Sturge equally lived by his Bible, but then involved himself in a more down-to-earth fashion.

Following in the steps of Thomas Attwood, another leading Birmingham liberal, he tried to keep going the alliance, or the possibility of it, between middle class reformers and working class Chartists, to secure through organised meetings and petitions such a weight of public demand that Parliament would have to concede manhood suffrage. He also stood four times for Parliament (refusing to make use of the usual bribes, or even to ask for votes, as similarly did Joseph Pease) in the interests of the same programme. But his scrupulousness, his moderate temper out of keeping with demagogic agitation, and the social balance of power factors beyond his control, never allowed him practical success. He could not compete with a Chartist like O'Connor for the loyalty of factory operatives, he could not prevail on O'Connor himself. The movement grew more violent and collapsed. Sturge, like the other Chartist leader, Lovett, turned to the need for better education for the working class as a whole, and through his influence in Birmingham put the Adult School Movement into the forefront of reforming interests. There was after all so much to be done, a reverse need never persist

60 *Memoirs*, p. 292.

for long. And in all he had shown Friends where, if their life was to have integrity, from the silence of worship to conduct in the world, they should be active too. His example, his stature, could not be gainsaid.

This was made the more evident by the supporting performance of John Bright. Of course Bright was more of a national star, but from a Quaker point of view he doesn't quite measure up, for all his Miltonic perorations dramatising the right course of action, to the concerned quality of Joseph Sturge. He was, perhaps conditioned by Parliamentary needs, the artifice required for commanding effect, inclined to oversimplify issues, to reduce every question where possible to the contest between the bad old landlord's order and the good new manufacturers' one, and in consequence give too much moral weight to the motives of the latter. He started off, as a public speaker, with an overwhelming sense of grievance against the oppressive Tory Establishment, and doubtless most of what he said was true, leading fruitfully to such measures as the abolition of Church rates (1868), the Universities Test Act (1871), the Disestablishment of the Irish Protestant Church (1869), and the Irish Land Acts of 1870 and 1881; but to counter this, because an orator needs must raise an Angel against the prevailing tyranny, he sanctified the capitalist order at its current Benthamite stage of development, which led him to oppose Factory legislation from 1844 to 1850, and to bring all together too much unction to the repeal of the Corn Laws (1849) and to the retention of India and Ireland as British, in his last Parliamentary years. Such fervour was equally explicable in terms of what was good for Lancashire cotton spinners was good for the whole world. His oratory was so persuasive—Lord Salisbury said ... " He was the greatest master of the English oratory that this generation has produced " [61]—that to some extent it overpowered him too.

[61] G. M. Trevelyan, *Life of John Bright*, 1913, p. 383

Nonetheless, when theme and power were riveted by a stroke of universal insight, he could be a great awakener of the national conscience, and a reminder to Friends of their prophetic tradition. With Bright in Parliament calling for the franchise, till first town then country workers obtained it, in 1867 and 1884; with his challenge such as that of " Let us try the nation. That is our faith, that is our purpose, that is our cry—Let us try the nation ",[62] ringing through massed audiences of Trade Unionists, whom he also called on to " speak out for peace " for then " there would be no war ";[63] in the educative tenor of many of his speeches, for instance, on the responsibilities of voters; most particularly in his linking of reform to a restrained foreign policy, leading to his great peace speeches, his pleas for a constructive use of national resources and for consideration above all for the ordinary man, that was ultimately his plea for Christian values— then Friends in their various walks of life could not but feel that they too should be making some relevant public testimony. How demure they could suddenly see them- selves to be. Here was the searching public voice scarcely heard among them since the time of Burrough. Thus, like Sturge, Bright powerfully led them to start looking at them- selves from a new angle, to start repositioning themselves.

As a body they did not change overnight. Both Sturge and Bright came in for a good deal of old-fashioned reproof. London Yearly Meeting was doggedly conservative, still whispering in its Epistle of 1843 that " We trust Friends may always be found among those who are quiet in the land ", and, as late as 1885, it could still raise a powerful contingent of those who considered that the literal word of Scripture gave sufficient answer to all man's problems, and that any other view was " advanced and dangerous ". Reforming activity was still branded as " unsanctified

[62] J. E. T. Rogers, *Speeches by John Bright*, 1868, Vol. 2, p. 211.
[63] H. Y. Leech, *Public Letters of John Bright*, 1885, p. 213.

zeal ", as " creaturely activity "; it was asked if such-and-
such a Friend was not " running before he was sent ", in
danger of being " consumed with sparks of his own kind-
ling ", for surely, as all comfortable Friends could see, " the
time had not yet come ".

This, however, was not the feeling among those whose
Adult Educational work, or whose work for the franchise,
or for Temperance, had taken them into the slums; or,
following the Franco-Prussian War, the Boer War, and
the various Balkan upheavals, of those who worked for
civilian war victims. Man was in need of help from man
(self-help was not enough), through immediate practical
measures and in a universal reconciling spirit: here surely
lay the natural line of expression for a living Quaker faith.
Few could emulate John Bright, at his best rousing the
whole nation to a sense of its moral obligations (though
from 1833 till 1918, about forty Friends entered Parliament,
their loyalty gradually inclining from Liberal to Labour,
a willing gesture from a small Society); but in the Municipal sphere, in education, in the broadening of international
work, the example of Joseph Sturge could be followed by
a goodly number of Friends. It was therefore not surprising that the next champions of the new liberal approach
should rise from another family that had followed up this
line to the hilt, the Rowntrees of York and Scarborough.

It was in John Stephenson Rowntree's essay of 1858,
" Quakerism Past and Present; being an Inquiry into the
Causes of its Decline in Great Britain and Ireland ", that
the new awareness was not only voiced, but also launched
the most decided criticism yet of conservative Friends and
the state to which their attitudes had brought the Society.
As an analysis it was only partially successful, for though it
inveighed against all the symptoms of conservatism—the
dead Ministry, the narrow education, the caution over dress
etc, the restrictive Discipline—it did not trace this to the
socio-economic drive that had governed Quaker life since

the seventeenth century. But it served good purpose, for it encouraged thought; it gave an intellectual dimension to the activities that Friends now felt drawn into; and it strongly assisted, was the occasion of, the mood demanding a reconstitution of the whole Quaker set-up. Within three years the Society had been liberalised, made democratic to a degree that the earlier merchant-banking caucus would have branded as anarchic. Though of course economically times had changed; credit was no longer the key problem; for this reason the entire structure of mid-Victorian society was undergoing liberalisation.

Once begun, such a movement grows in strength. Since 1843 there had been two English Quaker journals providing a forum for discussion, and in 1867 a third was added. The stand of the American liberals, the Hicksites, was being better appreciated. And, the new sense of social responsibility, empirically based, was of all the most formative factor. Quakerism was again renewing itself, and this time on viable lines. In 1884 three Friends published a book called "A Reasonable Faith", which restated the early Quaker thesis, basing the guidance of life firstly on the corporative experience of God in prayer: in effect a rebuttal of Gurneyism, of the 1878 Ohio Epistle, of the philosophic counterpart to social conservatism. The advance was proceeding on all fronts. It was now possible for liberal outsiders, readers of Darwin and Spencer and Huxley, finding that they still required something more centrally spiritual in their life, to turn to Quakerism as possibly the most honest medium for further search. Of these, Caroline Stephens was the spokesman through her writings. The Society was indeed regaining the open face of its early years.

Once again a Rowntree realised, however, that all was not as it should be. Possibly, in the Society at large, the change was still too slow. But in 1895, at the Manchester Conference of Friends, John Wihelm Rowntree pleaded

for an increased quickening of spiritual life, for more
directly helpful ministry, within the several meetings for
worship. He saw that a contemporary idiom was lacking
there, that the clichés of fifty years before were a distorting,
often a death-dealing medium for the experience that
Friends were now readier to face in all its possible diversity,
due to the freer life among them, and that without overhaul at this point all their other advance would be in vain.
He believed that the Pastoral solution in America was also
not the responsible one; but that Friends must each one
learn how to further, in living language, the communion
they shared. This, where words broke out of the silence,
was still the touchstone of all else.

He personally suggested, however, that this situation could
be best rectified through a series of Summer Schools, next
a permanent Quaker Settlement (Woodbrooke, at Birmingham), where at least a nucleus of Friends could study—
current trends in biblical criticism, in science, philosophy,
sociology: a sort of refresher course in modern thought—
and so shake off their more restrictive shibboleths. This
might free them for the undogmatic drawing close to the
shared Spirit within; and it might start some of them off
for the first time into the ministry. He felt that here lay
great promise, both for Friends and for others (perhaps
those who had turned their backs on all churches) who
could find a vital religion still in the exercise of a Quaker
meeting.

These then were the developments, spilling into the
present century, that had led the Society finally to re-
examine the very heart of its existence, the practice of the
meeting for worship. Its history had come full circle. Yet,
it is enough simply to state John Wilhelm Rowntree's
diagnosis (rising undoubtedly out of the deepest concern),
and the sort of cure he advocated, to see that the main
thinking of that time was still shying away from the kind
and degree of social commitment required by integrated

Quaker life. Study however admirable, especially for those
with time and money, was not perhaps the chief requirement of a Society still in the main embedded in exclusive
bourgeois existence. The language of prayer would remain
academic, would simply turn from its old religiosity to
something over-purified, if it were not also fertilised by a
sense of shared social purpose with the mass of fellow
citizens (increasingly, with all mankind), that, not holding
the worshippers back from God, neither left them content
to be too piously introverted while others needed their civic,
or international, co-operation. Not that Friends were
wholly blind to this, as the century just ending testified;
but as yet it was only half-recognised, an involvement only
half-accepted, their preference still for some biblical or other
readjustment, something usually that money could buy,
that would settle things without too much change in the
overall composition of their lives.

Doubtless, further development would have come from
within. Quaker faith had been freed enough to work
now constantly on its practitioners. But as it happened,
pressure was applied from without. The war of 1914 tore
into the bourgeois fabric, into which for over two hundred
years Friends had so diligently woven themselves. At its
end, all perspectives had changed. Friends in fact were
assisted by this in the direction they needed to go.

CHAPTER III

QUAKERS AS WORLD CITIZENS, 1918–58

(a) *International Service*

THIS latest period of Quaker history started significantly, both in England and America, with a number of Friends once again in prison. They had refused to be conscripted for war. Though undeniably they too were compromised in the acquisitive, spiritually evasive life of the societies to which they belonged, that had made this explosion of war inevitable, at this point they reasserted—against their own accumulated shortcomings as much as against the autocratic State or the surrounding chorus of worldly interests—the primacy of the timeless quest for the Light of God in every man, to keep way open for that through seeking unity with all people, whatever the particular circumstances or personal sacrifice involved. This set them against the current of events and the mass mood of their nations, and pulled them out, as nothing yet had done, from their positions of privilege and quiet conformity. They found themselves back in the common gaol. But it equally returned to them the freedom, for self-enquiry, for right action, so well known by early Friends.

If Quaker Yearly Meetings and their most concerned younger members had not made this stand, then the Society of Friends would have forfeited its prophetic function, would have again shut down its channels of insight, perhaps this time irreparably so far as its formal existence went, to be merged in the general phalanx of churches, views tempered to the world. As it was, a new era opened.

The decisive step had been taken by London Yearly Meeting in 1915. By then, because much of the Society's life was still in a confused rather false condition, the accretion of the previous two centuries not yet sufficiently dislodged by the most recent winds blowing through it, many members were supporting the war, recruiting and manufacturing munitions, and indeed trying to sway the Society as such to their individual course. At least two hundred and fifty nominal Quakers had enlisted (by the end of the War one third of those eligible had joined H.M. Forces), and others looked for some compromise move. In reply, the Yearly Meeting (the voice of the Society as distinct from the conscience of any one member) reaffirmed its Peace Testimony and the eternal basis from which that sprang. The large meeting house, at that time still at Devonshire House, was crowded day after after day to the doors. "The sense of the meeting" rose unmistakably—helped, prepared for, one must remember, by the constructive developments of the nineteenth century and the renewed vitality flowing from those—and the central Quaker course was set.

Next Friends, faced by conscription and the hint that they alone, due to their history, would be granted exemption, had refused, actually for the first time, to accept such special treatment. Both in Parliament and outside they had called for a broad exemption clause, thus ranging themselves with all those who, no matter how they explained their faith, stood for the awakening of mankind's conscience over this crucial issue. Though by statute this was achieved, in itself a remarkable advance in the thinking of a nation-state, the Tribunals in practice worked steadily against this broad front of objectors, so that, quite apart from those allowed to continue in agriculture or ambulance or relief groups, there was about thirteen hundred and fifty non-Quakers besides one hundred and forty-two Quakers sent to prison or Detention barracks, where again it was the non-Quakers who were especially victimised, so that seventy-one of them died from their treatment. Friends stood by them all through, actively supporting such organisations as the Fellowship of Reconciliation (interdenominational) and the No-Conscription Fellowship (Independent

Labour) in public work for peace, by promoting the widest publicity in the more liberal sections of the Press for the trial of each objector giving the gist of his defence, by arranging a system of prison visitors—when Quaker meetings for worship were again held in English prisons—and by helping financially in the support of families. Friends themselves didn't suffer quite so much, though five of them were among the thirty objectors transported to the front in France, court-martialled and sentenced to death, a sentence afterwards commuted to ten years penal servitude.

Finally, in 1917, Friends openly defied the censorship regulations, carefully notifying the Government and the Press of their intention and reasons, by continuing to print and distribute pamphlets not submitted to the censor. Meeting for Sufferings in December recorded a Minute . . . " that Christianity requires the toleration of opinions not our own, lest we should unwittingly hinder the workings of the Spirit of God. Beyond this there is a deeper issue involved. It is for Christians a permanent duty to be free to obey, and to act and speak in accordance with the law of God, a law higher than that of any State, and no Government official can release men from this duty."

This claim was publicly judged, in April of the following year, when the Chairman and the two Secretaries of the Friends Service Committee were tried at the Guildhall in London for issuing one of these pamphlets, and were in fact all imprisoned. But, the trial was well reported; it was followed up in the daily press and in periodicals with articles devoted to past Quaker defence of spiritual and civil liberties; and, on the occasion of the trial, when the magistrate retired to consider his verdict, Quakers present led the court into moments of silent worship during which vocal prayer was offered. The Manchester Guardian described this as " a throwback to the seventeenth century."

This, if deserved, was praise indeed. It was exactly the

quality of early Friends that modern Friends needed to discover anew as the ground for the forward march of the Society.

As yet, however, it was too soon to say how far they were succeeding in this. The war generation has started well, despite the evident contradictions and confusion, by the clarity of their main decision, which in effect had repositioned the Society, redefined it both for its members (an awareness that was gradually to spread through all Quaker meetings and their life) and in the eyes of the rest of the world; they had incidentally linked up again with the more radical elements socially, a fact that would lead to further rethinking of their overall position; and they had kept up their effort to reach the public at a level of conscience deeper than that of the nationalistic barrage. They had thus reached out to more inclusive goals than those of their more immediate elders, and were in consequence all the time strengthening the first new rush of spiritual vitality. But as yet all was in the early stages.

Also, in the way of service complementary to their stand against the war, yet denying no individual need their assistance, they had sent a civilian ambulance organisation to France (FAU), that was to serve there for five years; they were caring for enemy aliens in Britain; and from 1914 onwards they had built up, wherever the governments would permit, a relief organisation for civilian victims in Europe. This last service started in France, especially in the Verdun area, with emergency food, clothing, and medical help for refugees, then developed into the rebuilding of homes, the provision of seeds, tools, and stock for farmers, the opening of co-operative stores. By " 1918–19 there were more than five hundred English and American men and women, trained and untrained, in as many as forty-five centres, ministering to the extraordinarily varied needs of a population who had lost practically everything by war, and were endeavouring to piece together their broken lives." [1]

This relief work spread to Holland, Serbia, Austria, Hungary, Poland, Russia, and finally to Germany. Children were especially cared for. Near Vienna and Warsaw cows were supplied to farmers on condition that, till the animals were in this way paid for, their milk would be sent free to the city children's hospitals. Students were helped, typhus fought, farmers aided to re-plough their land. The approach was always a co-operative one, and increasingly side-by-side with that of other voluntary relief teams, the aim being to help the dispossessed to stand again on their own feet as quickly as possible.

The most searing task of all was faced in the 1921 famine in Russia . . . "At first I could not think why so many stood in pathetic rows, straight up against the wall, motionless and without a smile, sometimes just staring in front of them as if they were already dead. Then I found that the stove warmed the wall just there, and that was why. With the customary courtesy of children, many even of these little sufferers responded with a wan smile to our farewell—Do Svedania! (Au revoir). I think you have never seen a child's smile, till you have seen it on the face of one who is near death's door from hunger " . . . " We had noticed a little fellow of 9 or 10 years of age who had come to the kitchen for 2 rations, neither of them for himself. He stumbled away across the snow, hugging the can of soup and cup of cocoa with two bread rations buttoned under his coat. I thought the child would collapse any moment. His face was colourless, the lips drawn back. He was shivering and crying tearlessly, as so many do. We went with him to his home, and found his mother trying to cook some grass flour, adding twigs of wood. The soup and bread were handed over to the two younger children, and the boy stood watching them, following

1 A. R. Fry, *A Quaker Adventure* (Abridged Edition), 1943, p. 19.

every movement of the wooden spoons, but not attempting to take anything for himself. Later, we saw him struggling once more across the snow, slipping and stumbling, and still crying quietly. We asked that if possible a ration should be given to him, but he is only one of the many as yet unfed." [2] Ruth Fry, who was Honorary Secretary of the Friends Relief Committee, found that, contrary to English press reports, the Soviet authorities were both wonderfully co-operative, themselves after all contributing a high proportion of the relief given, and scrupulously honest over foreign supplies. She also noted that they described Quakers as "psychologically incapable of espionage!" [3]

In Germany Friends' initiative in piercing the Allied blockade with supplies of food and clothing, first for infants and nursing mothers, was the start of widespread relief work there (later to be remembered kindly by Nazis), and the overcoming of the terrible hatred engendered by the war, and marked the main entry into this field of the American Friends Service Committee (AFSC). Somewhat parallel development to much of that outlined above had been taking place in the Society in America (examined in the second part of this chapter) and the spearhead of this was the AFSC, and from this time on, through this Committee and its counterpart in London, American and English Friends worked increasingly together, in relief jobs, then in the emerging structure of their international service.

It had been thought that the relief work would wind up shortly after the war (then, by 1923 at the latest), and it did then fall away for a time: but only to mount again in the 'thirties, and then increasingly through the devastation of the 'forties, and still in this present decade for Korean and Hungarian refugees and to meet other smaller

[2] *A Quaker Adventure*, pp. 50–1.
[3] *A Quaker Adventure*, p. 48.

emergencies. Its particular sense of urgency was never allowed to fade for long. However, Friends did not find in such work, nor in its growing emphasis on the rehabilitation of the sufferers, the limit of their concern (as it became increasingly clear to them) to bring people everywhere more together in a spirit of service and reconciliation, so to induce wherever it might follow, that profoundest spiritual unity which, as they themselves had been stirred again to see, was the guiding condition for human life. They were not, that is, mere humanitarians; they were members of a religious Society very much put on their metal by the challenge of world conflict and disorder, that had suddenly burst all previous bounds.

Carl Heath, who had joined Friends at the age of forty-seven in 1916, coming to them through the work of the National Peace Council and War Victims Relief, gave expression to this deeper commitment in his plan for the establishment of a worldwide chain of Quaker centres, first of all in Europe, to be open to all comers for fellowship and international activities as these might arise. He wrote . . . " Our Settlements (or Embassies) must stand first and foremost for the Message of Life, the reality and universality of the Divine Indwelling; secondly, for study; and thirdly for Service; and we look to people coming to us as well as our going out to them." [4]

This first embryonic description was taken up by London Yearly Meeting in 1918, leading to the formation of a Council for International Service, with Carl Heath as chairman, and before long with the promised participation of AFSC in the work projected. Heath was a man of great perception, who reflected the most alert tendencies of the reawakening Quaker community, and he guided things so that in 1927 the elder Friends Foreign Mission Service (which had been born of the evangelical burden of the previous century) was gathered into the new approach, all

[4] C. Heath, *Quaker Embassies*, 1917, p. 50.

now to become the charge of a Friends Service Council (as continued to this day), of which he became secretary. The scope of this Council, with its accent on service, thus extended to Asia and to Africa; and his own especial concern was increasingly for the situation in India, leading in 1931 to the formation of the India Conciliation Group, of which he was made chairman, and to further close contact with Gandhi. In the same year he promoted the first of the Annual Conferences of European Friends, a development that by then rose naturally out of the life of the European Centres and the new Yearly Meetings formed. Thus, in 1937, with the second World Conference of Friends, and the setting up of a standing World Committee for Consultation, of which he became first chairman, it could be seen how central his life had been to this whole trend that was expressive of the third, potentially most hopeful, period in Quaker history. He died in 1950, saying that Friends still needed far more self-discipline if, in an increasingly authoritarian world, they were to practise their faith successfully.

Turning back to the European Centres, these were established in Paris, Berlin, Vienna, and Geneva (also in Warsaw and Moscow till 1931, and in Frankfurt and Nurnberg until German Friends took them over in 1934) and they grew in life till the Second World War broke out, to be re-established in the postwar period. For a large part of their existence their energies, willy-nilly, were directed to relief—in all of them during the early 'twenties, then in Paris 1932–37 for German Jewish refugees, then again from there (1938) for Spanish refugees, in Vienna 1934–38 for victims of the 1934 Revolution and in the latest period, 1956–58, for Hungarian refugees; while since the last war in Germany (and the dispersion of Centre work to Cologne and Brunswick, and the Rest Home at Bad Pyrmont) there have been the continuous needs of clothing and re-employment for displaced Ger-

mans. This work, bulking so largely, has thus tended to
become (in Friends' minds often as much as in that of the
Press, Governments, or the public) the main description
of Quaker international service. Friends are best known
for it, and their impartial functional reputation has resulted,
for instance, in the AFSC becoming the leading American
agency for handling relief funds and goods. People still
trust their money to them as they did in the eighteenth
century. "I am overwhelmingly convinced, declared Mr
Citrine, that it is utterly impossible as it has been all along,
to do any adequate relief work except through an organisation like the Friends ":[5] so, in Vienna in 1934, the International Federation of Trade Unions dispensed its cash
through the Quakers. Again, for the Jewish refugees, a
Paris Centre worker wrote . . . " Our Center is the only
non-Jewish Committee in Paris giving relief, and has been
chosen by the Christian Churches in the United States,
England and Switzerland as the Committee in France
through which they will do their refugee work." [6]

Such work is of course an essential commitment for any
Centre called on, and a primary channel of service for some
workers, and in general a most valuable school, for them,
and for the recipients, because of the interdependent spirit
of partnership fostered, often between people of very different background and assumptions, as the work takes
shape. It not only heals, it opens up new understanding,
a new sense of the unity of man. It has sparked off such
kindred work as that of the IVSP, whose founder, Pierre
Ceresole, later joined Friends. It is practical, full of the
sobering realities of an unremittingly harsh world. Though
it has also had the danger of inflating the reputation of the
Society of Friends as a whole, for which it is not a primary,
but an unsought, an emergency expression. To judge
Friends by their relief activities is to get them out of focus.

5 *Daily Herald*, 20th April, 1934.
6 *Friend's Intelligencer*, 29th February, 1936.

The Centres, therefore, never ceased to develop more permanent activities: as havens of study and discussion free from political or national bias; through running student clubs and hostels and exchange travel schemes, as the meeting points for students from across all frontiers; and as the starting points of individual efforts to pour oil on menacing situations. For instance, in Vienna in the 'thirties the Centre was the one place where leaders of the rival parties could meet, in the hope of averting bloodshed. In Berlin, Corder Catchpool from 1930 to 1936 used his powers of reconciliation, in Germany itself on behalf of Jews, in Lithuania on behalf of Nazis. A recent example of such work continuing is that of Horace Alexander, moving out from the Cenre in Delhi to mediate between Pakistanis and Indians.

From the start the Centres were team undertakings, with a growing proportion of indigenous staff, as, through attending the meetings for worship or through reading the Quaker literature or through participating in the relief work, more local people became Friends or close sympathisers. There was never any aim of recruiting members, simply of drawing together with those who were already kindred in spirit or who might suddenly realise that this way of life and worship suited them. Most of the small Quaker, and Mennonite, groups on the Continent, that George Fox had sent letters to and which Stephen Grellet and others had visited, had during the nineteenth century, when under pressure for military service, emigrated to the United States; so that really from 1920 onwards European Quakerism made a fresh start.

The most active group (not unnaturally, looking back to the sixteenth century) was soon that in Germany, leading to a separate Yearly Meeting by 1925, with a network of local meetings spreading across the country. (German Friends maintained their witness through the Nazi régime and the Second World War, and to-day contribute among the most searching viewpoints found in the Society). Other groups arose, and Yearly Meetings were formed, in the Netherlands (1931), in France (1933), Sweden (1935), and Switzerland (1944); and the small residual Quaker communities of Denmark and Norway began to grow again; and there were isolated meetings in Greece and Italy, and even in Majorca in Spain. All these groups were self-sustaining, because the centre of Quaker life anywhere is the local meeting for worship, and its church business is almost equally decentralised; yet it was natural and inevitable that the separate Yearly Meetings should also move closer together. Hence their annual conferences, their close liaison with Centre work in their own and neighbouring countries, their growing sense of belonging to the one world community of Friends.

All these countries were acknowledged equals, and all heirs to the Christian faith. In Asia and Africa however, in the vast colonial territories, some Friends, in the main Americans, of decidedly evangelical outlook, had been operating as missionaries: helping, that is, to counteract the exploiting greed of traders and governments, through the provision of schools and hospitals, yet, insensitive to the faiths and cultures of the dependent peoples, except to adapt various currents of fear to the implanting of evangelical dogma, themselves taking up an invidious rôle as unwitting destroyers, one-sided indoctrinators, bringers of selective charity, arbiters of right and wrong, so that though they could register recruits to the Christian fold (alas, often with a different creed to the infallibly proclaimed in the next valley) these recruits had been alienated from their centuries-old techniques of adjustment to each other and to metaphysical realities. Admittedly, the strident western world was forcing Asians and Africans to do this on every front, and awareness of that and their hunger for every kind of new knowledge would condition their response to missionaries; even so, it must be doubtful how deep their

new nominal allegiance went, and how long it could prevail before they reverted to some indigenous pattern of
thought and feeling (often more subtle psychologically, or
more understanding socially, or with a more profound
spiritual witness, than what missionaries feel driven to offer)
from which they could learn at their own speed, and, most
important of all, in their own responsible communal framework, from Christian faith and insights, practical as well
as mystical, as part of man's common religious heritage.
Friends approaching them on this basis could together with
them seek out "that of God in every man". Less easily,
however, on the old basis.

Fortunately, the new spirit among Friends and the
experience this provided in Europe following the First
World War began to take effect further afield, though
only at first in India, where equally the indigenous pressure
for it was the most advanced. There the older missionary
work, in Central Provinces, was contracting. The Friends
Service Council, therefore, already in touch with Gandhi
and giving its support for the release of political prisoners,
and helping Indian students in Britain, began to send leading Friends to India, to lecture on Quakers principles and
to feel out openings for a more acceptable service: which
resulted, in 1935, in Hilda Cashmore opening the Rasulia
Rural Centre, which, non-proselytising, was an experiment
in settlement work. Its basis was co-operative for all vil-
lagers taking part, and soon as much an Indian as an
English concern, and it was a meeting place for those of
different religious persuasion, who met there in Quaker
silence. It became the most advanced point yet along the
new path of Quakerism.

War cut further developments, only in turn quickly to
offer another opening for Friends. The fear of Japanese
air raids on Calcutta brought a small Friends Ambulance
Unit team under the leadership of Horace Alexander to
help with any civilian casualities, and, as events turned

out, this team found its main employment combating the
effects of a cyclone and of famine in 1943. From the start
contact had been made with Gandhi (then demanding the
withdrawal of all British authority) and the relationship
of the FAU to work in India properly established, so that
the subsequent enrolment of a number of Bengali volunteer
workers, many of them women, went ahead smoothly,
leading on to the establishment of long-term rehabilitation
schemes, such as industrial craft centres and the construction of a model village, which schemes the co-opted Bengalis
soon felt able to take over. Great encouragement was given
to the women to keep going a regular child welfare scheme.
Ultimately a Quaker Centre was set up in Calcutta.

Following Indian independence, and the division with
Pakistan, a second Quaker Centre was established at Dacca
in East Pakistan: to offer opportunities for similar social
service (such as the international work camp that has built
houses for flood victims) and to foster educational requirements; but pre-eminently, as in Calcutta, and Rasulia, and
at the further Centre in Delhi, to help create a spirit of unity
among all who might come there, and among all who could
be reached from there, in which spirit worldly difficulties
could find solutions, and the Light of God could be
induced, rigidities of dogma falling away. Horace Alexander for fifteen years has devoted himself to this work.
Again, there is no aim of making Quakers, of turning
Hindus or Moslems away from their faith to Christianity,
but of offering the silent Quaker worship, and the Quaker
concern to serve humanity, to all who can thus realise themselves and their faith the better through it.

At least the development in India then, following on
from that in Europe of which it can be seen as the apex,
both shows Friends of this latest period testifying to a
Quakerism as potent spiritually as that of their seventeenth-
century forbears, creative in the situation of its day, pruned
to the most direct revelation, and also, through their extend-

ing chain of Centres, bringing East and West into a practical partnership. To look at it for a moment thus is to see that the name Quaker has grown in meaning.

Leaving China for a minute aside, and only mentioning that in Tokyo, firstly through the lifetime service of an American Friend, Gilbert Bowles, and then through the care of the small Japan Yearly Meeting (established 1917) together with the AFSC, there is also an international Centre engaged in the same commitment as the others, then the other great area of interest rapidly emerging to take its place in the contemporary world is Africa. How have Friends fared there?

The answer would seem to be relative to the socio-political condition of the places where Friends have got a foothold. In Ruanda-Urundi (part of the " no-nonsense " Belgian dispensation) the approach, by Kansas Friends through a united Protestant Alliance, is still that of the evangelical missionary. In Madagascar (where France staged its first postwar demonstration of full-scale colonial repression, in 1946–8) evangelical English Friends, working together with the Paris Mission and the London Missionary Society, have stuck to much the same approach; though in the last few years, coincident with renewed Malagasy political pressure, and through heart searching in London Yearly Meeting, and through slight shifts of feeling within East Africa Yearly Meeting (established 1946), the ultimate change is coming into view. Thus, more control is being given to the Malagasy within the church structure, bush school education is being raised from the simple bible class level, and the first silent meeting has been started. Independence, equality, responsibility: one can see how these are entering in, and how colonialism, including colonialism of the spirit, is having to fade out. Friends, if they feel concerned to stay (as a Society, that is, not simply as seconded workers to a more persistently pastoral church) must learn the lessons of India (and of China) and forge the new kind of partnership.

In Kenya (politically fluid, with intransigent settler pockets, a more liberal government policy, and a louder African voice) this moral has been partly drawn. For the years of dominant colonialism the missionary approach, by American Friends serving under the American Friends Board of Foreign Missions, was considered adequate; and indeed so much money was spent and such excellent schools, craft training shops, hospitals, and dispensaries provided, and such a good well-watered site (Kaimosi, near Kisumu) was owned by the Mission for demonstrating improved husbandry, and most important of all, such care was taken in building up the Friends' Church (to-day with 26,000 members) through probationary periods for all would-be members, through a near-tribal degree of authority given to the Elders, and through the actual simplicity of the meetings held, that a more integrated Christian community was built here by Quakers missionaries than anywhere else.

Even so, looking to the future, one would doubt its powers of survival in its present form, if Kenya or East Africa as a whole became politically an African domain; and even now, in the decades of confused struggle, modification is being admitted, concepts of inter-racial partnership, and of involvement in the wider political scene, beginning to colour its ordained life. An important influence in this has been the advent of FSC workers, following the Mau Mau outburst, to work in the Thiba detention camp, in the new Mwea villages, and in the Nairobi community centre at Ofafa. They have reflected the new Quaker approach (the one most likely, moreover, to be successful with the detribalised urban African); and since then the participation of African Friends in the development at Ofafa is taking the process a step further. East Africa Yearly Meeting stirs with a new appreciation of Quaker interdependence, of its own equal place and potential contribution to Friends' world community; perhaps to some

extent symbolised for it in 1956, by the construction of a
new ward for the Kaimosi hospital by an international
work team, and by a meeting that year, together with
Pemba and Madagascar Friends, under the chairmanship
of an Indian Friend, Ranjit Chetsingh, en route from
America to India.

Down in South Africa (the regressive area politically)
things, alas, are quite otherwise. The two hundred and
twenty odd members of Southern Africa Yearly Meeting
(established 1948), which also covers the Rhodesias, do
what they can individually to better race relations, but any
ordered sizeable moves towards inter-racial partnership
seem to be little better than a mirage. Early in 1958, two
English Friends, Myrtle and Philip Radley, after some
years with coloured students in London, went under concern to Cape Town, to see what they could do about this.
The problem is clearly one that leads towards patient work
with the Government, the Dutched Reform Church, the
white public, as well as with the Africans; and one, moreover, linked to the conduct of race relations and to political
developments in the continent as a whole. In fact Friends
in Africa, few and isolated (there are a few others in
Uganda, Ghana, Nigeria, the Gold Coast, and of course
Pemba), and in the process there also of re-educating themselves, like all Westerners, with regard to the indigenous
society, have as yet only been able to launch one or two
minor pilot schemes that in any way partake of the character of the more established Centre work.

However, this situation is hopeful because, from the
point of view of Friends, the area is open to their concern
—they can go there; but that does not so readily apply to
the vast dominions of the Communist powers. Among
these previously they were only established in China to any
extent, and of course there mostly on a missionary basis,
of the pastoral kind in Nanking, and of the more direct
Quakerly kind in Czechwan, where they had been helping

to run the West China Union University, at Chengtu; though also a Centre had been started in Shanghai that had done great service for stranded European refugees; and, during the Second World War, the FAU had operated its transport of medical supplies impartially for both the Communists and the Kuomintang. By 1952, however, Quakers, like most other Westerners, especially missionaries, had been obliged to leave.

Chinese Quakers, naturally, had stayed; and it is instructive that, under the Marxist régime, it was the Nanking Evangelical Friends, pastor-led, who were most easily understood by the authorities. Those in Chengtu and Chungking, with silent worship and emphasis on individual conscience, and the internationally-orientated Centre at Shanghai, fared less well.

It was because Friends wished, not only to extend a hand of friendship that in a small way might help to lessen tension between East and West, but also to make sure that the Communist authorities grasped Quaker aims and faith, that they sent two Missions, of English Friends sponsored by Meeting for Sufferings in London, to Russia in 1951 and to China in 1955. Both these Missions travelled widely and met for frank discussions with their hosts, and this initiative, as their reports show, had a good deal of the desired effect.[7] Then, in 1954, six young Russians came to England at the invitation of English Young Friends, who in 1957 sent their own party to the World Youth Festival in Moscow. Also in 1957 an international Mission of American, English, Swedish, and Danish Friends visited Poland; and in August of the following year Friends were able to hold an international seminar and work camp in Poland, as also at Kranj in Yugoslavia. There is now hope that the small continuing group of Polish Quakers, and much wider circle of sympathisers, will be able to contribute to other international activities sponsored by Friends.

---

[7] *Quakers Visit Russia* (ed. K. Lonsdale), 1952; *Quakers Visit China*, 1956.

Side by side with endeavours in this for the moment most restricted terrain, goes the work of Friends at the United Nations, where a small team tries to bring something of Quaker experience and insight to the problems facing the national delegates (Friends, in recent years, have even been running study groups for diplomats), and to relay information back from there to the Friends World Committee for Consultation. Friends Centre, New York, is a useful adjunct to this service.

In sum, one gets the picture of a relatively small but active movement spreading across the world of our day, advancing here, held up there, but all the time using a technique that expresses its innermost nature well and that also seems to draw other people in. Quakerism is no longer Anglo-Saxon. It is opening itself to African, to Asian, to European insights. Silence is a good basis of exchange. So is a sense of shared commitment, of racial and political equality as well as equality before God. At the Third World Conference of Friends in 1952, delegates came from twenty-five countries. Clearly, development is not all on a par, but the main Quaker trend is marked. And it began, definitively, with the deepening of insight at the time of the First World War. As much as anywhere it started with the return of English Friends to gaol.

(b) The Home Front. Conclusion

What about the home front? The reassertion of the Society's commitment to seek God through unity with all men, against the current of war and governmental decree, had led it to reach out across the world and build a dynamic organisation, that going beyond palliatives or any sort of patronage brought forms of service in which all manner of people, whatever their nation or race or creed, could join; and thus corporatively, as the Society of Friends, it had given practical expression to the essence of its faith and tradition.

But did it do the same at home? Seeking to live, as George Fox had put it " in the virtue of that life and power that took away the occasion of all wars "[8] what did it do about the social order in England and in America, about which for so long it had been largely complaisant, for which it had even helped build the sinews in its arch-capitalist days, but which was rife with all those elements of conflict and violence and injustice and greed that simply got magnified in international dispute, to which they directly contributed? Pioneering in service abroad, was it shirking the issue back at home? This could not just be answered by the life of any one Friend but by the Society's approach as a whole, by the degree to which it responded to individual concern, and thus in these parent countries established a framework, clear to the world and to its own young people, of Quaker social testimony. To what extent —equally to be evidence of the depth of its spiritual renewal —did it succeed in doing this?

It began well. The 1914 war cut deep, so that firstly in England the logic of a fundamental stand for its faith, that so to speak broke the truce with the Establishment it had entered into around 1720, landing its members back in gaol, caused it with a fresh simple honesty to face its social complicity hitherto and its obligation to change course. Again, some preparative work had been done by small groups of Friends, for example in the Friends Social Union since 1902, but now it was London Yearly Meeting, the collective voice, that set up a War and Social Order Committee (1915) enabling it by 1918 to set forth an eight point Quaker charter for a " true " social system.

This charter called for such a system to be directed " beyond all material ends to the growth of personality truly related to God and man ", knowing no " restriction of race, sex, or social class ". The pace of change implicit in the wording was gradual, but nonetheless it hit the bull's

[8] *Journal*, p. 65.

eye with its immediate prompting that " Our rejection of the methods of outward domination, and of the appeal to force applies not only to international affairs, but to the whole problem of industrial control . . . Service, not private gain, should be the motive of all work . . . The ownership of material things, such as land and capital, should be so regulated as best to minister to the need and development of man." This was the first non-bourgeois social statement it had made since 1660, though of course individuals, especially John Woolman, had had a good deal to say. But the Society as such, fearing to listen, had turned evangelical instead—thus doing plenty of good, but strictly on the terms of its continuing stake in capitalist gain and property holding. Now, in 1918, it was attempting a new start.

This framework of written principle was reaffirmed by London Yearly Meeting from time to time, for instance, in 1925 . . . " The chief purpose of life is defeated, both in our own lives and in those of others, when men's efforts are directed mainly to the acquisition, protection and extension of private property . . . We are concerned as Friends not only to live in personal integrity, but also to build up the common life of men . . . [and] we must not think to wait until all are changed in heart " . . . and again in 1934 . . . " In a rightly ordered community wealth would be held in relation to need, to service and to the fulness of life for all . . . we should not allow any apprehension of individual loss of privilege and power, any fear of a lessened security, comfort, and spaciousness in our own lives to qualify our acceptance of the ideal, or weaken our pursuit of it . . . If discipleship of Christ demands renunciation, it does so with the thought of a heightened capacity for life." To-day (November 1958) an open conference for Friends is being held in London, sponsored by Meeting for Sufferings, once again to review these principles, in the light of forty years' experience, and it would indeed be strange if the next Yearly Meeting did not in consequence set them out again. If deeply pondered, they contain (together with the lessons to be drawn from the three hundred years of Quaker history) all that is needed to make a start with a united Friends' social testimony.

However, these particular years represent the peaks of response to an almost continuous feeling among a number of English Friends—those returning from relief work in the 'twenties, or those working with the unemployed in the 'thirties, or those simply more aware of the quickening pace of adverse factors in the interlocked world of the 'fifties—that their Society has still not been explicit enough, so as to aid all its members to appreciate what is involved, nor as a body made much progress with carrying principles into practice. A good deal of frustration has been evident (even to the extent at this present moment of a certain throwing up of hands in despair, with cries that a Quaker social testimony is obviously impossible of attainment) and Yearly Meetings has bowed to the charge, in words such as those of 1938 . . . "Again and again we have to acknowledge our failure when it comes to practical measures " . . . as though the transmuting of belief into action is in this sphere too complicated for it corporatively to do much about. It is as if, having named its target, it has thereafter felt held back by the resurgence of doubt and apathy, and daily preoccupations, among the membership at large, and also through lack of seeing what actually the first steps should be. Rather as in the days of slave-holding, the imaginative leap (although precedent might be thought to exist elsewhere in the world) has, so the inference would be, proved elusive.

What further light can be thrown on this, and indeed does the above represent a too stringent minority criticism? Surely there has been some progress, that simply requires further logical development, some tentative equivalent to the action taken overseas, perhaps masked from the eyes of idealists by the general shift of English society into the Welfare State?

Well, one group from whom a lead could decidedly have influenced the whole membership has been that of the Quaker employers. They held a first conference in the key year of 1918, as a direct result of the investigations of the War and Social Order Committee into the part of the industrial order in the fomentation of war, and also in an effort to reflect the new more radically-concerned Quaker spirit of the time; and they afterwards repeated the holding of this conference once in each decade, with progress reports.

On the first occasion their deliberations were still saturated with the paternalism of the more profitable sections of the existing order, combined with a forward look to improved status for the worker, his primary share in the returns of the business and in some form of joint control, this to be facilitated by the better provision of housing, general education, specialised training, and so forth for him and his children. Quaker employers like the Cadburys', Rowntrees', Reckitts', were indeed pioneers in the introduction of workers' garden cities, profit-sharing schemes, works councils, management training courses, holidays with pay, welfare departments, and much else: all to ease industrial tensions, nurture a co-operative approach to the efficient functioning of the business, and through that perhaps evoke some improved industrial system in the interests of personality growth.

They did not, however, on this first occasion or ever subsequently, attempt directly to match up to the eight point Quaker social charter, considering this beyond their power . . . "We have sought in the course of our discussions primarily to discover and define the duties of employers within the present industrial system, not because we hold a brief for it or regard it as ideal, but because the task of changing it immediately is beyond the power

of individual employers or group of employers . . . as
citizens, we should work towards the alteration of the
industrial system in so far as we regard it as inconsistent
with the principles of our religion; but in the meantime
we cannot afford to neglect the urgent needs and the outstanding opportunities which confront us in our own
factories . . . have we yet ever fully tested the potentialities
of the present system, whatever criticisms may be urged
against it, as a field for applied Christian ethics?" [9]

They were ready, that is, to reform to the hilt, to learn
and adapt, to become the most progressive élite morally
within the capitalist system, but always on ground that
they had chosen, the final power remaining within their
class or group of families; and this, moreover, during two
decades when, whatever the reforms within the system,
grave unemployment came into being and war clearly
threatened again. No radical intellectual effort nor imaginative leap, initiating even a pilot scheme based on the eight
point charter, rose out of them.

At the 1938 conference one of their number, John Guy,
summed the situation up . . . "The positions we have
built up are so closely interwoven with property rights,
that I do not think we are willing to expose ourselves to
the chancy favours of a new constituency, nor to weaken
the force of self-interest on which we rely so largely. I
think that Quakerism has been brought very nearly to a
standstill in the economic sphere. . . ." [10] He did himself
afterwards put forward a few tentative ideas, but his contribution was not all that well received by the conference.

As he said himself . . . "As soon as we approach specific
measures such as we would devise if entirely without bias,
it is apparent that basic change is really somewhat repug-
nant to the appetites and mental habits developed under
the present system. To me they look like a large dose of

[9] *Quakerism and Industry* (Conference Report), 1918, p. 130.
[10] *Quakerism and Industry*, 1938, p. 28.

very unpleasant medicine. That income shall be drawn only from work and equitably apportioned, that the free consent of the governed shall be secured in industry as well as politics, and that openness of accounts shall give an equal chance to all interested parties may sound innocent and right enough, but they contain some very sharp teeth.

It is no use, however, asserting that the Eight Foundations are very pretty but quite impracticable; I believe that intelligently and moderately applied, they are quite practical but very unpleasant to established tastes. The alternatives are, however, still worse.

To make the professions we have publicly made and to acquiesce in the existing order is transparent hypocrisy; to lower those professions is to deny our deepest convictions, the faith of our fathers and our own." [11]

A year later war broke out. After that Quaker employers were overtaken by a Socialist Administration in Britain, by new organisational experiments on the part of non-Quaker firms, and by such pioneer ideas as those, for instance, being worked out in Yugoslav industry. At the 1948 conference and since they have been taking stock of this.

However, to conclude that they failed to give any lead at all to the Society towards implementing the principles accepted by the 1918 Yearly Meeting would be to discount unfairly the value of the steps they did take as excellent jumping off points for better empirical understanding, perhaps among the workers or managers they trained, of how industry could be run democratically; also they provided openings for the increasing number of Quakers who felt concerned to take up welfare and labour relations work; and, most important, they fostered a good day-to-day atmosphere which, whatever the system, is primary. A lead, therefore, from this influential group, though devious and gradualist, and most likely to bear fruit in other lives, was not wholly missing. They oiled the wheels.

[11] *Quakerism and Industry*, 1938, p. 32.

A more frontal approach came following the emergency of the 1926 General Strike. At that point Emma Noble, a Friend who was the wife of a leading Trade Unionist, visited the Rhondda Valley in South Wales, where the entire working population of miners was unemployed, hungry, and neurotically depressed. She interested the Society to initiate local relief schemes, through the provision of materials and tools for Women's Sewing Groups and Boot-repairing Centres, and this led on (exactly as in FSC work abroad, and divorced too, and necessarily so, from evangelical overtones) to the setting up of a permanent Centre for the Rhondda, where the Nobles became wardens for the next eighteen years.

This Centre, Maes-yr-haf, directly working among a population of 160,000, started courses in adult education (by 1939 " more than 475 grant-earning classes and courses of lectures were successfully held, and thousands of single lectures ",[12] later, by 1952, to be assured of a regular grant from the Glamorganshire County Council), instruction in dress-making, weaving and pottery-making, and physical training; and also counselling work was undertaken throughout the district. For unemployed single men Occupational Clubs were started, which developed into a larger system for all unemployed persons (by 1939 " there were sixty-six clubs for men, women, and young people, with a total membership of some 9,000." [13] " ' The Unemployed Clubs '," said Lord Lindsay of Birker (Chairman of the Unemployed Committee of the National Council of Social Service), " came out of Maes-yr-haf and spread all over England and migrated to America." [14]

Maes-yr-haf was also the base in South Wales for the Allotments Committee of the Society of Friends, that, following the lead of John Robson, helped unemployed men to develop allotment gardens, a movement that even-

[12] W. Hazelton, *Maes-yr-haf* 1927–1952, p. 5.
[13] *Maes-yr-haf*, p. 8.
[14] *Maes-yr-haf*, p. 10.

tually covered England (in the peak year, 1935–6, 135,378 people were assisted), in turn leading on to an experiment in " group-holdings ", which in turn lead to the formation of the Land Settlement Association, through the help of the Carnegie Trust, which (1933–9) bought 9,817 acres and took 800 unemployed men on as trainee tenants.

In all this development Maes-yr-haf was not the only Quaker Centre, nor Emma Noble the only dedicated Quaker social worker, but she illustrated well the life of service given on home ground, against (others say) the impenetrable difficulties of a complex social order. Concern opened up a way; she lived to the full the possibilities, implicit with the Quaker search for unity, that were present to her. She showed, as the work overseas showed, that it is only by actually making a start (of course, on an acceptable basis) that more becomes possible, till suddenly practice is ahead of principle. Also she opened up the way for a great many others to join in; and she has inspired Friends of a younger generation to seek new openings for service. All this, by individual demonstration, has enabled the Society as a whole to see that its social principles are not impracticable, nor the right motive spirit lacking, and to keep it moving towards the formulation of at least a minimum social testimony that could be said to stand for Quakers as a body.

But as yet it has not done this. To the query why should it, there is firstly the answer that having set out principles in a season of heightened spiritual insight it destroys self-respect if it doesn't practise them, it loses its authority and appeal for other people, especially when in the relatively more detached foreign field it has gone some way ahead; and secondly, if it fails its insight, pretends it didn't really hear (and takes refuge, as some Friends would still like, in an evangelical cloud again), then insight, its life blood, may dry up. Older Friends may remember that during the years 1918–21, when it seemed as though the Society would, in social testimony as in peace testimony, take some big step forward, its meetings for worship were deeply gathered ones, and all who have engaged in some period of service know this to have been so then too; but otherwise it cannot be denied that there has been much thinness, vacuity, stopped power. Is not a main reason for this becoming by now apparent? Life activity is one, a double standard of truth is impossible. The future of the Society of Friends in England at some stage must, therefore, turn on its ability to go through with a social testimony, expressive of its religious faith, that as a group it will habitually practise. To plead that at least to-day it is more socially responsible than in the eighteenth century is hardly good enough; fresh insight sets fresh targets. The commitment at some point must be total. Only so can Friends remain Friends, and make their corporate contribution to growth in human capability on the world stage as a whole. And, not even their brave display in foreign Centre work can help them to skirt this issue for ever.

This equally, if not even more, applies to the Society of Friends in America. Turning to events there since 1918, in the first place that war did not present the Society with quite the same total challenge that it did Friends in Britain, partly because it involved America only towards its conclusion, and also because of a more liberal government attitude towards conscientious objection, based on memories of the Quaker stand during the Civil War and on observation of the current impasse in England; so that only thirteen American Friends served prison sentences, the rest who were objectors feeling free to accept State warrant for continuing work in agriculture or in European relief teams.

As in Britain, quite a few Quakers backed the war effort (nearly 3,000 served in the armed forces) but all meetings in their collective capacity reaffirmed the peace testimony—immensely strengthened at this point because, already, in 1915, a group of active young Friends, representing the two main fronts in the Society (the Orthodox were now known as members of the Five Years Meeting, the Hicksites as members of the Friends General Conference), together with a contingent from Philadelphia, had met at Winona Lake, Indiana, and put out a united message from " the Society of Friends in America " clearly restating their peace principles. This had been the landmark, from then on making possible a single strong witness for peace; and, moreover, the committee it had set up grew, in 1917, into the American Friends Service Committee (AFSC).

It was through this Committee that American Quakers, no matter what sub-allegiance they claimed, from now on served abroad, together with Friends of all other nations, in straight relief work and Centre activities. This greatly affected them. They got to know each other, and to know European Friends. Service together, they came to realise, was more fundamental than some confused inherited conflict. Moreover, from 1915 onwards, London Yearly Meeting had started to send its *Epistles* to all American Yearly Meetings, thus reversing its earlier rôle, to strengthen the unitive process; and in 1920 there took place the first All-Friends Conference in London. The Society, after all, was one.

So, these workers returning home wanted to see an end to division, and began to exert the pressure for reunion, the root-and-branch feeling as they called it, that has in fact never ceased since then. They did not of course have things all their own way. The most extreme among the Orthodox made a last attempt, in 1922, to bind Five Years Meeting to the letter of an evangelical creed, but, due largely to Rufus Jones and his young following of relief workers, they failed; and in consequence Oregan, Kansas, and then Ohio Yearly Meetings retired into independent lines of action. They were the largely rural, aggressively pastoral mission-minded meetings that had strayed furthest, as we have seen, from the early Quaker path: as Henry

J. Cadbury put it, as late as 1932, "there is in America a huge dull mass of denatured Quakerism, which is not conscious of its difference from other churches, and even less so of its international affiliations".[15] Even till to-day, though they have at least contributed to the work and funds of AFSC, their main efforts have continued to be given to evangelical revivalism at home and its missionary counterpart in central Africa, the Bolivian plains, and east China. They remain on the fringe of the new trend in the world Quaker movement.

This setback apart, the efforts, always pushed forward by AFSC and its ex-servicemen, to end the main divisions in the Society in America, if need be on a middle basis, reaped considerable success. From 1922 onwards, step by step, first anniversary ceremonies, then young Friends gatherings, then Quarterly Meetings were held together —"first time in a hundred years"[16] as these occasions were heralded; then came joint sessions of Yearly Meetings, provisions made for United Members, joint activities of every sort, one of the most significant of which was the establishment in 1946 of Philadelphia General Meeting in which all distinctions were ended.

Moreover, despite natural give-and-take, the usual basis of unity seemed to be increasingly weaned of pastoralised orthodoxy, with a marked re-appreciation, among Five Years Meeting members, of the older silent forms of worship, and much else. In a fairly recent progress report (1951) from them, Baltimore records . . . "a noticeable trend towards less dependence on a paid leadership, with more participation in meetings for worship and discipline by the membership generally. Friends have rediscovered the vitality that may be had in non-programmed meetings; less dependence is placed on the necessity of outward helps such as music and the prepared sermon; and such salaried

[15] Friends International Conference, Amsterdam, 1932, Report, p. 7.
[16] *The Friend* (Philadelphia), 20th April, 1922.

workers as have served in the Yearly Meeting in recent years have fitted in much more satisfactorily as secretaries than as pastors; in which latter capacity they formerly functioned " [17] . . . and Indiana records . . . " the increased use of silence in the Sunday morning meetings for worship, and with this a deepened concern for greater individual participation in worship " [18] . . . and New England records . . . " More than two-thirds of the Meetings were pro-grammed with a minister conducting worship . . . [but] open meetings for worship are steadily increasing and all Monthly, Quarterly and Yearly Meeting sessions are held on the basis of silence and periods of worship are held open to all to participate." [19]

This trend, admittedly, is most marked in the eastern seaboard cities, thus reversing the earlier pattern to put them in the van of liberal development, leaving the middle-west and middle-south clinging in part to ecclesiastic forms similar to those of their non-Quaker neighbours' churches : so that despite the real progress, still in train, towards unity on the traditional Friends' basis, there is still to-day about half the Society in America shy of recommitting itself to this extent. Add militant evangelical tendencies within the pressure on Friends (felt in England too) to join the World Church Movement (in which it is difficult to disentangle social and theological conservatism from growing appreciation of each unit's contribution to religious needs) and also lay authoritarian tendencies in American society, and the counter-forces to renascent Quakerism—inward, empirical, responsibly shared through seeking out the " sense of the meeting "—are still very much in the field.

It is, therefore, perhaps not too surprising that, so far as the existing social order goes, nothing in the nature of a united testimony, or much support for advanced principles,

---

[17] *Trends in American and Canadian Quakerism*, 1925–1950. 1951, p.9.
[18] *Trends in American and Canadian Quakerism*, 1925–1950, p. 21.
[19] *Trends in American and Canadian Quakerism*, 1925–1950, p. 32.

has been forthcoming from the Society in America. Friends have always been Republicans since the anti-slavery days, and for the most part enjoying the rural paradise of the middle-west have been puzzled to think of anything better. In the industrial east, in Philadelphia, New York, Baltimore, Social Order Committees on the English pattern got to work after 1918, and the Five Years Meeting of 1935 signalled a slight step forward in the literature being put out, and contribution was made to the social and economic reports of the Friends World Conference of 1937, but no strong radical interest, nothing that might involve material renunciation, was shown then; nor since. Perhaps American society is as yet too buoyant, and too cut off from the reality of the increasingly impoverished life of much of Asia, even of South America, for American Friends to feel ill at ease in this matter. Pastor-led worship, moreover, is not such as to kindle too many fresh doubts: it focuses attention upwards.

The slight progress that has been achieved has come, as in all these related fields, from AFSC pressure. The first need was to bring Friends together (AFSC organised the first American All-Friends Conference in 1929), then to open up still more energy, away from trying to save one's own soul, for service in one form or another; and always the demands of relief overseas, and the need to spread knowledge of the peace witness, seemed to consume the years. Along these lines much was achieved, through Institutes of International Relations, peace caravans, work camps, and the Wider Quaker Fellowship started by Rufus Jones; and abroad through relief distributions and then in the Centre and rural development schemes. To this work, in the States, must be added the very important watching concern of the Friends Committee on National Legislation, Yearly Meeting committees on Race Relations and Civil Liberties, and the more studious life at Pendle Hill College. There is no lack of fields for service, nor, as the 1955-7 trials of Mary Knowles showed, of challenge to stand firm by conscience,[20] within the United States itself.

It must nonetheless be asked if, there as in Britain, all these varied channels of service, without the backing of a basic and co-ordinating Quaker social testimony, are not inadequate and in a deep spiritual sense flawed? They mostly rose, in this latest period, out of a revitalised peace testimony, and spread through the growing initiative and universality of the FSC and AFSC, but to what does the peace testimony relate if not to equal witness against a social order in which the seeds of war are manifest? To what degree can American or English Friends, indeed any Friends, seek unity with their fellows, in Africa or China say, if they still show themselves as allied to social privilege and property interests that require force for survival? Can they be so self-deceiving? May not even their spiritual life, if practice in this social sphere does not keep pace with insight, suddenly turn sour on them?

What then should they do? First, they must become, or stay, honest regarding the problem. John Guy's words about "established tastes" and "unpleasant medicine" are relevant. As history shows it is very largely evasive to become absorbed in evangelical dogma: the decision that presses is a personal one in the material framework of life. History also reminds us that Friends in their first creative period displayed unlimited courage, not the least because of the help they extended to one another in moments of stress. In this present age if Western Quakers lack the guts or imagination to take the first renunciatory steps involved in a total life testimony, it is not impossible that Eastern Quakers, out of their different experience and tradition, could help with both ideas and strength to see them across that difficulty. Friends are building a world Society: why not tap that fact to the full? Why not be willing to ask for help? Why not learn both from other world faiths

[20] *The Plymouth Meeting Controversy*, Report, Phila., 1957.

(accepting that the marked impact, for instance, on Hindus and Buddhists of the Christian ethic suggests rewards from a two-way process) and from other social and political systems, if not directly through exponents uncongenial to Friends, then through other Friends or attenders at meetings, in Europe and India and elsewhere, whose lives are currently bound up with those other approaches to a world problem? For English Friends in particular, one can see that part of their difficulty comes through their chasing a social testimony simply with the sources of energy, dwindling in a predominantly middle-aged group, at their own immediate disposal. They want to tap the universe of spirit, but there are other antennæ besides theirs. This is also a matter of resensitising their vocabulary.

A practical step on the home front for Friends, with immense possibilities, would be the very wide extension of Quaker Centres, the model being those already tested overseas, or that of Emma Noble at Maes-yr-haf. Buildings exist in present meeting houses, some of which are variedly used, others being largely reserved for devotional purposes and zealously guarded by premises committees that still share the exaggerated property consciousness that was the undoing of Quakers during their long middle period. Friends, then, as a Society, could take a certain step forward with regard to their joint property, reactivating meeting houses as primarily social Centres (where worship would of course continue, but in the freer spirit known by Early Friends who used hired rooms, their homes, indeed the fields if need be, emphasising that the church was inward and not something built with stones), these Centres to be bases for Quaker service in the district, according to the district's particular needs. Such Centres need a resident warden, and each district usually only needs one Centre: which might entail the disposal of some very small or socially redundant Quaker property, the proceeds to be then available for the setting up of new Centres elsewhere, including new ones in Asia and Africa. If Friends' World Community is one, it is one in all such things.

The work of these Centres would vary, but certain aims might be basic. From them the public might look for facilities for study groups, lectures, unbiased information on national and international events (racial incidents, for instance), facilities from which Friends too could profit; but the primary concerns would always be more active ones, because, for instance, if you want other people to fall in with Friend's peace testimony, and practise civil disobedience in event of national aggression and go to gaol and stand up to a possible military occupation with nonviolence, then you can bring them to this state of mind, more surely than through pamphlets, posters, or even speeches, through involving them and their nervous energies in socially creative service.

Even in the Welfare State, there is growing need for this. Instead of Old People's Homes, it is kinder to enable old people to remain in their loved setting: only possible if some regular personal service is assured them, more comprehensive than that at the moment provided from Town Halls. The increased prison population, delinquents, social misfits, lonely coloured immigrants, need aid as never before, and the sort of social service begun by Friends Relief Service during the Second World War among evacuees, and to some extent kept up, could be expanded from permanently active Quaker Centres. As found at Maes-yr-haf, and one can again and again go back to this example for useful instruction, work always opens into further practical opportunities. The most obvious form of service, the one that catches youth's enthusiasm and wins easy public interest, is the work camp, that answers some small concrete need locally: in which in turn all Centre members could join, planning their district projects, together with non-Quaker volunteers (including delinquents on probation, coloured men, and any other isolates), and as widely as possible with foreign participants. To work in an international team is to begin to think internationally: this is the sort of local opportunity Friends could provide for the wider public: this is the best education for peace. Surely all those overseas activities by FSC and AFSC, that happened to be awarded the Nobel Peace Prize, could find equivalents on home ground?

Again to the query whether this should be such a prime concern of a religious Society, it can be asked in return: if in Meeting for Worship the guiding factor is reception of spiritual signals and their transmission through sensitive ministry, and if Quaker history shows that during periods of material acquisitiveness and social conservatism, ministry either went dead or cloudy, and is still without much power to-day, then might not lives more devoted to service liberate new strength for it? This ultimately, as Friends know, leads to the practice of the presence of God. Can anything be left to stand in its way?

No Friend is so busy that he cannot give time, re-allot time, to the above kind of service (and to the sketchy ideas mooted above, scores of others must be waiting for an opening); young people especially could with benefit give a year of their lives. A good way of inducing interest in adults would be to follow the example of Vinobe Bhave in India and ask each of them, or each family, and each Quaker firm too, to give up at once a proportion of their property—a kind of voluntary capital levy, that would psychologically better involve them, and provide immediate funds for the work, for the fares of international team workers, and for an extension of overseas Centres. If we want governments to give more for economic development in Asia and elsewhere, if we feel the public has funds to spare, we should, as a Society, do something drastic ourselves. Such voluntary gestures have wide effect. Friends have never failed to rope in sympathetic financial support where they have pioneered.

Moreover, this redirection of money—from needless expenditures and also from our westernised conception of a basic standard of living, for only when it hurts are we on the right track—affects not only social and international relationships but the giver's attitude to the ways in which that money was produced. If business men and traders surrendered a high proportion of their profit for specific international projects (large-scale technical aid development as well as small service schemes) and began to see the provision of this as a prime aim of their firms and of their whole working life, then the nature of the social order is by quite a large fraction shifted; but the best chance of this happening would be through the voluntary lead of individuals or groups, and the first here could be the Quakers. Social energies need redirecting, through example, through encouragement that is ahead of the law, for people's imaginations are captured through schemes, no matter how radical, they help to put in train themselves.

Just as the Society corporatively could put its properties to the maximum social use, so it could rethink the use being made of its many funds, and allied committee time, rechannelling these for the most pressing priorities. Intemperance, for example, is no longer quite the social problem it was. The most important item, however, for discussion would be that of the Quaker schools. They are outstanding of their kind, but enormously expensive, and they further social privilege. Would it not be much healthier if all children went to the one national school system, as day pupils, as in most parts of the world? If this were accepted for Friends' children (quite apart from the saving in subsidies) then Quaker influence would still be maintained for them in the home, even more so indeed, and secondly through the local Quaker Social Centres, which could then increasingly offer activities for all age groups. The Society would not suffer from some such readjustment (most of its active blood in this century has come to it out of non-

Quaker backgrounds): it would on the contrary be opening its doors more easily to working class children.

There would, therefore, appear to be steps that the Society of Friends, both in England and America, and elsewhere, could without much further ado take towards implementing in practice such social principles as it has already put forth. Will it reach the point of doing this—without more wars, or social revolution—and so consolidate, at home as abroad, the fresh leap forward of 1918? If it does, then in one sense it will only be removing the obstacles to its mystical life built up, at times with the energy of beavers, in the main since 1689. It will be putting a deviation right. It will still be left with its prime commitment, to be discovered and tested by each new Friend: to help the break-through of God's Spirit, as practised most purely in Meeting for Worship.

Yet service for man is the gateway to the effective practice of Meeting for Worship. They are inseparable, each lighting the other.

INDEX